ANDY KIRKPATRICK

COLD WARS

CLIMBING THE FINE LINE BETWEEN RISK AND REALITY

Andy Kirkpatrick

Cold Wars

CLIMBING THE FINE LINE BETWEEN RISK AND REALITY

Vertebrate Publishing, Sheffield
www.v-publishing.co.uk

ANDY KIRKPATRICK – COLD WARS

First published in 2011 by Vertebrate Publishing, an imprint of Vertebrate Graphics Ltd.
This paperback edition first published 2013
Copyright © Andy Kirkpatrick 2011.

VERTEBRATE PUBLISHING
Crescent House, 228 Psalter Lane, Sheffield S11 8UT.
www.v-publishing.co.uk

Andy Kirkpatrick has asserted his rights under the Copyright, Designs and Patents Act 1988
to be identified as author of this work.

This book is a work of non-fiction based on the life, experiences and recollections of Andy Kirkpatrick.
In some limited cases the names of people, places, dates and sequences or the detail of events have been
changed solely to protect the privacy of others. The author has stated to the publishers that, except in such
minor respects not affecting the substantial accuracy of the work, the contents of the book are true.

A CIP catalogue record for this book is available from the British Library.

ISBN: 978-1-906148-46-1 (Trade paperback)
ISBN: 978-1-906148-37-9 (Ebook)
10 9 8 7 6 5 4 3 2 1

Every effort has been made to obtain the necessary permissions with reference to copyright material,
both illustrative and quoted. We apologise for any omissions in this respect and will be pleased
to make the appropriate acknowledgements in any future edition.

Designed and typeset in Adobe Garamond Pro by Nathan Ryder – Vertebrate Graphics Ltd. – www.v-graphics.co.uk
Printed and bound in the UK by T.J. International Ltd, Padstow, Cornwall.

For Ella & Ewen

Contents

Acknowledgements

I owe a big debt of gratitude to many people in this book, both in the writing of it, and in the living of its stories. I have tried to be very honest in my views of people back then, much to my detriment I expect, and I hope friends like Kenton Cool, Ian Parnell, Leo Houlding and others forgive me for my flawed opinions and pig farmer psychology. They remain superstars and the best of their generation.

Most of the people described in this book are partners of the wall and partners of life, and I owe them all a debt for taking me along, especially Paul Ramsden, Nick Lewis and Robert Steiner.

Some people are left unnamed in the book when a story was too important to omit (I couldn't bring myself to give you a new name), and some important stories and incidents have been left out. Some people don't wish notoriety of any sort, while others are only mentioned when it's unavoidable. This is the story of me, not them.

When writing this book I tried hard to make it an improvement over *Psychovertical*, not wanting it to be my 'difficult' second album. You need to write a book to know how it's done. Thanks to Ed Douglas for doing the edit, no small task, no matter how many times it had been through the spell checker. Ed scares me a bit because he has a super-powered brain (he'd make a good Bond or Superman baddy) and knows stuff about grammar and stuff. I lived in fear of reading his comments on the chapters he sent back for more work.

A big thanks go to John Coefield and Jon Barton at Vertebrate for taking on such a project during hard times in the book world, and for being so patient (it was only a year late!), as well as their designer Nathan for indulging my meddling with the front cover (it *is* better without the squiggles).

Thanks to my friend and ex RE teacher Rob Sanders for reading through my chapters as I wrote them, as well as Tim Maud, Chris Harle and many others for feedback (sorry it made you cry in the Adidas cafeteria Tim).

Thanks go out to all those cafes I've frequented over the last year. I guess for every page in this book a cup of tea was drunk.

I'd also like to thank all the people and companies that supported me through the adventures in this book, including: First Ascent, Patagonia, Black Diamond, Petzl, La Sportiva, the British Mountaineering Council, the Mount Everest Foundation, Outside and Snow+Rock, as well as Geoff Birtles and Ian Smith at High Magazine (another pair of very patient men), and my old boss Dick Turnbull.

Thanks to my Dad for reading the draft of the book, a hard read I know, but I hope you see it as much as a love letter (in a man-love way) as an indictment (I dissect my past out of interest, not to find fault).

Thanks to my kids Ella and Ewen for putting up with a dad who calls himself a writer (honestly writing *is* work) and for being inappropriate at times (you're not adopted). I hope when you grow up and read this book you won't judge me too harshly – like most adults I had no plan, and so just made it up as I went along.

And lastly, although she is noticeable by her absence in this book, my thanks go to Mandy. This book was written for her (even though she'll never read it, which is good, as she'd tell me it was sub sixth-form crap). I just wanted her to know it was never easy.

Preface

A few months ago I went to Switzerland for the launch of the German translation of my first book *Psychovertical*, a book that ends a few hours before this one begins. At the event, full of serious and academic types, an old white-haired Swiss lady came up to me and asked politely if I wasn't a little young to be writing my autobiography. The question really threw me, especially considering that *Psychovertical* ends when I'm still only twenty nine, with nearly ten years of stories of trips and climbs left to tell. She was intimidating in a teacher sort of way, and I daren't even tell her that it was only part one in a planned trilogy!

'Oh I think when you read his book you will see Andy has many stories to tell,' said Robert Steiner, the translator.

'But you are so young,' said the lady unconvinced. She looked as if she was in her late sixties and no doubt had many stories of her own to share.

'It's not an autobiography,' I said, laughing off her question, while feeling a bit embarrassed at the very idea, having never thought of it as such. 'It's just a story about a climber,' I said, trying to sound humble.

Still feeling a bit uneasy I was led into a huge hall filled with people, all waiting to hear me speak about my book. I'd been warned by Robert that they may give me a hard time, as Swiss-German people tend to view people like me – who seem not to hold their lives too dear – as a little crazy, and not in a good way.

I stood there on the stage, looking out at all these serious climbers, wondering what to say, how to explain myself, my book and my view on life.

'Hello,' I said, Robert translating as I spoke. 'My name is Andy Kirkpatrick. I am mentally ill.'

The stern serious audience broke into laughter. I was saved.

Psychovertical was a book about a man who is struggling: against the wall, against himself, but who wins through. The story a hundred thousand word answer to the question: '*Why do you climb?*'

Cold Wars asks a different question: '*What is the price?*'

Yosemite

June 2001

It had taken eleven days to reach the final pitch, the wall beneath my feet skyscraper high, every inch climbed by me alone. Every day had felt like it could be my last. Out of my depth but unable to back off, it had been just me against the wall – toe to toe. Now we were done, the summit a few metres away, just an overhanging roof for me to cross, an easy crack from which to dangle. The Reticent Wall, one of the world's hardest climbs, the climb of my life. And it was almost over.

The thought stuck in my head. 'The climb of my life.'

The wall had taken everything I had to give, and in doing so made me see everything I had to offer as a climber, as a human being. The wall became a mirror, and in it I saw my life in complete clarity. Up here, a low-achiever, a guy with no prospects, with a dead-end job and in a marriage that wasn't working, could really be somebody. Up here you could transcend the life you had. Once I got down, the world would see me differently. Maybe even I would be convinced.

I moved out to the crack, feet swinging, the two weeks spent up here still no antidote to the dizzying exposure. For ten years I had been pushing so hard, climbing in the Alps, Patagonia, Norway and here in Yosemite, consumed by a burning drive that seemed at odds with my character. The truth was I felt I had nothing to lose in a game with the highest stakes.

Halfway across the roof I allowed myself to look down and feel the waves of fear. All my heroes, the gods of climbing, had finished their climbs out across this very same feature. And as the fear swept across me, again and again, I knew what it meant to be superhuman.

'Hi. I'm down. I'm safe,' I said, standing at a phone booth in Yosemite Lodge, my legs still wobbly after the long descent from the summit of El Capitan, my feet throbbing from eleven days stood in slings. It was late evening in the UK. I could hear Ella in the background singing, home from nursery. I imagined Mandy sat on the stairs where the phone lived. I could see her sat with her hand on her pregnant belly, our second child inside.

'Did you do it?'

'Yes.'

'Do you feel better?'

'Yes.'

'Do you want to make a go of it?'

'Yes,' I said, trying not to cry.

It seemed I was brave enough to solo one of the hardest routes in the world, but was too scared to tell her no.

I sat in the Yosemite Lodge cafeteria, sunlight streaming through the windows, thick branches swaying in a slight breeze, their leaves brushing the glass. The big room was almost empty.

Dirty plates stood piled up beside me on the table from breakfast and lunch. I hadn't moved from this spot all morning, happy to just sit there, reading my book, looking at the trees and other people as they came and went.

I had never felt so much peace within me.

This time yesterday I was on the crux of the Reticent Wall.

I could so easily be a corpse now; being hauled up by the rescue team from the ledge I started from yesterday, smashed to bits, my story that of a climber who went crazy and tried to solo one of the most serious routes in the world, and how he came unstuck, overreaching, dying.

It was the only way such a story could be played out.

The route was beyond me.

But I didn't die.

I did it.

The leaves brushed against the glass. People laughed around me. I thought about the falls.

I thought about how much I wanted to back off.

I thought about how close I was to the edge.

I thought about the fear.

I knew I was going to die.

I wanted to die.

I did it.

I did it. I did it.

'It's the Kirkpatrick,' said a voice I recognized, and I turned to see Leo Houlding and Jason Pickles walking over to me. In their Hawaiian shirts, shorts and shades they looked like rock stars – which they are.

'Where you been?' asked Leo, one of Britain's best young rock climbers. Skinny and good-looking, Leo spent a few months every year out in the Valley climbing. He was someone who only lived the dream.

'Climbing,' I said.

'Well, I guessed that,' said Leo, rolling his eyes, his manner always assured. It was something you could forgive him for, as he was justified in his self-confidence, his skills as a climber touched by magic.

'Not much...' I said, preparing to tell them.

Leo interrupted. 'Well, me and Jason have just freed the West Face of Leaning Tower,' he said, pulling a catwalk face, no sign of the usual British reticence, his words like a challenge.

'I've just soloed the Reticent,' I replied, deadpan.

'Oh,' said Jason, looking at Leo with a smirk.

Leo's face was blank for a moment, as though awaiting confirmation it wasn't a joke.

'Well done that man,' he said finally, shaking me by the hand, a smile on his face.

'Good effort,' said Jason, the tension suddenly gone.

'Looks like you've lost lots of weight,' said Leo, poking me in the tummy with a finger.

'I'm the self of my former shadow,' I said, stealing a line from the great Mo Anthoine.

'Have you met Pep?' asked Leo, pointing over at the Table of the Gods, where all the superstars sat. 'You should talk to him. He did the Reticent with his girlfriend Silvia a while back.'

We walked over to a table I'd never dared approach before, everyone on it a face, the young superstars, tomorrow's heroes, and the legends, all sat chatting and laughing, oozing cool. These people had been places – in body and mind – that few can imagine.

'Everyone, this is Andy. He's just soloed the Reticent,' said Leo, his hand on my shoulder.

I felt embarrassed, knowing it would be impossible to excuse myself as they all turned to me, looking like Benny Hill.

'Hardcore dude,' said an old guy in sunglasses.

'Way to go,' echoed a younger guy wearing funny specs.

'Well done, Andy,' said a girl who looked about ten.

'Oh it was nothing really. Even Leo could have done it,' I said, sitting down at the top table for the first time.

'Pep. Andy. Andy. Pep,' said Leo, as I took my place next to a good-looking Spanish climber, a guy I knew a lot about already. Pep Masip was one of the stars of big-wall climbing.

'Andy, I have read some of your writings, it is a pleasure to meet you,' said Pep, shaking my hand. 'How was it?'

We talked about the route for a while, which pitches were the hardest, which were the most beautiful, where we thought the crux was.

'What have you got planned for this trip?' I asked, excited to hear what this hero was up to.

'I wanted to solo Native Son, but I changed my mind,' he replied, Native Son being a hard climb, but not as hard as the Reticent.

'Why did you come down?' I asked, thinking there must be some good reason.

'I changed my mind.'

'Changed your mind?'

'I'm just tired.'

Leo asked Pep about Amin Brakk, his last climb. The wall was in Pakistan and he'd climbed it with his girlfriend Silvia Vidal, one the best big-wall climbers around, and Miguel Puigdomenech, who had also been on Reticent with them. They had to share a portaledge. Halfway up the wall, Silvia and Pep had split up.

'Blimey!' said Leo, both of us trying to imagine how you could do that, and carry on.

'We had a lot on our minds, so it was not so hard,' he replied.

They had run out of food, underestimating the length of the wall, and climbed on starvation rations, their bodies consuming themselves until they reached the top, the descent taking a further two days. The route had taken thirty-four days to climb.

'It was not good,' said Pep, 'to take so much from your body. I have not been the same since.'

'Tell me, Andy, are you married?' asked Pep, changing the subject.

'Yes.'

'Do you have children?'

'Yes, I've got a daughter who's three, and another kid on the way,' I said.

'Is it hard to do such things as this when you have a wife and kids?' he asked.

'It's hard on Mandy, my wife. She always thinks I'm going to die.'

'She sounds like a clever woman, your wife,' said Pep with a smile. 'How many times did you nearly die on the Reticent?'

'Only once,' I said, thinking back to my hundred and fifty foot fall on the second hardest pitch, a fall that should have been terminal. 'Maybe twice,' I added, remembering the storm, when I almost froze to death. 'A couple of times,' I said, as more near misses came back to me.

Pep raised his eyebrows. He had a decade on me. He knew the score.

'It's not dying that is the problem,' he said. 'Climbing is like a lover, and your wife knows this. Whenever you are together, no matter how much you love your family, your thoughts are only of your lover, of climbing.'

The deer sprinted out of the woods. Spooked. Into the road. Impossible to miss. Car doing fifty. Mandy beside me, her bump showing. Ella in the back, asleep in the car seat.

I knew I would hit it – saw its giant eyes. It knew it too. We were both heading for disaster on the road to Scarborough.

Everything, as it always does, slowed down. No time for fear, no time to freeze. Foot off the accelerator, going for the brake, knowing it was too late, the bones in my foot still bruised from the wall, hands tightening on the wheel, strong from hauling, knowing that I had to hold our course, not lose it on the busy road, trucks and cars speeding towards us on the other side.

We were going to hit the deer.

We met. A blow. Deceleration. It was like pushing against a soft wall, like wet clay, the deer bending around the bonnet, a bag of meat and bone, the glass breaking, our bodies shooting forward and then the seatbelts snapping us back.

Mandy had screamed as my foot hit the brake – too late. The deer unwrapped itself from the bonnet in slow motion, spinning off, legs liquid, into the oncoming traffic, missing the cars and stopping on the edge of the road.

I held on.

The car slowed.

I held on. In control.

Pulling in, onto the grass verge, the cars behind slowed as drivers turned to see the deer.

We'd stopped.

'Are you okay, Mandy?' I said, looking at her, her pregnant belly proud of the seatbelt.

'Oh God I can't believe what's just happened,' she said, panicked.

'Are you okay?' I asked again.

'Yes… yes, I'm okay.'

I turned around to check Ella. She was still asleep.

'Stay in the car,' I said, and got out, the traffic now at a standstill, other people getting out, everyone walking over to the deer. I joined them, saw it lying in the dirt, tongue stuck out, its chest rising and falling. I waited for its last breath. Dying. Dead.

Walking back to the car I checked the damage. The front was bent, the lights on one side smashed. I opened up the bonnet and checked the engine, pulling out bits of bodywork that were getting in the way. It looked fine.

Getting back in, I asked Mandy again, 'Are you sure you're okay?' I put my hand on her bump.

'Yes. Are you?' she replied.

'I'm fine.'

I started the engine. It sounded all right. The traffic had begun moving again, a green Land Rover pulling in to where the deer lay, a man in wellies jumping out.

I pulled back out into the traffic, and drove on towards Scarborough. Mandy burst into tears.

'I can't believe how calm you are,' she said, sobbing. 'You're so calm.'

A few days ago I'd been on the crux of the Reticent Wall.

'What's going on dad?' said Ella, waking up.

I turned up for work on the Monday morning, and stood behind the counter selling boots, telling the story of my holiday to as many people who would listen. My feet were still sore from the wall, my hands still swollen and scabby. I yearned to be back there, away from mundane things. I had been transformed into something magnificent. Now I was normal again.

'What you been up to, youth?' asked a customer I'd known for a long time, once a hard man of the Himalaya, but now just coasting to a standstill. When I first met him he'd just returned from climbing Everest. I was nineteen. He was the first person I'd ever met who'd climbed it, and I shook his hand as though he were an astronaut. His handshake was steel, his body hard, and he had a wicked grin on his face. Back then.

Now his handshake was soft – like his body. His hair, once military smart, was unkempt, his clothes crumpled and baggy. There were stains on his shirt – dribbles of baby food. He was a mess. A shadow. Now I was the strong one. I told him about the Reticent and felt I was sticking a knife in him.

'I'm thinking of trying Latok with a couple of mates,' he told me. Latok being one of the world's plum hard summits, a route the very best had been trying to climb for decades.

I scanned his bloated face, his belly obvious even beneath the baggy shirt he wore to obscure it, presumably from himself as much as others. His kids were at school, but you could still feel the weight of them on him. He was deluding himself. He was over the hill at thirty-five. His feet wouldn't leave the ground again.

'Good luck with that,' I said.

'What about you?' he asked.

'Something dead hard,' I replied.

'I might give climbing up,' I said to Mandy as we sat beside the river. Ella paddled in the water, the sun casting shadows around us.

'That would be nice,' she replied flatly. 'Why do you say that?'

'I don't think I can keep it up,' I said.

'Me neither.'

I stood in the living room with Ewen, my baby son, born only twelve hours before, in my arms. Mandy slept upstairs.

I stood there and watched planes smashing into buildings and becoming flames, on that perfect September day. First one tower fell, then the other, live, on television. It was the first day in years when I didn't think once about climbing.

'I think I'm off,' I said to Dick, the best boss I'd ever had. My days of shop work were at an end. 'I'm going to make a go of it as a full-time climbing dude.'

'Can you afford to leave?' he asked, obviously concerned, more as a friend than a boss.

'With my talks, my magazine column and other stuff I can leave and just focus on climbing. Also, I think maybe I'm past my sell-by date working in a climbing shop,' I said. I loved working in Outside, loved working for Dick Turnbull and being with all my mates, cycling out to the Peak District every day. I never once didn't look forward to work. It was well paid, for a job in a shop, offered loads of holidays, paid and unpaid, and made my passion my job. Dick and his shop were cornerstones in the life I'd built for myself.

'I love working here, but I know that I have to leave,' I said.

'Why?' asked Dick.

'For one, I hate it when people say: "Are you still here?" Also, I'm too comfortable. I could stay here forever. You don't really get anywhere in life when you're happy.'

'It's up to you,' said Dick.

'Oh, and I've also just been approached by Snow and Rock about being sponsored by them,' I said, Snow and Rock being one of the bigger outdoor chains in Britain. 'It would look a bit odd to be sponsored by one shop, while working in another.'

'So this is your last day then?' said Dick.

'I guess so.'

As the music played, the coffin containing Mandy's grandfather slipped away through the curtains. She sat beside me in the front pew. I was holding her hand. She was crying. We hadn't held hands for a long time. These days it was one of Ella's hands in mine, and the other in Mandy's. It was Ella that joined us as a family.

We walked outside and stood amongst the graves as she tried to stop crying.

'What were you thinking when you saw his coffin?' she asked.

'That maybe the next time I went to a funeral it would be mine.'

'Me too.'

Dawn found us beneath Fallout Corner, a classic hard mixed route about three pitches long on a frosted-up crag in the Cairngorms. I was due to give a talk in Inverness that night to raise funds for the Torridon Mountain Rescue Team, and had asked Ian Parnell and my dad to come along.

I rarely saw my dad. My parents had split up when I was six, and I moved from Wales to Hull with my mum and brother and sister. My dad had his own life, and I suppose dads were different in the 1970s. Even so, he had left a huge hole that was never filled, only papered over. I never consciously hated him for it, and as I got older I began to understand better how a dad could not see his kids. I could see how a child can still love an absent parent; the love is deep within you. But now, with kids of my own, I found it harder to understand. Although, instead of pity for my younger self, I felt sorry for my father: it was Dad who really paid the price.

I pulled out my harness from my rucksack and noticed that it held the same pieces of gear, including a skyhook and several 'birdbeaks,' from the day I topped out on the Reticent Wall six months before.

Six months without any climbing at all.

'How hard's this route, young'un?' asked Dad.

'It's a grade six I think.'

I set off up the first pitch, Ian taking pictures while Dad belayed, looking a little as if he hadn't belayed anyone for a long time, standing in a mess of ropes in borrowed crampons.

'Do you want me to stop while you sort that out?' I called down to Dad, worried as I watched him pulling at a tangled puzzle of knots with no obvious sign he was actually belaying me.

'Oh, it's OK. Keep going, I'll sort it,' he said, head turned down in concentration.

I carried on, scraping and scratching above him, twisting the picks of my axes into cracks until they stuck, then pulling up and repeating, my calves feeling heavy and weak.

'You do know I haven't been winter climbing for ten years,' he shouted up to me.

'I feel the same,' I shouted back.

On my travels I'd met a lot of people who had met my dad Pete while he'd been in the Royal Air Force, either when he was a physical training instructor, or later as one of the longest-serving team leaders in the RAF Mountain Rescue. Each told stories about a man who always made an impression, generally a good one, even if he came across as a bit mad. Most tales would start: 'One day, me and your dad…' and go on to describe some major epic. One bloke I met told me about paddling across the Irish Sea with Dad in a double kayak, and how my father had turned up in just his running gear – without waterproofs or drysuit – and worse still with nothing to eat.

'I'll just have some of yours,' he'd said.

It also transpired, rather like with our climb in Scotland, that he hadn't paddled a kayak for a decade. They made it, but had to crawl on their hands and knees from their kayaks to the ferry booking office to find out when the next boat back to Holyhead was.

It took me many years to put my finger on just what it was about my dad – and in turn me – that created so many stories of epics and near-death incidents. In the end, I put it down to blind optimism. That's also why he was the perfect man to run a rescue team. He always believed victims could be saved.

Safe at the belay, Dad followed, climbing up below me, a grin of concentration across his face. To pull himself up, he hooked his axes into the gear, which, although not strictly ethical, was certainly effective. I thought it impressive that not having climbed for ten years, he was still happy to follow his son up a hard route. Dad had taught me to climb in the first place, leading me up the sweeping Idwal Slabs in Snowdonia. This was so long ago I couldn't remember it clearly. It had been a long time since we'd climbed together.

I suddenly realised he was my oldest climbing partner.

'That wasn't too bad,' he said, as I clipped him to the belay. The two of us looked up at the pitch above – a hanging slab, thin and scary-looking.

'Glad it's my eldest leading though,' he said, smiling.

Unlike me, my dad kept most of his stories to himself. I thought this was down to some kind of Yorkshire hard-man kind of thing, not being brash or showing off.

'Actually, I just can't remember anything,' he admitted.

Yet every now and again, a little story would pop out, often to my amazement. One such tale emerged when I was telling him about a piece I'd read by a guy who'd survived the Fastnet race tragedy in 1979, when fifteen sailors died in a storm. It was the largest maritime rescue operation since the war.

'Oh, I was caught up in that storm,' said my dad, as though he was talking about a brief shower. 'It was pretty bad. I was on a small sailing boat on a training trip from a joint services centre. We were in the same area and ran for safety to the Isle of Wight. But because so many others had done the same thing we ended up mooring beyond the harbour walls. During the night, the boat was moving up and down like crazy. Stupidly I went out to check an unusual noise on my own. It was pitch black and stuff was flying everywhere, and I ended up falling overboard. Worse thing was I fell between two boats, and I still have no idea how I didn't get squashed. Somehow I managed to pull myself back on board.'

I could picture him perfectly, staggering back down into the cabin, his mates jeering at him. 'Trust Kirkpatrick to fall in.'

It occurred to me on hearing the Fastnet story that my dad had not only taught me to climb. He also taught me how to have epics.

The pitch was delicate, moving up a steep wall, crampons balanced on horizontal breaks as I fiddled gear into cracks that were coated in a thin layer of ice. It was very slow going, as each two-second move would take ten minutes of thought, preparation and general fannying around.

'Have you seen the time?' Ian shouted from below, his tone indicating that he had, and that he suspected there wasn't enough left to finish. We had to be in Inverness by seven. I had a talk to do.

Ian's partners, as being one of the few people daft enough to climb with me, and we'd done a few trips to France ice climbing. Things came to a head when we tried something hard, the Maria Callas Memorial route on the North Face of Les Droites. It was winter, and the route awaited a second ascent. The Maria Callas was state of the art and I was hungry to try the hardest route I could. Most good climbers know their place, and would not dream of trying such a route. Not me. I was an upstart – and so was Ian. In a way we were both outsiders, neither having done a traditional apprenticeship, and that's why we got on. When we climbed with proper climbers our ignorance shone through.

What compounded our choice of route that winter were the terrible conditions in the mountains, with tons of snow and high winds bringing a death a day. The low point for us was the death of Jamie Fisher, and the near death of Jamie Andrew, who would have both hands and feet amputated after surviving a week near the summit of Les Droites. It made no difference what had happened; it simply had no effect on me. I didn't know Jamie, and neither did the mountain. I felt indifferent, as we walked all the way up from the valley, since the cable car was shut down, ignoring the risk, just fixated on the summit.

We started in the middle of the night but progress was poor up the bottom of the face. I thought Ian was climbing too slowly, coughing and wheezing as he went. He was too weak, and because of him I knew we were going to fail.

I hated him. I hated him for being posh. I hated him for having so much time, and how for him failure meant nothing. He had another month here in the Alps after I went home. For me, this was it. I hated him for being weak because I knew how weak I was, and hoped he could carry me up the face with him.

I caught him up as he stopped, and asked him blankly what the problem was.

'I don't feel well Andy,' he said, coughing.

'That's fucking winter alpine climbing,' I spat back, only to catch myself, realising where I was, and with whom: a dangerous face; a friend who expected nothing from me.

We went down but something was broken. I'd had high ambitions for our partnership, but after that it was dead, for the short term at least. Instead I just watched – green with envy – as he went on to put up the kinds of routes I coveted, in Alaska, Greenland and the Himalaya. It was what I deserved.

Rushing down from Fallout Corner, we made it back to the car as it grew dark and since we barely had time to make the gig, we just piled in and drove off without changing from our climbing gear. Then I realised I'd neglected to ask exactly where the talk was being held, only that it was somewhere in Inverness. We made it to the talk, and only half an hour late, and I did the first part dressed in all my climbing gear, changing into my jeans in the toilet for the second half. I think some people thought my costume was part of the show, and seeing as all the proceeds went to the mountain rescue team, no one was too unhappy.

That night we drove back towards the Cairngorms, eating fish and chips as I drove, my dad in the front, Ian in the back listening on his iPod to what sounded like someone doing DIY, his music tastes always eclectic.

'Do you think it went well tonight?' Dad asked.

'Yes, I thought it was okay. Did you?' I suddenly wondered if my performance had been below par.

'I always think it's good. You're my son,' he replied, an uncomfortable silence building until I laughed his affection off.

'What is the most you would like to make from doing talks,' he asked, knowing that I already charged around three hundred quid.

'A thousand pounds?' I replied. 'Yes, a grand, that would be great, although I'd probably be happy to talk for free. Getting paid is just a bonus.'

'Well, if you're ever going to get that much money, then you have to make sure you're worth a thousand pounds.'

I guessed it was his way of telling me to pull my finger out, dress properly – not in climbing gear – and find out where the venue was. It was a suggestion I wouldn't forget. You can *seem* shambolic and crap, and it's funny, but if you can't change, or at least conceal it, then no one would ever take you seriously. Being taken seriously was what I wanted more than anything. I knew he was right, but I felt a little defensive, thinking that he was just as much of a fuck-up as me.

Someone my dad worked with once told me a story about his team getting called out for a crashed jet. Its fuselage lay intact in a field and the team set up a cordon so no one could approach the wreckage until crash investigators could be flown up there. It was a big deal. The investigators had a huge responsibility to check for anything that might explain why the aircraft had come down. When they turned up, my dad, as team leader, escorted them to the site and then moved aside to let them begin their investigation. After a while there seemed to be a bit of a commotion. Dad was called over, the experts standing and rubbing their chins while perusing a metal cylinder about four inches high and three inches wide, balanced on top of a piece of the fuselage. They were clueless as to what it was, and wondering if it had any bearing on the crash.

'Do you know what this is flight sergeant?' they asked my dad.

'Oh, I'm sorry,' he said. 'It's the lid off my flask.'

That night, not wanting to sleep in the drizzle in a car park, we dossed with a friend of Dad's from his RAF days, a guy called Tom Jones, who although not being *the* Tom Jones, was just about as loud and full of life – and Welsh. We sat in his kitchen drinking tea and talking, more stories coming out about my dad, including him getting hit on the head by a rock in the Dolomites, and how, on seeing the state of him, with blood pouring from the wound, his partner had fainted on the belay, and my dad had to look after him instead.

Tom's son had been in a bad car crash and suffered a brain injury, leaving him partly paralysed down one side of his body. As a former physical training instructor like my dad, Tom had decided he had to keep his son active, and so bought a tandem. He fixed his son's paralysed foot to the pedal, and the pair went off on epic bike journeys. 'The one thing you have to do, when you stop, is put your foot down on the right side, otherwise he'll just face plant,' said Tom, laughing.

Sitting there in Tom's warm kitchen, listening to the stories, I felt like my father's son, especially as most of their tales turned on how my dad would make some fuck-up, then save the day by his willingness to not accept the fact that he was screwed. Next morning we headed back up to Fallout Corner but a warm front had passed through during the night, and our climb had defrosted, the ropes hanging lank and damp. The only thing to do was climb up them, get the gear, and abseil off. We drove south that night – the chances for winter climbing being zero – dropping Dad off in the Lakes, where he worked.

The roads were quiet as we continued on to Sheffield, and we talked non-stop, more to stay awake than for conversation.

'What you got planned next year?' I asked Ian, although not wanting to suffer the envy of knowing.

'I'm off to Alaska with Kenton Cool in the spring, and the Himalaya in the autumn. What about you?'

'I've started to think about going to Chamonix and trying to solo the Lafaille route on the Dru,' I said sheepishly, ready to rein back on my boast with a dismissive remark.

Ian nodded his head as if to prove he understood the gravity of what I had planned, while pulling the type of face that signified I had an evens chance of dying in the undertaking – to attempt a second ascent solo of the hardest wall in Europe. But I knew I had climbed harder routes in Yosemite, and that technically I could match Lafaille, the best all-round climber in the world, on that route at least. What I didn't know was if I had the balls to hang out on a frozen face for a week or two.

'I'm not sure about soloing though, it's just an idea,' I added. 'It would be much better to do it as a pair.'

'I'd be up for it,' said Ian.

And that was it.

ONE

Dru

February 2002

'Deux... tickets... to... la... summit. Un way,' Ian said slowly to the woman behind the thick glass. She looked confused. 'Un way,' he repeated, pointing up with his forefinger, towards some imagined summit in the sky. 'One... way... We go to climb the Dru.'

The woman sighed at his poor grasp of French and shook her head slowly, as only a French ticket woman who has spent a lifetime listening to her language being abused can. She waited for him to have another go, but thankfully he said no more. They both looked at each other. Ian pointed up again, which was really of no help, as most people at the bottom of a cable car in a ski resort want to go up not down.

Losing patience, as the queue built up behind him, she gave an unhappy slow shake of her head, pressed some unseen button, and two small tickets appeared. Ian grabbed them: 'Mercy!'

'That's the hardest part over with,' I said as he walked back, tickets in hand, and we hoisted our huge haul-bags onto our backs, each weighing almost as much as we did, making us stand out among the bustle of early morning skiers.

'I hope not,' said Ian.

The Lafaille route was perhaps the biggest available objective in Europe at the time, said to be the hardest big route on its hardest big wall – the Petit Dru's West Face. There were plenty of other hard climbs around, to repeat or put up, but the great thing about the Lafaille for us was none could be done so relatively cheaply, with Chamonix being only a day's drive from home an important consideration.

Jean-Christophe Lafaille, France's premier mountaineer, had finished the route the previous winter, pieced together both with partners and alone up the blankest section of the wall, a grey skyscraper towering over the Chamonix valley. He started off on the bottom section climbing with others, before continuing solo as the project dragged on, finally completing it over nine days. The final push had been made under the gaze of the media, with helicopters flying overhead. Lafaille was a poster-boy for French alpinism, a mystical figure – a survivor – and the French press followed his career closely. The route ended with a dash to the summit as a storm closed in, an added urgency being the fact his wife was expecting a baby. Once down he declared his new creation to be perhaps the hardest big-wall route in Europe, daft really, seeing as he hadn't done all the others. But since this was Lafaille speaking, most people took his words to mean that even if it weren't the hardest, it would be very hard indeed.

Most hard routes in the Alps wait many years, sometimes decades for a second ascent, the mystique of the hard men, or man, who climbed them too much for most to overcome. Most climbers view those at the forefront of alpinism as being superhuman, and it takes a long time to build up the group confidence necessary to attempt to follow in their footsteps. It's often young tigers, looking to build a reputation, that repeat the biggest climbs, rather than established heroes, who fear failure on their rivals' routes more than death itself.

Yet once a climb is repeated, there is invariably a rush to make further ascents. The mystique is gone. Overnight, a climb can go from something that is only whispered about, a project that everyone imagines doing sometime, to being a trade route, guided, soloed and diminished in the minds of all, with that god of a climber suffering the same fate.

We too were young tigers of a sort, eager to make a mark, and overcoming such a route was more than just an act of climbing. Like most such efforts it was a statement. Chamonix contained the highest proportion of top alpinists on the planet and for me and Ian – two nobodies – to get the second ascent would be quite something.

Shuffling through the echoing concrete corridor in a long queue of skiers towards the cable car, my shoulders ached under the huge load of gear. My haul-bag was bigger than a dustbin. I made a mental checklist of everything we needed to climb tomorrow: bivouac kit, climbing gear, ten days' food, fuel and portaledge. The one thing we didn't have was a first-aid kit. Such things always seemed a little defeatist.

I knew getting to the bottom of the face would be a nightmare with this kind of load; a real exercise in toil, made worse by the fact this was our second trip up, and we knew just what we were in for. Nevertheless the weight on my back felt great. It meant I was doing something positive towards something amazing.

A few days before, we'd taken the same route with equally heavy loads: up the cable car to the top of the Grands Montets, a peak that stands beside the Dru down which people ski to the valley. From there it was a short traverse to a band of cliffs, which we descended to the Nant Blanc Glacier. Crossing that put us at the bottom of the Dru. Only in the Alps could you walk *downhill* to your mountaineering objective.

On that first trip it hadn't seemed quite as easy as it sounds. We found ourselves trawling through deep snow and around big crevasses before we could dump our loads in a rock cave close to the bottom of the face. Each step was made worse from knowing we'd have to make it again in a few days' time. It had been dark and growing cold as we stashed our gear, and I'd been glad not to be setting off just yet. Going down for a few more days would help top up my psyche for the toughest challenge of my life. In winter, everything takes twice as long and requires ten times more energy, and so, on that first trip, it had been two in the morning by the time we made it back to Chamonix. Just getting our gear to the foot of the mountain had felt like a route. It was clear why it had taken Lafaille so long to complete his climb.

The cable car door slid open and people began to file in, the guard giving us puzzled looks, having seen us heading up with the same sized load only two days before. I assumed such people were used to seeing climbers doing the oddest things in the Alps, a playground for the unhinged.

The door shut and we began to ascend, the tiny cabin filled with excited voices, everyone looking forward to the coming day's skiing, the quality of the powder, which lines were 'in', who was doing what. Ian and I kept quiet, staring out of the scratched plastic window and bracing ourselves for the hard work to come.

For some reason I had no sense of fear about the climb, which was unusual. I felt instead a calm confidence that I had the skills, the gear, and the partner to do it. Like climbing El Capitan this route would be brought down by a thousand little cuts, not a single blow. Some would have said the route was out of our league. If you wrote up a list of heavy hitters who should have been trying to make this second ascent – professional climbers and guides living in the mountain's shadow – we'd be several hundred entries down. Yet here we were.

Success sometimes comes down to just giving things a try.

I thought back to Ian's assertion that I was the most ambitious climber he'd met, and that he must have been right, and that maybe instead of feeling embarrassed about it, I should embrace it and accept it was true.

The cable car reached the halfway station and we piled out, half the skiers shuffling out to the slopes, the other half queuing again to go up to the top, where only the best skiers dared to venture. A gentle wind permeated the building as we took our place within a maze of steel barriers, like cattle in a slaughterhouse, waiting for our turn to go. It was nothing more than a breeze, yet it cut into us, everyone zipping up their jackets and pulling down their hats. I wondered how much colder it would be 'up there,' how this would seem tropical on the wall.

Ian took shots with his heavy Nikon, looking like someone's dad with his glasses falling down his nose, not your typical super-alpinist, except maybe a British one. I doubt there had ever been a less cool climbing team. Neither of us looked ripped or skinny. We're both short-sighted and everything we wore, no matter how expensive, became lumpy and dishevelled. Ian looked like a tramp. I looked like a garbage man.

On our first trip up, Ian had me model some clothes for a catalogue he was illustrating, trying to kill two birds with one stone. The problem was I was too fat, and nothing fitted, requiring him to find angles which hid zippers that couldn't be shut and seams that were fit to burst. I was always envious of climbers who looked like climbers, who looked the part, irrespective of whether they could climb or not. I'd probably be just as happy looking like a good climber than actually being one. Maybe what I really wanted was a life that gave you that kind of body, a life of just climbing, to become a thoroughbred of rock and ice, rather than a donkey, useful enough, but stubborn and plodding.

The queue jostled forward and we entered the upper cable car. Inside it was quieter now, many of the skiers psyching themselves up for some hard runs, the odd one or two with axes strapped to their packs, heading down to the Argentière glacier to climb, to tick off a route that day and be back home for supper. There is nothing more satisfying than climbing a big route and reaching the pub that evening. Especially in winter when no one wants to spend the night out, because of the obvious misery, and the need to carry lots of extra kit. Seeing them standing there, comparing their tiny daypacks with our gigantic haul-bags, I thought about the reality of spending so long on a winter wall, hauling up everything we needed to survive, sleeping in our folding portaledge with nothing more substantial between us and the Arctic cold than a sheet of nylon.

Most climbs are completed at speed to avoid exposure to the elements, but on a big wall it generally comes down to grinding it out, literally inch by inch, one hard pitch potentially taking as long as a thousand metres on a mixed face. I'd never spent that long in such harsh conditions. How would I cope? Could my fingers survive climbing such a technical route in the cold? Would we be able to remain strong partners? All I knew was that if others had done so, then so could I.

The cable car lifted out of the mid station, out over the glistening pistes dotted with skiers, and up towards the summit of the Grands Montets, the top station looking like a Bond villain's lair. I thought back to a story an engineer told us in the station one winter, about being trapped there for a week in a huge storm, and how the roof blew off. They hid deep inside the building's bunker-like foundations, only daring to venture into the upper levels to piss out of the door. I guessed such storms were rare, but wondered how our tiny folding portaledge would cope, its narrow alloy tubing and nylon our only hiding place on the wall.

The Alps opened up before me as we rose. Watching familiar landmarks float by beneath, nose pressed against the plexiglass window, I thought about all those fruitless trips taken in this very same aluminium cabin, a space soaked in the ambition of so many, my own often ending in nothing more glorious than a slow stagger back down to the valley. But then there were times when my ambition had been realised. It seemed so long ago though – a lifetime. What was it that kept me coming back, and trying harder and harder climbs? Why not just come and enjoy it, climb those day routes, learn to ski and make climbing fun?

The cabin slid between the steel arms of the top station, the doors slid open for the last time, the passengers clattering out, their clunky ski boots dully bashing their way down more concrete corridors and out into the dazzling light. Standing on the viewing platform, they gasped as they took in the view, breathing air so cold it stung.

The Dru came into focus, a tower of rock, sharp and forbidding, its North Face almost black, the only detail picked out by a spider's web of ice. The West Face lay on the other side, a grey canvas of walls and slabs, scarred by rock falls, many so big they created mini-earthquakes that made needles jitter on distant seismographs. When you told people you were going to climb the Dru they invariably asked if it was still standing.

The Dru had captivated me from the very start of my climbing career, and only a decade ago I'd stood on a frozen street in Chamonix, a proto-alpinist with zero experience, and gazed up at it, that grey tower block, in the cold light of dawn, wondering what it would take to climb such a thing in winter. Now I knew, having climbed it once before via the Dru Couloir. The route took two tough days, and the answer to my question was simple:

it took everything. Imagining myself back then, standing in the street without a clue that one day I'd be back to try the Dru's hardest route in winter, seemed outlandish. It had taken more than just a leap of faith, but a leap of reason too. I marvelled at what life could bring you. That alone seemed reason enough to try what seemed impossible. Climbing is not about winning, or reaching the summit. If it were, no one would climb. It's about having the self-belief to try.

The skiers descended awkwardly down a flight of metal stairs and began clipping on skis for the descent, while we walked up to the high viewing platform to take a few last pictures, and put off the grim walk for a few more minutes. We only had to reach the bottom of the Dru that day. There was no rush.

Walking up the stairs I could feel my heart beating faster from the altitude, leaving me breathless at the top. The Argentière glacier spread out below us. I looked over at the North Face of Les Droites, tracing the kilometre-high face, which I'd soloed a few years before, and its twelve hundred metre Northeast Spur, my second winter alpine route. Each was like a test, the solo teaching me the value of self-belief – *you won't fall* – the Spur illustrating the value of simply being stubborn and not giving in – *you WILL make it* – climbing the route over four days with a broken stove, and consequently almost no food or water. I imagined all the climbs that led up to this one, climbs in the Alps, Patagonia and Yosemite, each teaching me another lesson. The Lafaille felt like the final test, but experience showed it would slip in along with all the rest, just another step towards something I couldn't see yet, just over the horizon.

'Right. Let's go,' said Ian, and down he went, boots clanking on the metalwork, while I followed. We picked up our haul-bags and our old tracks leading to the Dru.

The route down involved dragging ourselves through deep powder to the edge of some high cliffs, then climbing and abseiling down these to a jumbled glacier. With a normal rucksack it would have been a simple walk, but with our monstrous bags the whole thing was an act of endurance, each little way-mark – the first abseil, reaching the glacier, the toe of the Nant Blanc Face – an objective in itself. The trip was too exhausting to comprehend as a whole, but each chunk put us closer to our goal.

Crevasses on the glacier dwarfed us as we took turns ploughing our route towards the Dru, following our old tracks mostly. Mindful of the extra weight in our haul-bags, we shuffled along unsure if we were on solid ground or some slender snow bridge. The bags, which we'd haul up behind us on the wall as our life-support system, were made from slick vinyl fabric, designed to slide up walls without catching. But if you fell on snow you'd take off like a rocket, strapped to your very own bobsled.

Both of us wore plastic snowshoes, but instead of allowing us to float on top of the snow, they simply tripped us up, designed more for gentle rambles through the woods than hardcore alpinism. Luckily for me, Ian was the only one to fall down a crevasse, saved by his bag wedging in the hole. At last we waddled down to our cache hidden in a jumble of boulders, the Dru soaring above our heads, the West Face lit up by the setting sun.

'Want another brew?' Ian asked. He sat up stiffly in his sleeping bag, like a vampire emerging from its coffin, his head bent sideways to avoid banging it on the roof of our cave, heavy flakes of snow drifting past outside.

'I wouldn't say no,' I replied, lying with my head just out of the way of the snow, which had been falling for two days.

The weather was becoming a problem, since each day we waited in our cave we ate up more of our supplies, food we'd busted a gut to haul to the mountain. We knew that Chamonix, with its food and entertainment, was only a few hours' walk down the hill, a tempting option after two days of nothing but tea and roof staring. But going down and coming back would also use up our most precious commodity of all – time. Not to mention having to do the hellish walk in all over again. By sitting put we could get on the route, only a hundred yards from our cave, the moment the snow stopped. Assuming it did.

Filling up a pan with snow I passed it to Ian and he stuck it onto the stove.

Lying there, you could just make out the base of the Dru's battlements, its height drifting up and up, until the snowflakes grew too thick and barred our view of what lay above. I thought how this waiting period could prove valuable, the Dru growing used to us, and us to it. The space we inhabited was utterly silent, nothing but the sound of yourself, the rustle of clothing moving, the beating of your heart, the boiling of tea.

'Here you go,' said Ian, passing over my metal mug, the tea inside almost transparent, the teabag the same used the last two times, the milk on ration. 'At least it's warm and wet,' he said apologetically.

'Like a good woman,' I added.

Ian groaned.

Ian was easy company, undemanding, not hyper through inactivity, more sloth-like, like me – fleecy and cuddly, but in a manly way. He never had a sense of urgency about him, always relaxed and calm until he started to climb. He was like no climber I'd ever met. I guess he thought the same about me. His biggest asset seemed to be a lack of any fear whatsoever. He could climb like a man who had nothing to live for, and although there were many climbers better than him, he topped the rankings purely due to the fact that – from the outside, at least – he had what looked like a death wish. Unlike some climbers who climb with grace and confidence, balletic footwork or Herculean strength, Ian climbed like someone who believed the gods were on his side, no matter what. I often imagined that he was so successful because he tricked the mountains he climbed, this shabby looking tramp racing up the walls before the rock had a chance to take guard. I also really liked him as a friend. Ian was one of the few people I knew outside of climbing.

The topic of Lafaille came up, the man in whose shadow we well and truly stood, whose every move we planned to follow. He was a legend, and it was easy to see why so many climbers viewed him as one of the best climbers in the world, pushing each climbing discipline – rock, ice, alpine, and Himalayan – as he rose in the sport. He had begun like many of us, just rock climbing on his local crag, only he was much stronger – albeit shorter – than most. In a few short years he reached the forefront of sport climbing, the safest discipline, clipping lines of bolts as he reached the very highest standards. Lafaille had climbed one of the world's first sport routes graded 8c, and soloed routes of 8a. Most climbers would have been content with that. Instead he took up alpine climbing. In only a few short years he was soloing the hardest faces in the Alps, following in a tradition of many great French climbers, putting up new routes and pushing the boundaries of his new discipline, establishing himself as a star not confined to safe, sunny cliffs. He was seen as a great new talent, and was asked to attempt a new route on the South Face of Annapurna in Nepal with Pierre Béghin, France's premier Himalayan climber.

Lafaille was twenty-seven, Béghin forty-one, their objective a new line climbed alpine-style on one of the world's biggest faces. The climbing was extremely hard, and for four days they moved up the wall, one night spent hanging in their harnesses, until bad weather stopped them close to the top. With no option but to descend, Béghin set up an anchor, a single cam in a crack, and set off down. The cam ripped, and Béghin fell two thousand metres to his death. Lafaille watched as he saw his partner fall, knowing that he too was in all likelihood dead, since Béghin had taken both ropes and all their hardware with him. Lafaille was alone, in the swirling cloud, standing on a tiny ledge, as alone as one human being can be. It seemed a death sentence. But with no other option, and a wife and child waiting at home, Lafaille had to try. He took some thin cord from his harness and tied himself to his ice axe, so if he slipped it might stop him. Then he started down.

Climbing down seventy-five degree ice, he reached their tent, and a stash of gear that included twenty metres of thin rope. This Lafaille used to abseil down the steepest sections below, cutting up the tent's poles to use as anchors. The distance he abseiled each time was tiny compared to the scale of the wall, and the risk unjustifiable to anyone but a man who was already dead. But despite all that, he kept his faith that somehow he might survive.

During the second day of his retreat, as though things weren't bad enough, a rock spun down from above, striking his forearm and snapping both bones. Reeling from pain, he cut away his jacket as his arm swelled. Lafaille was now a thousand metres from the base of the climb. Knowing he could go no further, and believing others would come to rescue him, he waited for two days on a small ledge, watching the flash bulbs from trekkers' cameras each night.

Yet no one came. At nightfall on the day after his accident, Lafaille took his life back into his own hands, and began climbing down again, using his one good arm and relying on moonlight to find his way. Five days after Béghin's death he reached base camp, amazing a Slovenian team, who had reported him dead. Lafaille's wife Véronique had already been told the news.

'How could you climb after that?' I asked Ian. 'How could you journey so far into your own death, like a dead man climbing, come through it, only to go back for more?'

'Maybe climbing's worth it?' said Ian, taking a sip of his tea. 'Why are we sat under this rock, ready to follow that same man up his hardest alpine route? I don't think we're so different. On the Reticent you must have thought you were going to die didn't you?'

'A few times,' I said, nodding.

'But when you didn't, what did you do?'

'I kept on climbing, but then I was trapped, it was all I could do, I had to keep going. Once you get back to the real world you have a choice,'

'You could always have stopped on the Reticent, but you just didn't want to,' said Ian.

I drank down the tea, leaving the last gritty dregs, then laid back again and contemplated the act of climbing.

'It seems so simple when you're doing it doesn't it' I said. 'And yet we seem to always be looking for an excuse.' Ian said nothing, and I wondered if it was only me who was looking for an explanation.

Outside, the snow fell.

Climbing up the corner, I bridged out, crampons scraping and scratching, the rope pulling hard at my waist, causing me to curse my poor choice of gear placements below. It would soon be dark, and I seemed stuck, too much drag keeping me from making it easy. It was our second day of climbing, the bad weather having cleared the previous afternoon, but tonight would be the first sleeping on the face.

I tried to move up, and force the rope to follow, but it wouldn't budge. Down below I'd obviously done a bad job of extending a piece of gear – or several, since the pitch started with aid, but ended with free climbing in crampons. I forced out a few inches, calves burning, with no place to rest, then holding on with one hand, pulled the rope up with all my strength, holding what I'd gained in my teeth as I reached down again. In this way I gained a few metres of rope and holding a huge loop of slack in my mouth, moved up and reached a sloping ledge.

'Safe!' I shouted down, the sky growing dark, night almost on us. Scrabbling to find some gear for a solid belay, I ended up with nothing I really trusted, a crap peg, a sling on a dubious spike of rock, some cams wedged between two wobbly blocks, nothing great, but with so much drag I couldn't do anything else. I just had to hope it would take Ian's weight and the much greater load of two haul-bags without ripping out.

I clipped a long sling through everything, drew it to a single point and tied a figure of eight knot, clipping the haul-line into it via our locking pulley.

'WILL BELAY HERE AND HAUL,' I shouted to Ian. 'YOU JUG WITH BAGS TO STOP JAMMING!' A tiny yell back suggested he had understood.

The weight of the bags slowly came on to the belay as Ian lowered them from his, the slings growing tight as they took the strain, the pulley creaking. Nothing ripped out.

I started hauling – exhausting work – the tiny pulley too small for such a load. We'd left the big one at home because it was deemed too heavy. Now it felt as if I was pulling a car uphill, a car with flat tyres, and a hill covered in speed bumps. I hauled in the darkness, the rope only slipping through the pulley a few inches at a time, every inch a mile it seemed to me.

Stooping for a rest, I peered down, hoping to see the bags in the beam of my headtorch, but saw only the white static rope disappearing into the dark, knowing they would not appear until I'd given up looking for them.

On I hauled, my waist hurting from the strain, wishing that Ian would hurry and help me, that with so far to haul this climb would set new standards of pain. On the Reticent Wall a few months before, my bags had weighed in at over a hundred and fifty kilos, but they were a doddle compared to this.

The rope lurched, and the load seemed to lighten, but then I heard a thunderous bang as something heavy crashed down the face. The bags had clearly been hung up on something that was now at the bottom of the face, something big and heavy.

'Ian? You okay?'

I got no answer so just kept on hauling.

Ian appeared, and jugged up to the belay, looking hot and flustered. He stepped past me and began pulling at the rope.

'The bags are still a long way down. I'll pull while you counterbalance them on the end of the haul-line,' he said.

Using me as a counterweight, Ian pulled the rope, clipping his jumar close to the pulley, while I slowly dropped downwards, foot by foot, as the load lifted. Sometimes being a fat knacker has its benefits.

As I descended, I pulled up on the live rope, the rope coming up from the bags, expending all the energy I had to get the bags to where we needed them, until with a jolt I stopped moving down, my own rope coming tight to the belay. I'd jug back up and start again. All the while there was the discomfort of knowing we were putting a huge strain on a belay I didn't trust in the first place; the only consolation being that at least if it held we'd know it was sound enough to sleep on.

At last the bags appeared, one huge, the other just big with the portaledge attached to it. The portaledge unpacked to the size of a large tabletop and was inevitably harder to set up when tired. We grumbled away at each other while trying to get the tubing slotted together, both just wanting to crash out after a long day. Finally, with the ledge set and our nylon bed taut, we fed it into the expedition flysheet, made from heavy-duty fabric and designed to totally enclose the ledge and keep us out of even the worst storms.

Ian leant against the belay as I took control. It was my bloody ledge. 'You've got it upside down,' Ian said. I pulled the ledge out, flipped it over and tried to insert it again. 'Now it's the wrong way round,' he said wearily, sounding like my old driving instructor, notifying me of my errors without telling me how to correct them. 'You bloody do it,' I snapped, shoving the ledge towards him, clearly beyond this simple task. Ignoring my childishness Ian held the ledge, telling me to hang onto my end, before slipping the bed in without any more fuss. 'You get in and I'll pass you the stuff from the haul-bag.'

The portaledge was pitched at a poor angle, leaving less room than normal, which wasn't much anyway. The thing was designed more for vertical walls than mountainsides. Nevertheless, with the stove purring and snug inside two sleeping bags, I felt calm return, that sense of being on top of things, rather than them being on top of me.

'Sorry for shouting,' I said, as Ian measured out a few spoons of hot chocolate.

I pulled out the night's food bag, containing: one small bag of nuts to share; one packet of couscous to share; a small packet of butter each; one instant soup and two hundred-gram bags of muesli for breakfast. It had seemed like enough when packing in the valley, but now it didn't seem quite up to our hunger.

'We should get to the big snow terrace tomorrow,' said Ian, warming his hands against the stove, snow melting for tea. 'From there the climbing should get more interesting, and a lot steeper, which should make hauling better.' Having so much stuff seemed to increase the work load and slow us to a snail's pace, but it also gave us the confidence and ability to hang out if things got rough. It was easy to see why it had taken Lafaille so long.

Someone had described this kind of climbing as having a 'guaranteed outcome', and it was sort of true, but that guarantee came from the vastly higher workload you took on, something I doubted many would want to tolerate. So far, the best job was to lead, as belaying was long, cold and tedious. Hauling was an exercise in slow, exhausting torture by haul-bag. The best thing about this kind of climbing, compared to racing up a face with a tiny rucksack and a handful of food, was the sense of engaging in a long, hard-fought battle with the climb, a war of attrition and logistics, rather than gymnastics. I had no doubt that in the week, or weeks to come, our resolve was going to be tested. It was this that I looked forward to the most.

We reached the big snow terrace late in the day, time slipping through our fingers yet again. Night was at our heels. I kicked up the slope to the belay getting my first sense of the wall above. It had seemed steep on the two hundred and fifty metres of rock below, but the face really did tower up above us now, plumb vertical and overhanging in places. I thought about how intimidating it would look to any climber, and wondered if Lafaille had soloed it because no one else would climb with him. It was hard to make out where his route went, but there was certainly a great deal of blank sections, up which a climber might knock out a very hard line. The thought of being up there made me giggle with excitement.

I reached the base of the wall, the bags hanging fifty metres below at the edge of the slope, set up a solid belay, fed the haul-line through the pulley, and shouted for Ian to lower them out, just as we had all the way up so far. The pulley took the strain. Looking down and holding the rope, I began walking back down the mountain, pulling the bags through the pulley, the rope locking when I stopped, the mass of luggage sliding up nicely on the slick snow.

I felt a sense of pride in my work, of being competent at this art of big-wall climbing and the meshing of so many skills. We could set up a nice little bivy here and really get to grips with the climbing above tomorrow. The climbing below hadn't been really hard, but it had helped iron out a few problems that could have proved disastrous above. Now we were on our way.

Ian appeared at the lip, and took his time sorting out the rack, seeing that the hauling was all in hand. The bags slid up until they were halfway to me, when they suddenly stopped dead. Looking down I saw they were hung up on a spike of rock, and so I pulled harder, straining with my legs while pulling up with the rope. I'd had the top bag the longest, having been up El Cap with it ten times, the only sign of damage the worn stitching, while the bag attached below was pretty new, and held all our bivouac gear and the precious stove. One or both of them was stuck, and so I jerked my body, hoping they would pop off the rock, not wanting to have to climb down and do it myself.

They remained stuck.

'Ian?' I shouted down. 'Can you sort out the bags?' He was fiddling with his camera now.

'In a minute,' Ian shouted back, lifting the Nikon to his eye and capturing the wall above in the beautiful glow of evening light.

I stood impatiently, wanting to get the ledge sorted before dark.

'I'll do it,' I said, untying and clipping into the haul-line, sure I wouldn't fall off, then climbing down to the bags, grabbing the top one and pulling it hard. It remained stuck. I pulled harder. The top one weighed close to fifty kilos, the bottom one half as much, with the portaledge in its own bag attached to it. I pulled again, only very hard. There was a ripping sound of very worn stitching giving up the ghost. To my horror and disbelief I watched the bottom bag and the ledge slide away towards the edge.

For a moment I thought that perhaps they might get stuck on something and be saved. After all, the bastards had become stuck every other time they moved. But no, this time they seemed to welcome the activity. The bag and portaledge swept down the slope, shot over the edge and fell, silently, all the way to the bottom of the face.

Ian looked up at me with tears in his eyes. All our hard work, the climbing, two walk-ins, all of it was for nothing. The portaledge was destroyed, all our bivy gear gone, darkness now all but upon us.

'Don't worry,' I said. 'It's not as bad as it looks.'

'No,' I shouted back, wanting to add how it was hard to look at your watch when you were clinging to the rock for your life. 'But I think we've got time,' I added with typical Kirkpatrick optimism.

'I don't think you have,' he shouted back, his tone now authoritative, even dictatorial, like a teacher explaining something to a misbehaving pupil: 'It'll take an hour to get down, and an hour to drive to Inverness and it's nearly four now.'

'Oh,' I said, looking down at the two of them between my legs.

My dad just kept smiling.

We scurried back to the car having left our ropes tied to some nuts at the high point, the plan being we would come back tomorrow and finish it. Ian hurried along, axes dangling haphazardly from his rucksack, his trousers patched with tape, his National Health Service glasses askew. It was hard to believe he was one of Britain's greatest living alpinists – or soon would be. Like me, he had some optimism engine that powered him on, only his ran much hotter than mine. From the first day I met him I thought: 'You'll not be alive long.'

Thankfully, he's proved me wrong so far.

We'd only climbed together a few times, and to begin with I didn't like him, as he seemed posh, or at least posher than me, as most people are. I only found out later that he'd had elocution lessons and this was the reason for his good diction. He'd also been a bell-ringer, which I found endearing and funny, often telling people, 'Ian's a bell-ringer,' and pointing out this wasn't a euphemism for something else. One thing we shared in common was having both been a bit arty. Ian actually was an artist, and had gone to art school. Then both of us had swapped that passion for the love of climbing, making me wonder if climbing wasn't just another creative pursuit.

The first time we climbed together was in Yosemite in 1998. He was a few years older than me, so seemed like an old man, but he proved his metal when we climbed a route called Lost in America, on which, as was my usual want, I almost died, pulling off a large rock and pitching into the night.

Ian had held my fall.

What I saw in Ian was what I saw in me, a kind of uncompromising and scary drive. Only mine was compromised. I was a husband and father, and he was not. In many ways Ian was who I could be. He was the man who stayed behind when I had to go home. He had no limits or limitations. Unencumbered by the baggage of love and fear, Ian's rise would be meteoric. As for Ian's view of me, all I know is that he'd described me as the most ambitious climber he'd met.

After Yosemite I viewed Ian, along also with Jules Cartwright, one of

Two

Lafaille

The conductor on the cable car raised his eyebrows as we walked up the stairs for the third time in a week. Ian and I shrugged our shoulders as if to say 'Yes, it's us again,' and he léd us into the cabin and slid the door shut. His eyes never left us as the car lifted from the station. Perhaps he thought he'd met the fastest big-wall climbers ever seen in Chamonix, knocking off two walls in only a few days. Or maybe he assumed we were carrying huge loads up his *téléphérique* for charity.

After the bags fell and thumped into the snow below the wall, I had misled Ian when I told him things weren't as bad as they looked. I'd simply recalled it was possible to traverse across the slope we were on to escape the face more easily than heading straight down. Apart from that, things really were as bad as they looked.

Hauling up the remaining bag, I realised that the strap connecting it to those we'd lost had ripped from its stitching. I clipped it into the belay as Ian joined me. There was no question of going on. We'd lost the ledge and all the bivy kit. The remaining bag held mainly food and fuel. We had two choices: we could chuck this bag off too, meaning the trip was over; or we could leave the bag here, go down in the hope the ledge had somehow survived the drop and climb back up next day via the easier North Face to regain our highpoint.

By stashing all our gear here we would be leaving a bond, forcing our future selves to return, something our future selves would probably not want to do at first, especially if the ledge was knackered, and we needed to go all the way back to the valley. But at least we would still be in the game. So we shoved all the ropes and rack into the remaining haul-bag and began our retreat.

It was midnight by the time we'd traversed the slopes and abseiled down the North Face, leaving a rope behind over the steepest section to speed our next effort. I traversed back to the base of the wall and using the beam of my headtorch searched the area until I found the impact crater from the bags. Following the trail they'd made sliding down the slope, I found them a few hundred metres from the wall. The bags seemed intact, and the sleeping bags and bivy gear were okay, but a brief inspection of the ledge by torchlight confirmed that it was indeed knackered. Its aluminium frame was hopelessly bent and twisted. We would have to go down, meaning all the way down, and all the way back again, either to continue, or just to retrieve our bond.

The cable car arrived at the Grands Montets and we walked out, me carrying a rucksack full of extra food and fuel, Ian carrying a replacement portaledge borrowed from Andy Parkin, an alpinist and artist who lived in the valley. It was a very generous thing to do considering, but that's climbers for you. They wouldn't lend you a fiver, but they would lend you a portaledge worth five hundred quid.

As we clumped down the metal stairs, heading for our well worn tracks to the Dru, both of us knew that having invested so much, there was no way we'd be making this trip again. This time we would get to the top, no matter what.

'Watch me' called Ian, as he bridged up the corner, his ice axes twisted into a crack, muscling his way up to the belay, climbing the last 'easy' pitch. Now everything looked blank. And hard. And *steep*. We swapped free climbing for aid. I followed up on jumars attached to the lead rope, tugging at the haul-bags to keep them running free, those once fixed to the broken strap now attached with a stout loop of rope.

'Got a surprise up here for you,' said Ian, looking over the edge.

Clipped to the belay was a coil of thin, nine-millimetre static rope, which would come in handy, as well as a fancy-looking rucksack, both left behind by Lafaille.

'See if it's got any food in it,' I said, feeling ravenous, my hundred grams of Alpen twelve hours ago somehow not proving sufficient. Ian opened the rucksack and rummaged around, hoping like me to find and snaffle some booty. Inside we discovered: a locking pulley like ours; a pair of tiny rock boots; three toothbrushes; and lots of rubbish. Lafaille was famous for being very short, not much over five foot, and we guessed these child-sized boots could only be his. Plus, we could now add the fact that he obviously had very good teeth. We took the pulley, and threw off the rucksack, having no need for it, watching it tumble in space for a long time before disappearing.

'Do you think a body would fall like that?' I said.

'I guess so,' replied Ian.

'I wonder why he didn't throw it off himself. Maybe seeing stuff fall brought back bad memories.'

'Maybe,' said Ian.

'Have you ever wondered what it would feel like?' I asked, not taking my eyes from the spot where the sack had disappeared, waiting for it to appear on the snow slopes below.

'To what?' asked Ian.

'To fall like that. Off a wall. Into space.'

'I'd rather not,' said Ian. 'Why? Do you?'

'All the time.'

'Oh, this is nice,' said Ian, only his eyes visible as he lifted his head in his sleeping bag, finding that it, and everything else inside the portaledge, was now covered in snow. Bad weather had returned in the night, with snow pouring down the wall in vast showers, battering the fly. I'd lain there all night, feeling snug and smug, thinking we were invulnerable in the ledge, that the mountain couldn't touch us. It seemed I was wrong, and that it wasn't as secure as the one I'd dropped. Snow had forced its way upwards through two big holes at either end, covering everything. Pushing a hand out of his sleeping bag, Ian gave the flysheet a poke. Big flakes of ice, formed by our breath freezing on the fabric during the night, showered down on us both. 'This could be interesting,' Ian said.

The weather outside was crap, so we spent a few hours trying to clear up our little home, brushing the snow down the same holes through which it had come and then blocking them off with spare clothes, fastidiously putting everything in stuff sacks. It seemed we'd made a good choice bringing big synthetic sleeping bags, which could cope with damp conditions, each with a thin down layer inside for a boost in warmth. It looked like staying dry was not going to be an option. We had a petrol stove that could be hung from the ledge's suspension straps, and with this running the temperature rose above zero, giving a fair degree of comfort. The downside was that any ice or snow we'd failed to wipe or brush away would melt and drip onto us.

Ian had spent a week on the North Face of Mount Hunter in Alaska sharing a portaledge with Jules Cartwright, climbing a new route they'd called The Knowledge. I'd only used them in California. On Hunter Jules and Ian shared a single-person ledge, which must have been very cosy, as even in a double, room was tight. We'd only spent three nights in it so far, but already ledge sickness had begun, the other person always in your space, pushing against you in the dark. As the sickness took hold you'd imagine they were selfishly taking up all the room, uncaring about your comfort, whereas in fact they were just as squashed as you.

I had taken the inside, so I really did have less room, squashed between the wall on one side and Ian on the other. Ian had only me pressing against him. The downside for him was my berth tended to be the safest spot; any rocks falling down the wall would have a higher chance of hitting him. For this reason, every night, as well as sleeping in his harness, which was never removed, he also slept in his helmet. Just in case.

By lunchtime the weather was no better, and feeling bored, I suggested that I might go out and solo the next pitch, self-belaying to save Ian suffering in the cold.

'If you're sure?' said Ian, obviously impressed by my enthusiasm and thoughtfulness on his behalf. In reality, I felt sitting and waiting would just waste time, and that a little hard work in the storm might make the difference when the hard climbing came. We might get weather that made climbing impossible.

As I geared up, putting on all my layers, and doing up my boots, I said: 'You know what the Slovenians say when they're climbing hard routes in Patagonia? Do a little bit every day. I think that's what our approach is going to have to be.'

Outside our little shelter, with the snow pouring down in sheets, it did indeed feel very Patagonian, clipping on the gear I'd need and stacking my ropes, the idea being that I'd pay the rope out myself rather than have Ian do it. It sounded extreme, soloing on the Dru in winter, but in fact it was no big deal. I set off, climbing and hooking above the portaledge, heading for a thin crack.

'Say cheese,' said Ian, his head poking out of the bottom of the flysheet, camera pointed at me, the lens already picking up dots of snow. I made a thumbs-up sign and returned to the climbing, thinking that I must look pretty hardcore, like one of my heroes, the climber I aspired to be. It felt good making progress, and even a metre more was a metre less tomorrow. As is usually the case, the weather, which had sounded bad inside the portaledge, wasn't so bad once you got out in it. In fact, when moving, it was quite pleasant.

I knew the main crux pitch was somewhere above me, a hairline crack rated A5, meaning hard and dangerous, but it was impossible to see. The whole wall was covered in a layer of snow, which hid all but the biggest features. Our topo, the little diagram that guided our progress, was a photo of the face with a big green line up it, printed off the Internet the night before we left. It wasn't up to the job. All I could do was try and imagine I was Lafaille and go where he would have gone. The only problem was he could see where he was.

I'd never been much interested in climbing new routes, even though this seemed to obsess most climbers. For me climbing had never been about pandering to that part of the ego, to plant a flag. For me it was more about reaching new summits within myself. I needed to follow in the footsteps of my heroes and gods – to climb their routes, rather than my own. On the sharp end the mind is stripped bare, so what you see, what you touch, and what you think mirrors their experience. For a brief moment you glimpse what it is to be them.

At the end of the rope's length, I set up a belay and abseiled back down to the ledge, hoping Ian would have my tea on, knowing he'd probably just be reading his book. It was almost dark.

'Hi, honey, I'm home,' I said as my feet reached the ledge.

'How was it?'

'Not bad, but I couldn't see the crux with all the snow.'

'Well done,' said Ian as I dove back under the flysheet, trying to keep most of the weather outside, brushing myself down before I pulled out my sleeping bag.

'I guess someone had to do it,' I said, unzipping my gaiters and clipping my boots on to one of the ledge's suspension straps.

'That's the thing, you didn't,' Ian laughed, shaking his head.

'Oh yes,' I said, smiling back. I guess I just wanted to show willing.

The storm lasted for a week. Every day and every pitch was faced in full Scottish conditions. Each foot of rock was swept to find what lay beneath. Somehow we missed out the crux of the route, the A5 pitch, and only spotted it, a short crack, as we abseiled down to the portaledge. I wondered if the way we'd gone wasn't just as hard. Both of us had climbed much more difficult big-wall routes than Lafaille had. Often we'd head up the harder sections, chosen to match our expectations of where the route should go, only to find we'd overlooked his line and climbed new ground instead.

On the second stormy day our pulley had slipped out of my gloved fingers. It seemed a strange piece of luck that we could replace this crucial item of gear, without which we'd have needed to retreat, with the very same model of pulley we'd found in Lafaille's rucksack.

The rock was very compact and Lafaille had been forced to drill two bolts for each belay. For some reason we never discovered, he had unscrewed the nut and hanger from them, leaving either a small steel stud, or worse still, a tiny 5mm hole that was almost impossible to see. Several times we'd make a desperate move only to look down and see a bolt without its hanger; and those were the ones we spotted not covered with snow.

I'd come prepared for this, bringing nuts and hangers that would fit these holes, only somehow we'd dropped them all. Now, at each belay, we would have to improvise, looping a wire over a stud and just trusting friction and the weight of the load to hold it in place, or else finding a peg or nut instead. Equipping these bolts became our biggest problem and belays were always a scary affair. Luckily we had Lafaille's length of white static rope, and so we could leave the portaledge and all the heavy gear on a good belay, and skip the belays we thought might rip under the strain with an extra long haul. In effect we were climbing capsule-style, moving a camp up the wall. It was a great system, allowing us to rap down at the end of a cold day to the comparative comfort of our ledge.

'Ian, have you checked your feet lately?' I asked. My head lay a few inches from the end of his sleeping bag and the smell was almost too much to bear.

'Why, do they smell bad?' he replied from the other end of the ledge.

'It's like sleeping next to a cheese counter,' I told him, pulling the edge of the sleeping bag up, so my own stink hid his, my bag smelling fusty and damp, having gotten wet, then frozen and thawed repeatedly since we started.

'They don't feel good; I think my old frostbite's acting up. I think your boots are a lot warmer than mine.'

Ian's feet were one of my main preoccupations on the wall, along with hunger and cold, a little bit of cheesy spice that reminded me that there was no escape from the horror. Even when my stomach was full and I was toasty in my sleeping bag, there would always be that smell. Every night we would get back into the ledge, take off all our gear, light up the stove and defrost. Being warm and cosy was a bit of normality, and it was spoiled when Ian took off his socks to rub his feet back to life.

Food was another big problem. Our diet was fine for a two-day alpine ascent but no good for a protracted climb. I could actually feel my body wasting away by the day, getting a sexual thrill from running my hands over my chest and abdomen. I no longer felt like me. Breakfast was a sad affair, and began with me picking out all the raisins from my eggcup portion of Alpen and giving them to Ian. This was a loss of calories, but preferable to puking the whole lot back up, my aversion to raisins trumping even my hunger.

By the time we were climbing out of the ledge my stomach was empty again, and it was only being scared that seemed to make me feel full. During my belaying stints, all I could think about was food.

There was no lunch. Teatime began with a cup of tea, then a diet portion of couscous. We'd brought single-portion packets of butter to boost the flavour of the couscous – one for each serving – but we gobbled them up like a piece of chocolate long before the water had boiled. I'd used Happy Shopper couscous to work out the portions, a hundred grams producing a good meal, but bought a fancy gourmet variety for the route, which wouldn't have fed a mouse. Our biggest treat was the small packet of peanuts, which held forty or fifty nuts. This would be emptied into a depression in my sleeping bag and divvied fairly; one for me, one for Ian, until there were two small piles each. A portion that could be eaten in one mouthful was then savoured, each nut as valuable as a diamond.

Eventually tea would be over, and everything would be packed away, the final act to put the piss bottle on top of the stove that hung between us. Unable to really move in the night, let alone pop out for a wizz, you'd just have to reach out, grab the bottle, take it into your bag and have a wee. The etiquette was if you used it, then you emptied it, as the contents would soon freeze, and no one wants the problem of having to thaw a bottle of piss.

That job over with we would burrow down into our bags and Ian would stick on a CD, our portable CD player and single speaker being our one luxury, the player stuck inside Ian's bag so the batteries didn't die in the cold. I think every night we listened to the same album, mostly down to the fact it was the only album we had: Ian Brown's Music of the Spheres. People say that music sounds good when you're high on drugs, but when you're high in a portaledge it's also pretty amazing. Music can take your mind to extraordinary places, but being in such a place already, it just took us home.

A week and the wall stretched away below us, the top of the climb now close, perhaps just two days away, as I set off up an easy looking crack. Above this lay the route's second crux, a jutting buttress of compact granite, like a ship's prow, the pitch rated A4. We knew nothing else about it. Our topo had by now disintegrated into tiny lumps of frozen paper within the washing-machine wetness of our pockets. Now we were simply on autopilot, climbing straight up, whether it was where Lafaille had gone or not.

Ian's belay was hanging in space, two cams in a corner, so I set off as fast as I could, partly because it would be dark soon, but also because Ian wasn't coping well with the cold. His feet were beginning to worry both of us, and not just because of the smell. On long belays he had to take off his boots and massage his feet to warm them. Often this would coincide with a mini-avalanche, making things worse, as the snow coated his socks and filled up his open boots. It seemed to me that other people's suffering is just abstract, and although I could fake concern, my only worry was about whether or not his feet would force a retreat. They say it's not worth losing your toes for a climb, but when they're not your toes it seems worth the risk.

The climbing was easy, probably the easiest yet, just a three-inch crack splitting the wall, and I leapfrogged the same two cams for protection, scary if you thought about it, but fine if you didn't. I could see the belay, just at the base of the prow, but to reach it I had to cross a shattered section, a tombstone-shaped chunk of rock jutting from the crack. Placing a cam below this I tried to reach past, grabbing hold of the flake's top edge to steady myself.

At once, it made a grinding noise and began to slip from the crack on top of me, pressing down on me until all its weight rested on my shoulder, stopping it, but pinning me there. If it fell it would probably hit Ian. I held it for a second, judging its mass, unsure how big it actually was, just knowing it was heavy. Carefully I let go. It slid further and I held its weight again. I was stuck.

I tried to work out how big the flake was, but could only see that behind it were several smaller blocks ready to tumble after it.

'IAN!' I shouted, trying to sound calm. 'There's a big loose rock here. I'm holding it but I'm going to have to let it fall. Can you move?' I already knew the answer.

'Erm... not really,' came the reply. 'How big is it?'

'Big enough,' I replied. 'I'm going to chuck down some smaller stones so watch out.'

With the flake still on my shoulder I reached behind it and fished out the smaller rocks and threw them over my shoulder. Each fell without making a sound, only a dull, distant 'thwunk' as they landed far below us.

I threw the last one, but this one hit something, probably the top of the corner above Ian, sending down a shower of fragments. Ian let out a yelp. He'd been hit.

While I couldn't see him I could hear him moaning. Fine, I thought, if he can complain he's still breathing. When all the stones were gone, I squatted down and took the big rock entirely on my shoulder, allowing it to roll out of the crack. As it did I stood up, and with a yell pushed it away as hard as I could.

It fell for a moment then hit something with a loud boom, followed by a cascade of smaller crashes and bangs that lasted for several seconds as the remains of the flake tumbled down the face.

I looked down. Ian was looking up. He'd stopped moaning. He was okay. The rock had missed him. I guessed he'd also forgotten about his feet.

I climbed on, reached the belay and stripped the gear on the way down. Now we were only two pitches from the top.

'Are your feet okay?' I asked, looking over the top of my book. Ian was sat rubbing his stinking feet longer than was usual, tea having to wait until he was done. Ian had once told me that he hated people who complained, so I guessed it was worth asking.

'I don't seem to be able to get my foot warmed up,' said Ian, rubbing hard at the yellow flesh. The toes were white and seemed dead.

I sat up on one elbow and watched, knowing how horrible it was, that moment between having cold feet, and the warmth returning, that uncertainty, not knowing if the blood will return, that your toes really are dead and will just rot away.

Ian rubbed on.

'Do you want to stick it on my stomach?' I asked, knowing it would be the only way to get the blood moving.

Ian looked at me, thinking I was joking, having spent the last few days doing nothing but complain about the smell. 'Really?'

'Yes if you want,' I said, knowing this was going way beyond the realms of normal friendship, way above sharing a girlfriend or donating a kidney.

'Okay,' said Ian, shuffling near, straightening his leg, his foot moving closer.

I sat up, and moved closer. Taking his foot in one hand, I lifted up my fleeces with the other, and pressed it onto my warm belly, feeling his almost dead flesh imprint its cold shape on my warm skin, sucking in my heat.

Neither of us looked at each other, the moment embarrassingly intimate: two men, never more than sixty metres apart, sleeping in the same bed and pissing in the same bottle, their bodies now... touching. I could tell he was keeping his foot rigid, the slightest toe wriggle beyond the pale.

And there we sat, until the blood returned, and dinner could be started.

As usual it snowed the next day, and it was a long jumar up the ropes to our highpoint. We were leading two pitches each go, so it was still my turn, and this would most likely be the second-hardest pitch on the route.

At the bottom of the jutting buttress there seemed only one way to go, up right to a thin crack. The problem was it looked hard and lay above a big ledge, the famous 'jammed block' on the classic American Direct. I climbed over and saw a peg high up with a karabiner on it. He had obviously been here. It was only later that we discovered this peg was an abortive attempt, and he'd lowered off it to climb up the *other* side of the buttress, a line obscured by snow as I looked up. Climbing on, I reached the peg, the crack above closing down to just a hairline, meaning I had to use one of the smallest pegs I had, a birdbeak, a peg no bigger than a coin, shaped like a tiny ice axe, with a fingernail blade designed to be tapped into the thinnest cracks. With total concentration I moved up, piecing the pitch together, big clouds of spindrift showering down. The climbing was great, and not once did I think I would fall, or consider what would happen if I did.

The crack finished, but I was able to hook up some flakes until they too ran out. Looking down at the distance between me and the last beak, and below that to the last piece of gear that would hold a big fall, I realised I would go miles, but instead of feeling scared, I simply revelled at my own nerve and control.

A body's length above me the rock eased back, and I could see an obvious spot where Lafaille must have belayed. But between me and it there was nothing.

Except there always is.

I stepped up as high as I dared and found a tiny horizontal overlap in the rock, not a crack, just an upside down edge no wider than the top of a skirting board. Running my fingers along its length I felt a little hollow spot, a horizontal widening the size of half a penny. It appeared and was gone, almost small enough to miss. I looked through my rack and fished out a RURP, a square peg the size of a large stamp with the thickness of a credit card, one edge sharpened. It's name stood for Realized Ultimate Reality Piton, which had always sounded a bit daft to me, but now made sense as I pushed one edge into the gap.

The amount of metal it took was no more than a little fingernail. This was a joke placement, something I'd conjure up in the climbing shop by sticking it into the edge of the counter and asking my mate: 'What if you had to trust your life to that?' There was no way something so fragile could hold a thirteen-stone climber; and yet I believed it would. So I clipped my etrier to it, along with my daisy chain, and started to ease onto it. My weight twisted the RURP, this force being the only thing holding it in place. The hook below, clipped to the rope, would have no chance of holding me if the RURP now ripped.

Finally, all my weight hung from it.

It held.

I hung there for a moment, ignoring the urge to rush away before this time-bomb exploded, marvelling that someone could make something so little and yet so strong. I stared at it, the entire time expecting it to bend or break in front of my eyes.

It held.
    Reality had been altered.

I stepped up, oh so carefully, but for some reason took out my camera and took a picture to capture the moment.
    I stepped higher.
    The gap between my outstretched hand and the good crack was just one placement.
    There was nothing. Except, of course, there is always something.
    I fingered the rock and felt a little flat spot, fingernail sized, a little geological flaw that offered itself to me.
    I took my smallest skyhook, placed it on the edge, clipped in an aider, and stepped up, feeling no need to test the hook, just eager to get off the RURP.
    Bang! The hook popped. I dropped onto my daisy chain, the sling snapping tight onto the crazy RURP, and I waited for the gear-ripping ride to start, and for its end, as my body smashed into the jammed block.
    Only it didn't.
    The RURP held.
    'IAN!' I shouted looking down at him hunkered over at the belay, about thirty metres below me. 'Hey Ian! I just took a daisy fall onto the edge of a RURP. And it held!'
    Ian didn't look up, but simply began paying out rope, his brain too frozen to imagine my shouting could be about anything but a demand for slack.
    I stepped up, replaced the hook with a more pointed one, tested it this time, and finally made the last move to the good crack.
    Stuffing in two cams, I tied off the ropes and shouted for Ian to follow. Looking up, I thought the sight of the next pitch – his lead – should warm him up. It looked easy. As I stood waiting I noticed that small rays of sun were shining through the clouds as the sun began to set, and wondered if perhaps it was a sign that good weather was at last on its way – a bit late seeing as we only had one more pitch to go.

Ledge life seemed more desperate than ever that night. With the end in sight, our guard had begun to fall. Ian dropped his mug and his spoon and had to make do with an empty milk powder container, which promptly turned semi-liquid itself once hot water was poured in. He replaced his spoon with a peg. My head spun when the stove was running, but ventilation meant cold air, and so we just poisoned ourselves. Things got so bad we burped fuel vapour.

'Ian, we need to look out for each other,' I said, knowing that we were in a dangerous situation, that we had become too blasé about where we were, as if gravity no longer effected us. A few days before Ian had fallen out of the ledge in the morning, and only luck and a tangled rope had saved him, having neglected to clip in properly. If we weren't careful it wouldn't be a spoon that would be lost.

We woke in the dark and slowly tried to gather our wits about us, knowing that it could all be over today. Slowly and methodically we ate our starvation rations, put everything away, got our boots on, checked harnesses, the whole operation completed under the usual shower of falling ice. Ian went first, stepping out onto the ledge and slowly jumaring up as I waited below, my stiff sleeping bag draped around my shoulders until it was my turn to climb.

I lay there, everything around me frozen, sustained by a fading ember of comfort still burning inside. This could be our last morning on the wall, yet thinking so was foolish. Even if we reached the top of the route, the summit still lay another day away at least, probably two or three with all our gear, plus another to get down. We had one more night's food at most, but neither of us had broached the subject. I guess we had put the mountain to one side and focused on the route, that thinking beyond this was just too much. I couldn't dwell on the idea that even in success we would fail.

'Rope free,' Ian called, and I cast off my bag, swung my legs off the ledge, clipped in my jumars and started to climb. It was a clear day at last.

Ian racked up while I tried to find a comfortable spot, putting on the usual double belay jackets. The corner above didn't look hard at all, curving up and out over an overhang. Easy but very, very exposed, with the whole route under Ian's toes as he climbed.

'Guess I'll be off,' said Ian, placing the first runner and stepping up.

He climbed fast, and I filmed him, but there wasn't much to see until he got to the overhang and began thrashing around.

'I can see the belay,' he shouted down, 'just a few moves and I think I can free climb up to it. A couple of bolts.'

'When you get there,' I shouted back, 'make a big noise, as I'm filming, but I won't see you.'

'Okay,' he said, looking back up as the sun broke through the clouds. A few rays hit our upturned faces.

I felt a sense of relief, knowing that he was almost there, that we were almost there, that it was easy, and we were both safe, with no more stings in the tail. Never in my life had I tried so hard for something, or given so much. But it wasn't about the route. As is always the case, the gift was in the giving, that it was the pursuit of the climb that mattered, not the climb itself.

I looked up. Ian was almost out of sight, kicking free of his aiders and grunting up some unseen crack. I took out the video camera and tried to capture his last movements, and then the whoop that would follow, with the climb in the bag.

His feet disappeared.

A few bits of grit fell past.

Then some snow.

I tried to hold the camera still, imagining him reaching up for the belay, envying him the psychological release of clipping those fabulous bolts.

'I'm there,' he rasped. It was hardly the rebel yell of victory I was waiting for. But it was enough.

'The higher I get the better I feel' I shouted as I jumared up the last few feet. Ian came into view, standing on a wide ledge, the whole of the Alps spread out for us.

I flopped down and lay in the snow, my arms out, no longer caring about anything, just ecstatic that it was over, Ian laughing at my total disregard for where I was, my legs hanging over the edge. I felt drunk, no longer caring about anything. Nothing could touch me now or ever again. We had followed in the footsteps of a god. We were in his heaven.

'We're not going to the top are we,' I said, my eyes still closed, feeling the gentlest warmth on my face.

'No,' said Ian. There really wasn't anything to talk about.

'I guess we're going back down the way we came then,' I said, feeling the snow melting under me, one leg growing cold as the sun moved out of sight and the shadows returned.

'Yep. We might be back down for lunch tomorrow.'

You can't sit on sunny ledges forever, so I went first, aiding down the last pitch as the sun set so I could reach the belay. Ian joined me as once again the darkness fell. I felt paranoid, that we were going to undo ourselves through some minor error, the exhaustion returning. The next abseil was down the crux pitch, a plumb line. My toes could just scuff the rock as I slipped back down the ship's prow. The belay was out of reach and it took a few swings for me to grab the mess of ropes attached to it; a strand that led back down to the portaledge hidden somewhere in a mass of loops and coils. My headtorch was almost out of juice and I thought that instead of hanging there and sorting out the loops and knots to make it easier to retrieve the ropes, I'd leave them for Ian to sort out, now just wanting to get back to the portaledge. I felt for the thin strand I needed, attached my abseil device, unclipped from the belay and leaned back.

The rope didn't go tight. It just fed out.

I was falling.

'...?!'

With a lurch I stopped a few metres lower, my hand locked down on the rope. I let out a scream, as much at myself as the fall. I'd clipped into the wrong strand, a loop that was just hanging from the belay, but not directly attached. Somehow it had knotted up and held me. It could easily have just let me slip off its end. Quickly I reached for the correct rope, clipped a jumar in, and, resetting my abseil device, set off again. I didn't have the energy to consider it further.

Collapsing into the portaledge, I double-checked I was properly tied in before getting off the rope, and then brushed the ice from my sleeping bag while I waited for Ian. All sense of relief at getting to the top was gone; now I felt on the wrong side of safe, as if something awful would creep up and squash me now it knew my guard was down. Frightened, I switched off my headtorch and just lay there. Hiding.

I heard the slip of belay plate on rope, then the plastic clunk of Ian's feet as he arrived, seeing the beam of his headtorch flashing over their black plastic. I heard him sigh. He too was having a moment.

'You in there?' he said.

'Just warming your slippers.'

'One, two, three... Away you go!' I shouted, throwing our biggest haul-bag off the ledge.

It tumbled down, and down, and down, spinning over and over, twisting and falling. It fell free, filled with all our soft gear, or gear we didn't mind losing, until it finally struck the edge of the bottom buttress, and shot out away from the wall, lost from sight.

'I hope we find it,' said Ian, lowering the video camera.

'I don't really care. I just want to get down.'

'We've got one more thing to do,' said Ian, pulling out something small from his pocket, wrapped in plastic. 'I promised I'd throw this off as well.' Ian unwrapped a small plastic Superman complete with parachute. The figure was about four inches high.

'Is that a life-size model of Lafaille?' I asked.

Ian gave a guilty laugh, knowing he shouldn't.

Pulling out the plastic parachute, its dozen strings tied to the model's rubber shoulders, Ian threw it out over the drop. It fell for a second, then stopped as the chute filled with air, then rose up, past us, the tiny blue figure spinning in the breeze, until it slipped into a wide crack and just hung there.

We set off down, me going first with the little haul-bag clipped to my harness. Ian followed with the portaledge clipped to his. We picked up the line of the American Direct and rapped off its anchors, each one getting us closer to the ground.

All the way I focused on not making a mistake, making sure every knot was perfect, doing everything in my power not to fuck up now we were so close to being safe again.

I thought, as I often did, about the story Doug Scott had told me many years ago while sat eating breakfast in Fort William, the two of us having been the star turns at a climbing film festival. We sat in the empty dining room as his young kids played around under the tables.

'You always have to take care on the way down youth' said Doug, then in his late fifties. 'On Shishapangma I was done in and just wanted to sleep, but I knew I had to get down.' His alpine-style ascent of the peak had been one of the great first ascents. 'I kept imagining my mother telling my kids not to worry, that I was being really careful, taking care with every last step and that I would be home soon.'

I let myself be weak and thought about Ella and Ewen, for all our sakes.

Three hours after starting we reached the snow terrace.

An hour later we reached the ground.

I hit the snow and walked down until the rope ends slipped through my belay device, freeing me from the wall. I staggered on, my legs unused to the flat, unused to walking, carrying me away, dragging the haul-bag towards a mess of kit where the thrown bag had exploded. The bottom panel had blown out on impact. The bag's last journey would be back down the snow slopes to the glacier then up to the little station at Montenvers and the train ride down to Chamonix.

I turned around and watched Ian, kicking at the long red portaledge bag as he came down the slabs, until he too reached the bottom, and slumped in the snow. We just sat there. Both of us were knackered, the last gram of energy expended.

'We'd better get a move on if we're going to get the train,' he said.

The sun had begun to set and a cold wind blew down the Mer de Glace. We'd missed the train, our slow descent not helped by me throwing my haul-bag off the edge of cliffs that blocked our way, only to find the ropes we needed had been inside it.

'I guess it's only fair that it should end like this,' said Ian, pulling the bags under a large boulder, ready to be picked up later, the plan to walk down in just our clothes.

I took off my fleece jacket and stowed it with the bags, knowing I'd get hot on the way down, not used to moving hundreds, even thousands of metres an hour rather than a handful. We both stank, and the cold wind rushing over us felt like a wash. 'What's happened to your body?' exclaimed Ian as he switched on his headtorch, looking at me in a state of shock. I looked down, for the first time in ten days, at my body. My thermal top hung off what looked like someone else's torso. I had a waist. You could see my ribs. I'd been transformed by the climb. It was as if I'd set off fat and unfit, not looking the part, not fit to try the Alps' hardest climb, and come back looking just like you'd expect such a climber to look, like the climber I'd always dreamt of being. This was a hell of a way to go on a diet. My stomach grumbled. We had to get a move on, and set off down what would no doubt feel like a death march in our state, down the trail in the dark to Chamonix. Although I felt fragile, my head dizzy and spaced out, I also felt invulnerable, as if I could walk for a week without food, through storms and cold. There was nothing I could not endure after this.

We sat in the bar, the cleaner sweeping up from the night before. Ian and I were dressed in our normal clothes again, clothes that no longer fitted, each wearing belts improvised from a sling to stop our trousers falling down. Outside the door the early morning traffic moved slowly through a snowstorm, but inside it was warm. Just looking at snow made me feel cold, my body hyper-sensitised, as if it had held the line against a cold siege, and was now exhausted, and in need of tender care. I thought about my realisation on the Reticent Wall, that to survive on a hard climb you must treat yourself like someone you love. The Lafaille was proof; with love you could overcome most things. Love for yourself, for your partner, treating him like you must treat yourself; and for the mountain, as something to be loved, not hated.

Ian had the look of a veteran, face and lips chapped, his fingers swollen and battered, happy like me just to sit awhile, to set a mug of tea down and not worry it would spill as the other shifted, or fall from the table and tumble forever. In a month he was going to Alaska with Kenton Cool, another strong British alpinist. I wondered if he felt he was on a roll now, that the Dru had armed him for harder climbs, one built upon the next, or exhausted, the idea of another trip so soon too much to bear. I guessed he probably felt the latter. Both of us were mentally and physically shattered, feeling that limbo of not being on the climb, but also not quite back in the world, and missing both and neither at the same time. In a week our strength would return and the suffering would be just another pub story, only a slide to back it up, our camera smiles tricking us into believing it wasn't so bad.

Maybe it wasn't?

I looked forward to going home. Not once had I regretted being here, or wished to be home instead. It just felt right. Maybe that's how it's meant to feel. I knew though that when Ian left for Alaska, with no big climbs for me for another six months, I'd feel as if I'd been left behind.

In an hour we would drive home to England, but before then we had someone to see. He walked in through the door, his curly hair flecked with snow, his skin tanned and lined by a life in the mountains, mobile phone to his ear. I wondered if he would even see us, expecting to see someone else. That he'd walk straight past us, thinking we were skiers getting over a hangover – which in a way we were. But his eyes flashed as he saw us, his hand waved. Maybe he could see the mark of his route on us.

'Ian. Andy,' he said, walking over.

'Hello Jean-Christophe,' Ian said, standing up and shaking his hand, towering over him, like a schoolteacher and a child. I stepped up as well, feeling awkward to meet a hero in the flesh, this man we had tracked for fifteen days, attempting to think and act as he had, believing we could be his equal. Lafaille was indeed short, a pocket deity, only one with the hands of a giant, which he held out smiling. I put mine in his and expected a bone-crunching squeeze, something to confirm our rankings, but instead felt only his warmth.

We sat down and he asked us about the route, how we had found it, if we had difficulty due to the weather, which bits were dangerous and which bits were safe.

'We needed a better topo,' said Ian, laughing. 'We missed the crux pitch so we don't know how hard it was, but there was lots of hard climbing for sure. It would have been nice if you'd have left the bolts in.'

As Ian talked I could see something in Lafaille's eyes, a little fear from this fearless man. He really just wanted to know one thing: was it as hard as he'd thought, or were we going to make a name for ourselves, as many have done, by claiming it wasn't so bad. That was an easy trick to pull when you're two nobodies, worse still, British nobodies. Both of us had climbed much harder big walls than Lafaille, and so we probably *had* found it easier, shown by the fact we climbed it in such bad weather. If it had been as hard as he had said, this god, it would have been too hard for us mortals.

'I think it was very hard,' I said. Ian nodded.

Lafaille sat back on his chair and relaxed, and began to tell us about his real life, not about climbing. About trying to build his house, about his children and his wife's attempts to organize her man. 'Like you, really I just want to climb, but such things are difficult sometimes, no?'

We walked outside and I stood next to Lafaille while Ian took a picture, then a portrait of the man alone, the snow resting on his hair, the eventual slide looking slightly out of focus, as if it was misted over with the emotion of meeting him.

'These will make good obituary shots,' I said. Ian pulled a slightly cross face at such a vulgar remark, which Lafaille didn't hear, distracted by his phone ringing.

'My wife,' he said, rolling his eyes. 'I must go – maybe we can climb a wall together some day?' And with a wave he was gone into the storm.

Ian's photo, Lafaille standing solid outside the bar, snow flakes knocking the focus out just a touch, did get used a few years later, our hero, lost and never found on a solo winter ascent of Makalu.

'What a nice man,' said Ian.

And he was.

Three

Black Dog

It's past midnight and I'm sitting in A&E, under the strip lights, hair matted with blood, feeling woozy and sick from a cracked and throbbing head. Around me sit – or slump – the sick and deranged, all of us waiting to see the doctor, waiting to be mended. I look at the clock, and wonder if it's more than a coincidence that 'patients' rhymes with 'patience.' Four hours in, with only my fellow sufferers to read, I wish I'd brought a book.

I look at them, each with their own trauma. This room is a lens on mortality.

Over the last few months, as I've watched Ella and Ewen grow, death has come to preoccupy me, making me consider the risks I've taken, the ones I'm about to take.

But here, in these faces, I see another truth, one that soothes these feelings: that people suffer and die living safe lives just as much as dangerous ones. When people ask me how I can risk my life, the only answer I can give is: 'How can you *not* take risks?'

I would often think about my uncle Doug, a great man, a radio operator on Baffin Island, a hunter in New Zealand, dying in the prime of life, just about to enjoy his retirement. I told myself you have to live your life now, and not wait for some later date. Futures can be easily cancelled.

'Mr Samuels?' says a doctor, an old man standing painfully to follow him to the cubicles.

I look around the room at the others, many who looked used to A&E, pissed up, every night out ending here. Some are time-wasters, hypochondriacs, who are easy to spot trying to look ill while at the same time seeming at ease among familiar surroundings. I wonder why such people are drawn to hospitals, the one place most people try and avoid. Maybe they're lonely, looking for the warmth that attention brings, for someone to notice them, to take an interest in lives transparent to all but those paid to see them.

'Mrs Nugg?' says the doctor, the old man shuffling away, a new patient standing to follow him.

Half past twelve.

The day had started well, my first as a genuine, certified professional climber, signing my first contract with clothing company Patagonia. This was a proper deal, not just gear but money too, something I'd never dreamed could happen to me. I'd worked for Patagonia for a few years, getting clothes to test out, sometimes a jacket made from two different fabrics, one half made from fabric A, the other fabric B, making me look like a jester, or someone who made his own clothes out of remnants. Now I quite literally was the real deal.

Soloing the Reticent Wall meant little to anyone in Britain. I doubt there were more than twenty people who had heard of the route in the country. The Lafaille had been different. People took notice. Climbers had heard of Lafaille, and although his climb was little reported beyond France, its moniker of 'hardest wall in Europe' was shorthand magazine editors understood. Even the Independent covered our climb, although they did focus on why it had taken us fifteen days to climb just eight hundred metres.

Not everyone was so quick to pat us on the back. The editor of *On The Edge* magazine was quick to stir up a stink of contrived controversy, saying that we didn't go to the summit, and that better climbers would have free-climbed the route, which showed his ignorance of climbing beyond single-pitch routes in the Peak District. Ian was uncharacteristically enraged, but justifiably so considering the effort that had gone into the climb. Ian wrote a letter to the editor asking if he'd ever had frostbite, or slept in a sleeping bag with more ice than feathers, or jumared a rope you thought might break in a storm.

It was a good response, but the whole affair showed the lack of understanding of what was involved. It's why modern mountaineering is so poorly understood. Walking to the North Pole or reaching the summit of Everest are comprehensible, and can be shoehorned into a couple of paragraphs. Explaining something new, however, seems beyond the media, unless someone dies. If Ian had died, his stock would have been very high.

Despite all that, we had both turned overnight into minor climbing celebs, with people like Doug Scott and Chris Bonington saying nice things about us, and magazines running our pictures, which were pretty darned good even if I say so myself.

The highpoint for me came while queuing for the toilet at the National

Exhibition Centre in Birmingham. A total stranger coming out of the cubicle I was entering shook me by the hand: 'Well done on the Lafaille, mate. Awesome effort.' For some reason this meant a lot, although I wish he'd washed his hands first.

'Mr Green?' says the doctor. Another man stands.

I shift in my easy-wipe orange plastic chair. I've been sat here for four hours now, and my arse is as sore as my head. I touch the wound every now and again, feeling the huge bump, the split skin, imagining my fingers brushing the bone of my skull, telling myself not to be melodramatic.

I think back to the Lafaille, and wonder how hard it really was, and how much harder I could push things. We could push things, me and Ian. It had seemed pretty grim, the photos testament to that, the unseen hunger being the worst of it, but I'd been happy to be there, with none of the usual soul-searching.

Without that weight I could climb anything.

I could climb anything.

'Mr Kempster?' the doctor calls. He looks tired.

No one stands up.

'Mr Kempster?'

No one stands up.

'Mr Rasheed then?'

Someone stands, and the rest of us keep on waiting.

After getting back from the Alps I'd been asked to speak at a climbing symposium organized by the Alpine Club, a day of amazing climbers from around the world – and me – talking about their climbs.

I talked about the Lafaille and the Reticent Wall, which I guess were state of the art, and as hard as anything being climbed by other European climbers. Although having done them, I didn't see it like that. I wasn't proud of these climbs. I was only proud of the stories that stemmed from them.

After the talks, we were all transported to a pizza restaurant, its small bar buzzing with high-level climbing chat. I found myself standing in the bar, beer in hand, next to two of the most amazing climbers on the planet: Silvo Karo and Voytek Kurtyka. Silvo, with his cropped hair and barrel chest was a Slovenian who had set the benchmark for extreme climbing in the 1980s. It had been Silvo who had coined our Dru mantra 'do a little every day.' Every climb he'd put up was long, technical, bold and dangerous – and most remained unrepeated. His name had become shorthand for a 'death route,' the archetypal crazy eastern European. You'd imagine he'd be wild-eyed and longhaired, like a crazy Mexican from a Spaghetti Western. In reality he was modest and softly spoken, the routes he'd done not down to craziness, but talent, strength and experience in all the arts of climbing.

Voytek was Polish, and his list of achievements was enough to make any climber's jaw drop, starting with the first winter ascent of the Troll Wall, and then on to the Himalaya where he defined a new level of commitment, climbing the hardest faces in the purest style. He'd been one of a handful of climbers in the 1970s and 1980s pushing the boundaries of what was humanly possible – perhaps morally too, since some of his climbs looked almost suicidal.

Although Voytek survived, many of his contemporaries did not, something he shared with Silvo. Voytek had a striking face, like Rudolf Nureyev, and an ethereal quality that gave one the impression he wasn't really human at all. He was climbing's very own Achilles.

Standing there, between these two men, I felt myself diminished, as if I had nothing at all to say to them that could do justice to their greatness, neither able to ask them about themselves, or tell them about me, as either would diminish me further.

Instead I just stood there and felt myself to be invisible.

A young woman came up and began asking Silvo about his most famous routes, scribbling down notes as she probed him with the usual questions: 'when did you start climbing?' and 'have you ever had an accident?' The topic of his hardest routes came up, and John Porter, one of the symposium's organisers, explained to the journalist some of Silvo's climbs, and their context within the world of extreme climbing. Silvo was as tough as they came. The Devil's Dihedral was mentioned, Silvo's fearsome route on Fitz Roy, a route he'd climbed with the equally gnarly Janez Jeglič and Franček Knez in 1983. The climb had been nicknamed 'The Flushing Slovenian Death Couloir' by western climbers, twelve hundred metres of looseness and danger. Karo and his friends had doggedly pieced together the route over two months, retreating down fixed ropes between storms, the siege style testament to the climb's seriousness. 'It was hard,' was Silvo's one-line description.

If I climbed his route with Ian, in winter, just me and him, in alpine style, maybe I wouldn't feel invisible. At that moment, another climb began.

'Mr Kirkpatrick?' the doctor asks, emerging from the cubicles. 'Mr Kirkpatrick?' I follow him past the timewasters, hobbling, stiffening up.

'Sit down on the chair,' says the doctor, his manner robotic as he ticks his way through the sick. 'I see you've bumped your head,' he says, looking down at my bloody scalp like a man checking to see if a toilet is flushed. 'What happened?'

I'd not been on my bike for a long time, but decided that morning I would cycle to my historic meeting with Patagonia in Matlock, a distance of about twenty-two miles. There I'd have lunch with one of their top people and sign the contract.

As usual I underestimated both time and distance, and got hot and sweaty as my legs tried to remember how to go round, the bike feeling like a car that has stood for too long. Everything had seized up and not in a good way. I'd also lost my bike helmet, and cycling without one made me feel exposed, like driving without a seat belt.

Turning up damp, knackered and wheezing didn't seem a good start to my pro-athlete career, and I wasn't looking the part as I went into the meeting. Then again, I guess looking a state is part of my charm. I signed on the bottom line and we went for lunch.

It wasn't a huge amount of money and only a fraction of my old wages, but it was a start, and gave me a little more freedom to go climbing. As I signed I told Hervé, the French manager in charge of the British market, that it was odd to get paid to wear clothes, as when I was a kid my mum got money from the council to buy me clothes, and that risking your life didn't seem so bad if you looked good doing it. As usual, I spoke too quickly and he just smiled, having no idea what I was talking about.

Lunch over, I said my goodbyes and jumped back on my bike for the ride home, needing to be back by half five to take over from Jean, our child-minder. I was in for another hot and sweaty ride.

Cycling along that afternoon my imagination raced ahead of me. This was just the start. With more hard climbs I'd be able to get better sponsorship deals, and more money meant more climbing, because if climbing was a well-paid job, there would be no guilt involved. Signing a contract, just like climbing a hard route, had become just another step along the road. Already the excitement had gone, my mind on the next milestone.

I wondered if being sponsored would mean pressure to perform, but guessed nothing could trump my own motivation. But would it cloud my judgement, making climbing ever more goal oriented? I just had to keep a rational handle on things. Anyway, I was already a safe climber, and the more I climbed the safer I would become.

Bombing down the hill back into Sheffield, fingers gripping my brakes, I felt exposed without my helmet, thinking it would be just my luck to get killed hitting a pot hole on my bike, especially as I always made a big thing about climbers wearing helmets.

I often thought of the famous climber who had done many hard routes and climbed Everest, but who fell off a ladder in his bathroom while doing some DIY and broke his neck.

Death hid in plain view, not just in dark corners.

I kept on the brakes until a quarter of a mile from home, to the final little downhill before a short climb up to the house. Along two hundred yards of an empty road of terraced houses, the only sign of life was a parking car.

In a minute I'd be home with the kids. We'd go to the park and get an ice cream to celebrate.

I dropped into the top of the road and sped down, fingers off the brakes for once, feeling the rush of air through my hair, my stomach feeling weightless. Up ahead I saw the parking car find its spot and stop, the driver's door opening. I drifted to the other side of the road, accelerating now to get up the final climb.

I wondered why I'd not been on my bike for so long.

In the blur as I drew close to the car I saw the rear door open, but knew I had acres of room. I was safe.

I saw something black jumping inside

A dog.

Escaping.

Frantic.

In road.

Can't avoid.

No helmet.

I lay on the floor, unsure where I was, the world spinning in two different directions, a kaleidoscope slowly returning into focus. A blue sky. A terraced street. I couldn't breathe, but knew from experience I would. Experience born from too many falls from trees as a kid. Not dying, just winded.

One leg felt very heavy, maybe broken. Unable to lift it, I rolled over and tried to breathe, seeing my shoe was still clipped to its pedal.

It came back to me what had happened: the dog.

'Are you alright, love?' said an old woman, coming out of her house, looking just like my grandma, in a pinny, like a ghost, having died when I was kid.

'I've hit a dog,' I said.

'He landed on his head,' said another voice behind me.

'His head's really bleeding,' said another.

I reached for my head, my fingers trembling, and felt a warm patch of sticky liquid.

'Here love,' said another woman, the street now apparently bustling with concerned people, 'put this on your head.' She gave me some kitchen roll.

'Don't worry I don't have Aids,' I said, blood now everywhere, no doubt attempting to show I wasn't brain damaged, although this seemed to have the opposite effect. 'Is the dog okay?' I asked, unable to turn my neck.

'Don't worry about the dog,' another voice said, which didn't seem like a good sign.

'I've called an ambulance,' someone else chipped in.

'I'm OK really,' I said, standing up at the thought of having to go in an ambulance. I picked up my bike. 'I need to get home to my kids.' I tried to look fine by jumping in the saddle and trying to cycle nonchalantly away. Instead I just stayed on the spot, peddling like a clown, until I realised my chain had snapped.

'I think you should wait love, you were unconscious,' said the old woman grabbing my arm. 'Or at least walk.'

'I'm fine,' I said, wobbling away with a wave. 'Thanks for the kitchen roll.'

And that's all I remember.

Sometime later I turned up at home covered in blood, telling Jean that I thought I might have had a bike crash involving a dog, but I wasn't sure. Ella started crying, thinking I was going to die, my appearance instilling a continuing phobia of blood.

'It's not as bad as it looks,' I said, having not seen myself in a mirror yet to know it couldn't look much worse.

'You go home Jean,' I said, trying to sound calm.

'I think I'll hang on till Mandy gets home,' she said.

As I stood there the phone rang and I answered it, then put it down, only to find I had no idea what I'd said or who it was. The phone rang again. 'Are you okay Andy?' said a voice down the line. 'I've just had a very strange conversation with you?'

'Sorry, I didn't mean to be rude. I've just had a bike crash and landed on my head. I may have brain damage'.

'I fell off my bike and landed on my head,' I tell the doctor as he pokes at my head.

'That looks nasty' he replies. 'But it's not easy to stitch the scalp, so we'll leave it as it is. How did it happen?'

'I hit a black dog'

'A *black* dog? I thought black cats crossing your path was unlucky, not black dogs.'

'If it had crossed my path I wouldn't have been here'

'I suppose so.'

'I always wear a helmet, but not today,' I say, trying to show I take my safety seriously.

'And today a black dog almost crossed your path.'

'Yes, I guess it was synchronicity'

'Indeed,' he says. He opens a draw and brings out a leaflet – *Head Injuries: What You Need To Know*. 'Read this, and if you get any symptoms – acute headache, dizziness, clear fluid in your ears, things like that – then come back in. Okay?'

I take the leaflet.

'I guess you have a lot of injuries in your line of work?' he says unexpectedly.

'What do you mean?' I reply, not sure what he was talking about.

'Climbing mountains,' he says, smiling.

I can only guess he's a climber.

'No. I'm very safe,' I say.

'That's what they all think.'

I leave the cubicle with the leaflet. My meeting has lasted no more than a minute. The doctor follows me out into the waiting room, clipboard in hand, happy to cross off another name, no doubt hoping for a lull until the next rush around 2am.

'Watch out for those black dogs Mr Kirkpatrick,' he calls after me, and then looks round the room. 'Mr Bardwell?'

FOUR

Fitz Roy

August 2002

I kissed Mandy and the kids goodbye, eager to get it over with – to be gone. I would be away for less than four weeks, 'four weeks' sounding better than 'a month,' which to me was only a fraction of Ian's six or eight-week trips, but for Mandy was too long. Time is relative to the one watching the clock. Waiting for good weather in Patagonia it would drag; on a route time would pass in a flash, the day chased by the night. For Mandy it would be drawn out day by day, a single mother, having to carry the weight of two kids, plus wait for the bad news she always dreaded. I knew it was hard, and the right thing to do would not be to go; to never go anywhere ever again; to put such things aside for sixteen years, which meant forever. It's easy to say I know how hard it is, but that's just a lie. If I did, I wouldn't go, and so deep down I really didn't care.

I picked Ella up and gave her a hug, her tiny legs in their woolly tights dangling in space. I was glad she was still too small to know how long I'd be away, but I knew she'd miss me. Another climb had come around for Ian and me, the Devil's Dihedral on Fitz Roy, Silvo Karo's legendary challenge. We would be trying it alpine style and in winter. If we succeeded I would indeed be a superman. Just like Karo.

I caught the bus to the station, carrying a huge rucksack on my back, a bigger kit bag in one hand and a new fancy lightweight rucksack in the other, enduring the usual panic that I'd lost my passport, or forgotten something. I wished Ian were with me on the train, so I could relax. He was trying to finish some work and had decided to get the bus direct to Heathrow instead, to give himself more time. When I rang him from the station he said he was still packing.

The funny thing about Ian was that he said things with such authority that no matter how daft, you'd never question it. And so when he said, 'I'm getting the later bus, it goes direct to Heathrow, so I'll get there on time,' all I could say was 'Okay.' He was the same when it came to climbing, saying stuff like: 'I'm going to solo the North Face of the Eiger, the Matterhorn, then the Jorasses.' There would be no hint of doubt whatsoever.

I was utterly convinced Ian was good, because *he* was utterly convinced.

I got to London and had the usual battle on the tube, getting stuck in barriers, knocking into people, feeling the burn as I climbed up the stairs into Heathrow. I knew the weight of my gear was substantially more than my twenty-five kilogram limit. To overcome this hurdle we had a plan, one that unfortunately hinged on Ian getting to the airport on time.

Ian wasn't where we were supposed to meet, and wasn't answering his phone. I began to pace up and down, pushing my trolley, wondering what to do. After more ringing I got through. His voice was now edged with panic, and he'd started spreading the blame around, but was still exuding his usual confidence:

'The bloody bus is late getting there, but I'll get there in time, I'll see you at the check-in desk.'

Ian seemed to live on the edge, whatever he did. A few months before he'd planned a trip to Norway on a ferry, sharing a car with four other climbers. It was only when they entered the port, and were asked for their passports, that Ian remembered he didn't have his. He had to get the train home, find his passport, and fly out instead to meet them. He lived life at breakneck speed, something I put down to his age, and the fact he'd taken up serious climbing later in life. I also wondered if he suspected he'd not be around that long, so wanted to get things done.

I pushed through the crowds with my trolley, everyone going somewhere, my bags wobbling precariously. Inevitably, my new lightweight rucksack, custom made and sent from China only two days before, fell off the front and jammed under the trolley's wheels. I leaned forward and impatiently yanked it back on.

There was a ripping sound, and the sack's contents spilled out. One half of the rucksack was in my hand, the other jammed under the trolley. 'So much for lightweight gear,' I thought, stuffing the remains in a nearby bin, and repacking my gear into two carrier bags.

People often comment on how laid back I am, and how I don't get stressed. Yet it's a simple trick, really – just avoid it. The one thing that can stress me is travelling, mainly because my brain can't process dates and times well, meaning I often made a hash of it. Travelling with Captain Disaster compounded my underlying anxiety, and I became increasingly frantic as

I stood looking at my watch, the check-in queue for our flight to Buenos Aires growing shorter and shorter. I was trying to work out what to do if Ian didn't get there on time when in the distance I saw him, sweaty and running, looking deranged and out of place in a big duvet jacket and plastic boots.

Without a greeting we quickly re-sorted our gear and put our baggage plan into action.

Phase one. Ian held back while I went and checked in the correct weight of bags.

Phase two. I held back while Ian checked in the correct weight of bags.

Phase three. We wait a few minutes then each one of us went back again with a hand-luggage bag containing a ton of hardware – karabiners, pegs and so forth – looking panicked. We then explained to the check-in lady that security hadn't allowed our gear through and we had to put it in the hold. With the flight due to board, she rushed our gear through. Feeling very self-satisfied, we went through security with our real hand luggage, a bag of the correct size, only extra heavy since each one contained a rope.

'Sorry you can't take that on the flight,' said the woman at security, looking stern. 'And the same goes for you,' she said, as Ian's bag passed through the scanner.

'It's only a rope,' I said, forgetting the golden rule of authority, that it never backs down.

'Why?' said Ian.

'You could tie up the pilot with it,' she said, and so, rather embarrassed, and almost out of time, both of us had to run, hot and sweaty, back to check-in, and avoiding the same check-in lady, get a third helping of baggage.

I really wondered if all the stress was worth it.

The aircraft banked over Buenos Aires, the city sprawling below, both of us eager to get off after a long flight.

'What does your brother do?' asked Ian.

'He's a loadmaster in the RAF,' I replied, looking down at the grey buildings. 'He's on those old Hercules transport planes the RAF bought in the 1960s and have flown every day since.'

'Does he like it?'

'I think being in the military is tough, but he loves his job.'

As the flaps extended and the plane sank towards the runway, I told Ian a story Robin had told me about flying a celebrity into Kabul, about how she'd freaked out when a few miles out from the airport the whole crew had put on body armour, my brother checking his pistol was loaded, and his assault rifle close by. 'Why are you doing that?' asked the celeb.

'In case we crash land,' he said, matter-of-factly, both the star and her manager's face draining as he spoke. 'There are a lot of bad people down there who don't read *Hello!* magazine.'

'But the war's over,' said the manager. 'Isn't it?'

'Only on the news,' said Robin. 'Oh, and when we come in we'll be dropping steeply from high altitude and pulling up at the last minute. And we won't stop for long, so make sure you can debus as fast as possible.'

'Why?' said the celeb, her hands now shaking.

'Rockets,' said Robin, and walked off to check the rest of his passengers.

Ian laughed at the story. 'You'd have made a good soldier,' he said. 'All that suffering and danger, you'd have loved it.'

'I don't like ironing,' I replied, as the wheels kissed the tarmac.

We got a taxi to our hostel for the night. In the morning we'd be flying early to El Calafate, a small town from where we'd get a bus or taxi to the village of El Chaltén, a hamlet at the base of Fitz Roy. That was if the roads were open.

The taxi was small and so I sat in the back wedged in beside all our bags, the driver chatting away about the collapse of the Argentine economy. The peso had been linked to the dollar since 1992, meaning Argentina was one of the most expensive places to climb in the world, a crazy state of affairs. It was easy to see the economy didn't warrant such a fixed rate, as it seemed no one paid tax, and the big companies sent all their profits abroad. The year before things had come to a head and overnight the fixed rate had been abandoned, causing a financial collapse and a run on the banks. People saw their savings tumble to a fraction of their previous value and there was blood on the streets. The Argentines are a proud and noble people. I always got the sense they felt superior to other South Americans, perhaps more European too. That superiority was still there, but now carried a shabbiness with it. It was a shame, but it did mean Argentina was now as cheap as a developing country for hard-up climbers. Instead of eking out your money and going home skint, you could live like kings. Not that we did.

The taxi driver, like most Buenos Aires taxi drivers, was a veteran of the Falklands War, and told us how he'd been sent from the hot north of Argentina as a conscript to the islands, the Northerners being seen as troublemakers.

'It was a stinking place: no sun, no food, no woman,' he said shaking his head. 'And so cold, like stinking Patagonia.'

'Were you captured?' I asked.

'We were all captured, thank God, but you British were good to us, better than our army.'

His story reminded me about a guy I'd once known, an ex-Para, as tough as they come. I'd met another Para and asked if he knew him, as the subject of the Falklands War had come up and both of them had fought there.

'Oh yes, I knew him,' said the Para. 'The last time I saw him, he was standing on a pile of corpses firing bullets into them.'

We got to the hostel, probably named The Tango or something like it, since every hostel in the city has a name based on the theme of the tango: the Argentina Tango; Tango Buenos Aires or Tango Maradona. We paid for a room and carried all our gear in, which seemed like a lot for a lightweight trip, our bags piled up as though we were training for the baggage handler Olympics. Ian was still trying to finish some work for a magazine, so went downstairs to use one of the hostel's computers to type up his notes. Like me, he always seemed to have his back against the wall in the face of some deadline.

It was the usual place, full of young Israelis, Spanish and Americans, meant to be seeing the world on gap years, but invariably sat on the Internet all day or talking about how great home was. Most Israelis were fresh from military service, and seemed to be universally disliked in South America. I'd met a lot of Israelis over the years and liked them. Maybe that was because when I lived in London I'd known a lot of South Africans, who also have an arrogance, which tends to rub people up the wrong way. I often wondered if it came from being a besieged country, surrounded by enemies. The only way to cope when you're the outsider or the pariah is to have a superiority complex. Whatever you talked about it was generally better, longer or cheaper in South Africa or Israel, which generally begged the question: 'What are you doing here then?'

Yet I always envied them this confidence, as Brits are by and large bred with an inferiority complex, quick to apologise for everything and be the first to put the boot into all things British.

I almost got into a fight that first afternoon talking to a group of Americans and Israelis about suicide bombers – a touchy subject – saying that religious fundamentalism had nothing to do with it, that young men and women don't blow up skyscrapers or cafes because they want to go to paradise, but because life is hell, and they saw violence as the only way to change things, or else seek revenge. 'If an Israeli plane had bombed my house and killed my children I'd want to die, so why not die by killing Israelis or Americans?'

I noticed faces going red with anger.

'Fundamentalism is an excuse used by leaders to ignore the real causes of terrorism.'

Faces were now really red.

I decided to switch track.

'This Texan farmer goes to Israel and meets an Israeli farmer. He asks him how big his farm is, and the Israeli says: "A thousand hectares." The Texan says: "Boy, on my farm you can drive all day to the north and never reach the end of my farm. You can drive all day to the south and not reach the edge of my farm." You can drive all day east and west and not reach the edge of my farm. The Israeli farmer looks sad for the Texan and says: "I used to have a car like that."'

Cheesy gags really pissed them off, so I left Ian to his writing and went for a walk through Buenos Aires. They were the same streets I'd seen twice before, the city very much like any other. The world was becoming homogenised. Last time I'd been here I'd hung around for a week, leaving the mountains early due to bad weather. I'd stayed with two friends, who had a flat in the centre of the city. They'd told my partner Rich Cross and me that they lived above a disco, which excited Rich as he was going through a party-animal phase. Only it turned out that Disco was a chain of supermarkets.

I sat in a cafe and had some lunch, which, this being Argentina, meant steak and chips, the only food I could order in Spanish, along with eggs, which I'd had for breakfast. Sat there eating, I thought about how unadventurous I was, coming back to Patagonia three times on the trot, walking the same streets, even sat in the same cafe having the same food. I had no interest in going to all the places people travelled from the other side of the world to visit, being just as happy to go to the cinema. All that concerned me was climbing, just getting to Patagonia and going climbing. Everything else was just *stuff*.

Another day, another flight, another hostel, only this one had no connections to tango. In deep winter the town of El Calafate was all but deserted of tourists. The gift shops were closed, their windows grubby with dust. The only places open were the supermarket and the odd cafe. It felt like the Wild West down here, stuck on the edge of the world, Patagonia the last stop before Antarctica – like Cleethorpes on a weekend in February. We did the usual ferrying of bags from the taxi into the room, finding out that the road was clear to El Chaltén, and that a minibus would pick us up at six the following morning.

'That's the hardest part over with,' I said as we went back to our room to sort out all our equipment. We'd be setting off as soon as we got there, so everything had to be primed and packed, ready for action. Ten minutes later I realised all our plans had turned to dust.

'Ian have you seen the red bag with all the karabiners and nuts in?' I said, already knowing that it wasn't there and that it must be lost, but praying Ian might stand up and find he'd been sitting on it or something.

'Er, no,' he said, looking around. 'Have we lost it?' he said, raising his eyebrows, already knowing the answer. The 'have we' sounded more like 'have you'.

I stood in the middle of all our gear and mentally reconstructed what I'd done with it in the last few days: picking it up off the belt in Buenos Aires, hooking it on the trolley and then off the trolley into the back of the taxi and then… nothing. I'd left it in the taxi. It was gone, and without it so was our dream of Fitz Roy.

'Um,' said Ian, standing up and looking around the room, trying to remain positive. 'Maybe we can borrow or buy some krabs?'

I knew it was hopeless. The only climbing shop was several thousand miles away in Buenos Aires. No one was going to sell or lend us their precious gear.

'Yes, I have some equipment you can buy,' said the young bearded man behind the hostel's counter. 'I'm a climber.' Excited, we followed him into a back room where he started to search through some cardboard boxes, the room piled with junk left behind by a thousand absent-minded gap-year kids, until he opened one and announced: 'Here it is.' I prayed that out would come a big-wall rack of gear, expensive no doubt, but worth it if we were able to get our route done.

We held our breath.

Out came a single karabiner with two nuts attached, one the size of a large potato, the second no bigger than an ant's backpack. The man grinned as if he'd answered all our prayers.

We bought it anyway.

Next morning we boarded the minibus in the dark, our rucksacks thrown on the roof and tied down. Each one was full of state-of-the-art gear, designed for the hardest climb of our lives, but missing the glue that held a climb together – nuts and karabiners. Winston Churchill once said: 'When you're in hell, keep going.' It seemed the best plan of action.

Having climbed in over our sleeping fellow passengers, the bus set off on the road out of town and into the blackness beyond. Ian stuffed in his earphones and pulled his hat over his eyes, as familiar with such journeys as a man going to work on the tube. He'd spent a good deal of the last few years travelling to and from mountains, his luggage stowed on every form of transport from aircraft to mules. To him the thrill had long since gone, the journey something to endure.

In many ways, climbing far from home only brought the stupidity of such travel even more into focus. I could climb on the gritstone crags half an hour from my house, crags I loved like friends, every hold familiar from countless visits. Instead I spent a good percentage of my yearly wage travelling halfway around the world to a place where summits reached were the exception, and where the cold meant climbing wrapped in thick layers. All that just to step up onto the top of a lump of stone that no one knew or cared about, apart from me. Maybe the pointlessness of it all was what made it addictive, like building a train set in your loft, or collecting Dr Who memorabilia; the luxury of squandering time on nothing but a whim.

The ride was long and bumpy, the dawn, being so far south, arriving slowly through the misted windows. I watched the country slip by in the half-light, trying to shake my gear anxiety, to be happy that we'd made it this far, that just being here was enough. Yet it seemed so unfair to put in all this effort and to come unstuck due to the loss of one small bag. The devil is always in the detail.

A dark mood took hold, my thoughts as desolate as the landscape beyond the cracked windows, the scrublands of the pampas grey under an overcast sky. Then there was a murmur, a ripple of talk inside the bus, people standing up, or crossing the aisle, as on the horizon Fitz Roy appeared, the head and shoulders of a giant peeping over the horizon. My climber's heart began to race.

We roared into El Chaltén, even more frozen and empty than El Calafate, and got a bed in a friend's hostel, the only guests. In summer El Chaltén was a fleshpot, with big coaches coming in and out everyday, people from all over the world travelling in the hope of seeing the huge bulk of Fitz Roy and the needle spires of the Torres. Now there was only us and the cafes, restaurants and gift shops were closed and boarded up against the weather, a bitter wind blowing through the empty streets. Ruban, the owner of the hostel, shook his head on seeing me back again.

'When will you learn?' he said.

'I do not know if I want to sell my equipment,' the man said. Dressed like a labourer in his thick winter overalls, he stood at the table, his gear spread across it: six quickdraws and six nuts. 'It is all I have.'

Ruban explained to him how far we'd come, that we couldn't climb unless we used his gear, even though his rack was skeletal compared to the one we'd lost. He nodded the nod of a climber who knew how it would feel to lose their rack in such a place.

'Okay, you can take my equipment for free, but please, you must pay me for any loss.'

We packed that night, sorting out gear for our base camp in the valley, gear for our higher snow hole camp, and gear for the wall. Even with our baggage allowance shenanigans, we still only had a small amount of gear, so packing was quick. Glancing at our pathetic rack, I joked that at least it wouldn't slow us down.

With the devaluation in the exchange rate we found we had a surplus of cash and decided to save our legs by hiring a gaucho to carry our gear to base camp on horseback. In the past this had been too expensive, meaning a long fifteen-kilometre carry. This way we could wander in like tourists, taking pictures and enjoying the scenery.

The gaucho came round after we'd packed, to collect our stuff. He was a solid looking chap, with a moustache, dressed half like a cowboy, half like a pirate, with a coloured scarf wrapped around his waist from which poked a dagger. He smelt of damp horse and his hand, when I shook it, was thick and rough. He spoke no English but a price was agreed, Ruban helping to translate. Fifty dollars, which at twenty-five each was well worth it.

Walking in next day, the snow not too deep, Fitz Roy remained hidden behind the cloud. This wasn't ideal for Ian, who hoped to take some pictures to sell once we were home. Ian made most of his money through photography, and even though he cut his gear to the bone to be lightweight, this was generally negated by the huge amount of camera equipment he carried, including several different cameras, partly because he was a pro, and pros always had more than one camera, but also because he was accident prone. For this trip he'd brought a very expensive Nikon SLR, a Voigtländer rangefinder camera, as posh as a Leica, and a pricey Contax compact. The best thing about having a climbing partner who carries so many cameras is you always end up with some great pictures.

We reached the little shack that would serve as our base, essentially just a roof on legs, where we found the gaucho waiting. His two horses stood patiently in the snow, our bags beside them. We greeted each other and Ian gave him fifty dollars, but instead of doffing his stylish cowboy hat and riding off into the sunset as cowboys are supposed to do, he just looked at the money and shook his head.

'No,' he said.

He rubbed his thumb and forefinger together. We looked at each other.

'I think he wants more money,' I said,

'Well he's not having anymore, we agreed on fifty dollars,' said Ian, a man with more experience of being ripped off by the hired help. 'WE ARE NOT PAYING MORE,' said Ian loudly, shaking his head.

The gaucho looked at us, then he beckoned with his finger as he crouched down, both of us following his lead.

He took out his dagger, a mean looking blade, and with it wrote in the snow '$150'.

'I think we should pay,' I said, never being one for confrontation, especially with foreigners dressed like pirate cowboys and waving knives.

'This is bloody murder,' said Ian, pulling a face as he trudged up behind me, up the trench I'd slowly excavated with my feet as I kept doggedly pushing my way up the glacier. The plan was to get to our advanced base camp and dig a snow hole that day. I'd told Ian the approach to the Col of Patience would be easy and once we'd dug our cave we could wait comfortably for good weather, but things weren't turning out as I'd advertised. The snow was deep and soft, and even with snowshoes we sank down under the weight of a fortnight's food on our backs. To make matters worse it was snowing lightly and a mist cloaked the wide snowfield we were edging up. With no map, I was trying to work from memory.

'We'll be up there drinking tea before you know it,' I said, recalling it had only taken a day the last two times. My thighs kept pumping upwards, and I was glad of all my training. Ian started shouting behind me, and I turned to see him cursing at his rucksack, which he'd taken off.

'What's the matter?' I shouted back.

'It's my Nikon. I stuck it in the lid of my sack with my water bottle, but the lid must have had ice in it and didn't tighten. All the water's come out and gone in my camera.'

'At least you've got two spares,' I commiserated, trying to be positive about an error that would cost a thousand pounds to rectify.

Ian let out a frustrated scream, and then we moved on. We were only halfway when the sky started to grow dark, the days, like all winter days, unhelpfully short. Luckily for us I fell in a crevasse and found it would make a good home for the night, one wall rising over us like a breaking wave and offering protection. So we pitched our tiny red bivy tent at the bottom and settled in.

Inside, sheathed in our sleeping bags, we brewed up and talked about how tough a day it had been, wondering what all this would mean for our climb, whether there might be big car-sized snow blobs hanging above us waiting to fall, or if the route would be in condition.

Personally, I enjoyed the struggle. I liked that feeling of a little victory in every step, every metre of ground a battle won. I'd had a few months of being sat at home dreaming about nothing else but this climb, and nothing was going to stop me getting to it.

'I think it's buggered,' said Ian, opening and closing the back of his camera.

'I hope we're not pitched on a snow bridge,' I said, hoping the thought that at any second we might plummet down into the depths of the glacier neatly wrapped in the tent might take his mind off his loss.

'Didn't you check when you got here?' said Ian, my diversionary tactics working.

'No,' I replied. 'Did you?'

'It's not far now,' I shouted down against the roar of the wind and snow blasting against us as we swam up near vertical powder. I'd been saying this for two days now, flicking on my headtorch and looking upwards, looking for the end, another night coming on with us still not at the snow hole. It was almost dark and I knew we still had a way to go to the col, our trench stretching all the way up from the valley, like some bitterly won advance on the Somme.

'This is fucking ridiculous,' shouted Ian below me, the slope steepening towards a rock step, the last obstacle before the col.

It was, but we were also almost there.

Then the avalanche hit us.

'There's been an avalanche!' Ian shouted, helpfully informative as ever.

'I know,' I said, which I did, being the one in front, but glad that, as Ian now told me, 'It was only a small one.' We'd been held in place and not swept away thanks to the weight of our packs.

Digging ourselves out, we reached the band of cliffs that blocked our way to the col, our last hurdle.

'There should be a rope hanging down it!' I shouted, the storm turning up a notch. 'There is usually a rope,' I continued, foraging around in the deep snow but failing to find it.

'I can't see one,' Ian said through gritted teeth, looking left and right, and helping me dig. 'I'll just climb up'.

What followed was textbook Parnell, climbing with a giant rucksack on, in the teeth of a storm, with total confidence that he could do it, that he wouldn't fall.

And of course he didn't.

We staggered up to our longed-for oasis, finding the col at last. It was a desperate spot, just a snow scoop between two ridges, which in the storm was like the inside of a vacuum cleaner sucking up hailstones.

Blasted on all sides we crawled to an overhang of snow, where we guessed it would be deepest, and began digging the hole we'd be calling home for the next few weeks.

'I'll go first, you make sure the rucksacks don't blow away!' shouted Ian into my ear, as we knelt side by side. Ian then untied our one shovel from his rucksack.

Usually the one doing the digging has the hard job, but with only one shovel the one left to make sure the rucksacks didn't blow away had the short straw, quickly becoming cold with nothing to do. We took turns, digging away frantically for ten minutes while the one outside kept an eye on the time. The temptation was to stay inside the slowly expanding cave, where it was warm and quiet, shouting 'Just a minute' to hang on for a few more moments, while the one outside jostled forward for his shift.

Eventually the size seemed habitable enough for both of us to lie down head to toe. We dragged our gear in and closed the door with our rucksacks.

There was silence at last, just the hum of the storm outside the thick walls of our new home. Both of us brushed ourselves down, relieved to have made it to safety. The snow hole was too small, something we realised as soon as we'd relaxed a little, a common mistake when digging under duress. Now we were in it we could see that we should have spent a little longer enlarging it. It was sharing a single bed, only big enough as long as you didn't want to sit up, or move, a good place to stow a couple of coffins, but not two living climbers. Nevertheless neither of us wanted to go out while the other did some home improvements, so we just made do, sorting out our supplies, stowing food, gas and books around the damp walls to keep our sleeping bags off them.

We lit a candle, and this, combined with our body heat, brought the temperature nearer to something civilized. It was a great feeling to have made it to the base of the mountains. Fitz Roy was now only half an hour away across the glacier. We were safe and fully prepared for action.

For the next few days we stayed hunkered down, the storm raging outside as we made tiny home improvements: a shelf cut from the snow here, a piss hole there, making our snow cave a bit more homely. Not that I pissed in a hole at home.

Ian had brought along *Heavier Than Heaven*, the biography of Kurt Cobain, lead singer of Nirvana, who shot himself in 1994. It was not the most cheery book for an expedition.

'Does it have a happy ending?' I asked. Ian's eyes appeared over the top for a second before returning to the text.

I read *White Jazz* by James Elroy, my favorite writer, a man who rations his words like an alpine climber. I wondered if someday I might write a book, scale up the short stories I'd become used to writing to fifty times their size. If I did, I knew I'd have to write like Elroy, a man of few words that were emptied of verbose description, which has as little place in the mountains as in a noir L.A.

I always felt the Romantic view of mountains was only for the long retired or those who could only imagine what it would be like, for poets not climbers.

For me it was just a battle, and that's the only way you could write it up.

On the third day we woke without the dull hum of the wind. Digging away the snow that blocked the door, we stuck our heads out into a blue sky, but on scrambling out we discovered why it was clear – a cold so deep it almost sent us back inside. It was bitter, but bitter was good. Bitter meant stable weather, a big block of cold holding back the warm wet winds from the Pacific and Atlantic.

Fitz Roy stood before us, filling up most of the sky, unimaginably huge. Four times higher than Canary Wharf in London, a squat tower of granite fringed with storm-whipped eyebrows of snow. The mountain was so incredible it cried out to be climbed. I wanted to touch it. It was easy to see why so many climbers had wished their lives away waiting for the weather to clear, simply to have the chance to reach its summit.

When I looked at Fitz Roy, all doubts about what climbing meant to me vanished. It stood as an answer in stone.

On either side rose other peaks equally amazing and only diminished because of their place alongside Fitz Roy. Poincenot was the large fang to its left, which I'd climbed in the winter of 1999. Other peaks included Guillaumet and Saint-Exupéry, named after the pioneering French pilots of the early 1930s, as was Mermoz, its huge East Face sweeping down from a toothy ridge, the chain forming a climber's fantasy of what an alpine ridge should be.

We could easily make out our line on Fitz Roy, the Devil's Dihedral, the Flushing Death Couloir, huge snow mushrooms clinging in its darkest corners. It looked even more fearsome than I'd imagined, a climb you wouldn't wish on your worst enemy.

'I need to take a picture,' said Ian, crawling back into the snow hole, and backing out with his two cameras.

'Good job you brought spares or you'd have missed this,' I said as Ian lifted up his much beloved Voigtländer.

The shutter clicked, but the sound was far from normal.

'That's odd,' said Ian. He discovered the camera wouldn't wind on. It seemed the shutter had broken, perhaps from bringing it from the warm snow hole into the freezing air outside.

'Arse!' shouted Ian, his curses drifting out towards Fitz Roy.

'At least you've got the Contax camera,' I said.

We woke at five, had a brew and some food, packed up and left for the mountain, following tracks we'd prepared the day before, not wanting anything to go wrong.

It was super cold, and every part of our bodies was covered. Only our eyes were visible, my lashes sticking together when I blinked. We reached the huge bergschrund, dawn breaking behind us, the first rays of light illuminating the face above.

It was so big. Bigger than I remembered.

We were so small.

And we knew it.

We sorted out the ropes, both sixty metres long, one ten millimetres thick, the other eight, a choice born from bitter experience. In Patagonia there are no easy ways down. For every metre climbed, you add another metre that must be abseiled. In a storm ropes can become unmanageable, impossible to pull when frozen stiff, or whipped away from you in the wind, their ends becoming jammed behind some distant flake of rock. In Patagonia your two ropes are your only escape. A thick rope will fall straighter in the wind than a thin one, but a thin rope can be pulled through a far-off anchor more easily than a fat one. Having ropes of different diameters gave us one more small advantage. On my first visit to Patagonia in 1999 we'd abseiled a total of three thousand metres, so I guess I had a PhD in retreat.

Tying on, we set off.

Ian led with a small sack while I climbed behind with all our bivy gear in a much bigger sack, shouting instructions as I climbed behind. I seemed to be possessed by a manic urge for speed, no doubt because I knew the longer we lingered at the bottom of the route the greater the risk of being squashed. We moved together, and every time Ian slowed, or tried to place gear,

I'd shout up 'Keep moving!' or 'Don't bother with gear, you're not going to fall.' It was like our time on Les Droites again, Ian trying his best, while I bullied from behind wanting more than that.

Moving up an ice field on our front points, the ground grew more complex and so we began pitching it, me belaying while Ian climbed up a steep and difficult-looking buttress that ended at a snow ledge. He found a belay and I jumared after him, finding my own speed wanting under the weight of the sack.

I felt so small.

'Your turn now,' said Ian, taking the sack from me, a vast never-ending corner stretching up and up above our heads.

While Ian put on his belay jacket and made himself comfortable, I took the small sack and then racked up. This did not take long since most of our rack was now living with our taxi driver in Buenos Aires.

'Okay,' I said. 'Climbing.' I made a few free moves then stuffed in a cam and pulled up on it. The crack looked good but was gritty and dirty, no doubt from having a lot of junk falling down it from the summit. I climbed on, leapfrogging two cams up and up, one stuffed in and stepped on, the other removed, placed above me, and the action repeated again and again. All the while I knew if one blew while moving the other, I'd fall back to the belay, then on again for the same distance.

The crack widened a little and I stopped and looked down, taking a photo. Ian looked up at me, dressed in his blue belay jacket, one I'd designed, the face below sweeping away beneath us, the face I was willing to give anything to climb, the route I'd trained hard for. We'd climbed a long way in a short time, and could get up a few more pitches before dark.

I looked up.

I looked down again.

It was so cold when you stopped. It dug into you, fingers and face first, crawling down your back, biting, stinging, hurting, bitter like poison.

I was cold because I'd stopped.

I looked up and imagined what would happen if the wind came. It would be as cold as climbing on the moon.

I had never been scared of dying, never scared of suffering to some end. It was always worth it, to get to the top. But now I felt fear. This was a turning point in my life. How much did I want this? In that moment my headlong charge to be the best alpinist in the world stopped dead.

'I think we should go down,' I said, the words coming to my lips still half formed in my mind, as if some part of me knew my thought process too unreliable to make such a call, as if someone else was speaking on my behalf.

'I don't think we have enough gear to get up this, and I don't think we have enough to get down if we can't.'

Ian looked up at me and smiled.

'Okay.' Just like that I let go.

And so the long descent began.

We were back in the snow hole by midnight, neither of us saying a word about what we'd just done, or not done, crawling in and making ourselves at home again, reading another chapter as snow melted for a midnight brew before bed.

'What are we going to do instead?' asked Ian.

FIVE

Mermoz

I moved up slowly, aware I could fall at any moment, half hooking my axes on flakes of rock, half balancing on blobs of snow. If anything popped, so would I.

Then I heard Ian swearing below. Shouting.

'What?' I shouted back.

It sounded like he was talking to someone.

'WHAT'S THE PROBLEM!' I shouted down but got no reply.

With night only a couple of hours away, I still hadn't finished the first pitch, and already there was a drama.

'I can't hear you, Ian,' I said, and just kept going, the ropes feeding out easily behind me.

Having given up on Fitz Roy, the next most obvious objective was Mermoz, which had never had a winter ascent, and few in summer, with no easy routes to its summit. A vertical sweep of granite six hundred metres high, the most obvious winter objective was Andy Parkin's route, an unrepeated mixed climb up a prominent groove. Parkin had soloed it in 1993, a tour de force that very few had tried to repeat and without success, me included. I'd made my attempt in the winter of 2000 with Rich Cross and found the first quarter, which we'd done before a storm arrived, pretty challenging. It had reinforced everything I believed about Parkin, a climbing demi-God. Andy was also the man who'd lent us his portaledge after we dropped ours off the Dru, so it seemed fitting.

Reaching the end of the rope, I found an ancient bolt and clipped the piece of old tat tied through it, a remnant of some past siege. Then I brought Ian up. He looked flustered as he climbed, carrying all our bivy gear in one big pack.

'Who were you talking to down there, Ian?' I asked as he reached me.

He stopped and pressed his head against the ice. 'I took the battery out

of my Contax camera to warm it up and ended up dropping it down the bergschrund.'

'Ah.' Now he had no working cameras left.

'You can use my compact,' I offered. 'I'll use my SLR.' It seemed a generous offer, but wasn't really, as I wanted some nice shots of me climbing just as much as Ian needed shots to sell. The only problem was my cheap Olympus wasn't quite up to Ian's standards. Still, with it being the only one on offer, he took it. I guessed Ian had some camera curse, maybe having not bought some film from a gypsy or something, and funnily enough when we got back down this loaned camera never worked again.

It was dark already, and a few pitches higher I found a narrow snow ledge, the size of a small two-seater settee. 'We can chop this down and sit here tonight,' I said as Ian joined me.

'Oh God, I've had enough of horrible bivys this year. I'm sure we can find something better,' he said, looking around. This was fair enough. Only a month before he'd endured a sequence of gnarly nights on Denali in Alaska, including the bivyist's worst nightmare: the standing bivy.

He and Kenton Cool had opted for a one-man bivy tent to save weight, a plan that was light, but not as light as bringing nothing, which may have been a better idea when it came to squeezing themselves inside a tent built for one. To make matters worse the tent was a one-off, designed for a single Sherpa to camp out on the summit of Everest, and so was Sherpa-sized, unlike Kenton or Ian, who is more yak-sized.

This was not the end of their tribulations as the tent was only a mock-up of the one used on Everest, nothing more than a shop display, and so had cosmetic poles, which broke, and cheap non-breathable nylon fabric instead of Gore-tex, which meant their precious down sleeping bags got wet with condensation. Every night was a long, drawn-out icy torture. Then came the worst bivy, a spot too small to sit, and they had to stand inside the tent pitched on a vertical wall.

'Let's try down there,' Ian said, pointing in the fading light at a snow mushroom the size of a table below us, a hard-packed blob of snow stuck to the wall by who knew what. Ian climbed down and stood on it and when it didn't fall off the wall I climbed down and joined him. We stood there gingerly for a while, and when the snow mushroom still didn't fall off we hacked it down to make a bed, aware that at any moment it could disappear from underneath us.

I pulled out the bivouac tent, really no more than a Wendy house, a bag with two cross poles just big enough for two, and pitched it on the spot we'd cleared, with one end hanging over the edge.

'That's your end, Ian,' I teased, nodding at the fabric flapping in the light wind. We climbed inside, pulled out our sleeping bags, took off our boots and lay down, heads together at one end, our feet dangling over the other. It was only now – with us squashed together – that I noticed the difference in size of our sleeping bags. Ian had pulled his from a bulging stuff sack, grunting with the effort and slowly filling the tent, while mine came out with the ease of a condom sliding its wrapper, and with about the same insulation value. To make matters worse the days spent in our snow hole had not treated my bag well. Lacking a waterproof outer like Ian's, it had got damp, and I could already feel lumps of ice clogged among the feathers. Having picked the lightest option I could to save on effort, I had no one to blame but myself.

'That was a cold one,' said Ian from deep within the warm confines of his bag, as the alarm clock beeped away somewhere near his head.

I could hardly answer, having spent most of the night awake and shivering violently. Only the warmth stolen by pressing myself against Ian had kept me alive.

'Let's go,' I said, not sure if I meant up or down, but hoping that the weather was crapping out so it would be the latter.

'I think this is colder than Alaska,' said Ian, with the air of a man who wasn't particularly cold.

I'd never been to Alaska but it sounded warm.

'Looks like another clear day,' Ian said, peeping out from the open door of the tent.

The snow mushroom remained stuck fast as we packed everything away, the stove hanging from a nut in the wall melting water for tea as I stuffed the tent away. Its fabric shed frost like old skin. I was cold to the bone and wanted to get moving, but needed a brew first. I thought about dancing to warm up but decided against it, too afraid the blob would give way. So I just stood there, like a moody popsicle.

'You're quiet this morning,' said Ian.

Tea drunk and a muesli bar scoffed, I climbed up to our high point, brought Ian up, and let him pass to push the route on. Stiff with cold I was still glad it was his lead as he took the gear and stepped over me. Above him was a steep slab, just off vertical, with a slim vein of ice trickling down, the kind of trickle you get from leaky drainpipes in winter, a few inches thick and only a foot wide. The rock down which it ran was blank apart from a slight overlap way above, the wall kicking out a little beyond, making the ice higher hard to see.

It was the perfect pitch for Ian – bold, gearless death.

He tapped in the pick of one ice tool like a man hammering a very fragile copper nail into concrete, then the other, a little higher than the first, so as not to create a fracture line. Why or how ice stuck to nothing was a mystery, a mystery we had no wish to dwell on, just happy that it did. Ian was using 'mono-point' crampons, with just one tooth sticking out no more than an inch from each boot. He gently swung his boots at the ice.

Tap.

Tap.

He straightened up and took a breath, both of us expecting the ice to disintegrate.

'Okay,' he said in a soothing voice, perhaps addressing himself to the ice more than me, 'I'm off.' It wasn't a great choice of words, but off he went tiptoeing his way up the ice.

I fed out the rope, my head drawn in tortoise-like between my shoulders, my body racked with cold. My only comfort was the bomber belay, which gave me a rosy glow of security each time I looked at it.

Ian moved up higher.

'Any sign of gear?' I said, obviously a stupid question, although one meant as confirmation that I was taking an interest. If there were gear he'd have placed it. He didn't reply.

Moving higher, Ian stopped below the overlap, a sort of mini-roof, only a foot wide, but a place you'd hope nature would have left a crack.

'Thin up here,' said Ian softly, his expression as light as he could make it. He was now twenty metres above me, a body-breaking distance to fall.

'Can you see anything above?' I asked, again a stupid question, as if he'd forgotten to check out the ground above his head.

'Thin.'

I considered telling him that if it looked too dodgy he should climb back down, but I knew this pitch could be the key to the route, and that down might not be possible anyway. Plus, I had a great belay, so I was safe.

'Climbing,' said Ian gently, as if he was reminding himself that all this was for fun, rather than admitting he was trying not to die.

I held my breath as he placed his tools over the overlap and moved up, so carefully now, the ice so thin I could no longer see just what he was climbing. The rope fed out and out and out, its end creeping nearer and nearer, and with it my turn to follow.

I felt butterflies in my stomach.

'Peg,' he shouted down, and I craned back to see him balanced just one foot above the overlap, fiddling for a quickdraw then reaching out and clipping it into what looked like a thin knifeblade, probably left by Andy on his descent.

I heard the click of the karabiner.

The thick rope was pulled up a little.

Another click and the rope was clipped in.

'Any good?' I shouted cheerily, not feeling it.

'No,' came the reply. 'Climbing.'

The rope fed out again.

Out and out and out.

'Can you see a belay?' I shouted, no longer caring how stupid my questions were.

The rope fed out and out and out.

'Can you see a belay?' I shouted again. 'You're nearly out of rope.'

In fact Ian still had plenty of rope. It was me who was running out.

'Five metres left!' I called.

No reply.

'IAN, FIVE METRES LEFT!'

'Start climbing,' came the distant reply.

I let go of the rope, which made no difference since I was the belay now, and started to take out the gear, one piece at a time, hoping that giving him a few extra feet might just get him to a solid belay.

The rope fed out.

The rope went tight.

The rope went tighter. There would be no reprieve.

I pulled on my sack, cinched up my axe leashes and began to climb, not tapping like Ian, just hooking my axes into the holes that he had made, my heart well and truly where you'd expect it to be, my mind nowhere to be found.

Now we were moving together, only a single poor peg between us. I hung there, waiting for Ian to make his next move and release some rope, and then I'd hook my axes a little higher. The chances of either of us falling seemed very high indeed.

We were soloing.

I reached the overlap and peered round it. I could see Ian had stopped moving, his heels wobbling. One hand gripped the shaft of his ice axe; the other was fighting with a sling caught on his shoulder. He was trying to free it, a sign there must be some gear.

'Praise the lord,' I muttered to myself.

Only the sling was hung up on his rucksack, and Ian couldn't release it. He let go, and grabbed his axes again, steadying himself. It looked like he was barely keeping it together.

Deep breaths.

Ian dropped his heels and his feet stopped shaking. Then he let go again with one hand and tried another sling, tugging at it and grabbing his axe, tugging at it and once again grabbing his axe. From below I saw he must have put the sling over his shoulder before his rucksack, and so it was hopelessly stuck. He held onto his axe again.

'FUCK! he shouted.

A few sharp breaths.

He shook out his hand and tried again, tugging at the first sling again, each pull leaving him unbalanced but freeing a little more of the nylon webbing from whatever was trapping it. Finally it came free but for a moment I thought Ian had dropped it and was off, but he held on, regained his balance and with a cowboy flick cast the sling to one side over some unseen spike. The rope went tight, a karabiner clipped shut and Ian's body slackened.

'Safe.'

Never had the word been more apt.

We were going to live. Plus, I'd warmed up nicely.

Swapping leads for the rest of the day, the route getting steeper and steeper, we followed a corner system that split the vertical to overhanging wall, which proved just as exposed as the Lafaille, only this time we had only what we carried with us and no portaledge to hide in, totally committed.

Ian seemed to keep getting the hard leads, but he seemed to like it so I didn't complain. After all, he was a full-timer. My biggest worry was the lack of anywhere to sleep, just patches of snow somehow stuck into corners and bands of rotten ice. Shuddering at the prospect of both a night in my frozen bag, and having to stand up or hang in my harness, I pulled out all the stops to reach somewhere we could bivy, but the further we went the more desperate it became. The only relief was finding the peg Rich Cross and I had abseiled off from our highpoint in 2000. It seemed a lot of effort to retrieve a four-quid peg.

The sun began to set as we reached a cul de sac, the corner we'd been following tapering down to nothing, ending at a jutting roof. Two cracks led up, one thin the other wide.

With the temperature dropping fast, it seemed a good moment to put on all our spare clothes and thick belay jackets. Unfortunately, we already had them all on.

There was nowhere to sleep, just a steep patch of snow where the belay was, about ten metres below the roof, a foot or so beneath it seventy-degree ice pitched above a vertical drop.

'This is a bit desperate,' I said, trying to work out how we could rig somewhere to sleep. The most optimistic assessment was a sitting bivy, one above the other. There would be no shared warmth and no tent. I wasn't sure I'd survive that.

'There might be somewhere better on the next pitch,' said Ian, reading from the desperate alpinist's charter, both of us knowing that there never was.

'Okay, I'll carry on,' I said, pulling on my headtorch. Even if there was nothing, and even though I was knackered, the longer I climbed, the less amount of time I would suffer trying to sleep.

The crack was just wide enough to squeeze into, and I udged a bit, not trying too hard, just inching up, knowing the harder I fought the more chance there was of slipping out. The crack was very insecure, and I quickly knew that Andy, no matter how good, would not have gone this way.

I placed our largest cam and stopped.

'Ian,' I shouted, the face below me now pitch black apart from a pinprick of light from his headtorch, 'I'm going to clip the ten millimetre rope into this gear, then swing over to the other crack and try that instead.' Then I'd switch to the thinner, eight-millimetre rope to avoid any drag.

Ian lowered me and with a few strides back and forth, my headtorch flashing across the wall, I grabbed the thin crack. 'Hold me there, Ian,' I shouted, plugging in a cam.

Straightaway it was obvious Andy had come this way, as the crack was solid and just ate gear. Very soon I was up close to the roof itself.

I was glad it was dark, well aware of the exposure below me as I moved up using aid, placing a nut or cam, clipping in an aider and cranking up a little higher. Passing the roof on its left side, I saw that a few metres higher the crack came to a dead end, tapering down to nothing.

I knew there was a way.

Placing a solid nut in the last good spot, I clipped in the thin rope and stepped up in a sling, thinking I might have to start climbing free.

Nothing.

I hammered in a stubby knifeblade, just its tip going in no further than an inch. Clipping in another sling I stepped up again, knowing it was crap, but happy to try with a good nut just below it.

'Watch me, Ian,' I shouted and then moved up, pawing the rock, looking for something, for a sign of Andy, maybe a hook placement or a hidden…

Pinnnggg!

The peg ripped.

My heart lurched as I began to fall, but experience held my fear in check, knowing that in a moment I'd stop, the solid nut holding my fall.

Only I didn't stop, the rock carried on shooting past, splashed white by my headtorch, a jangling of gear, my body brushing the rock until it slipped away, out into space, the skinny rope slack.

Down I went.

'I'm not stopping.' The thought floated through my head. 'I'm going the whole way.'

But then it came, slow at first, and then a sudden, stretching stop, my body swinging back in, hitting the snow a few feet above Ian's head.

Silence.

I was alive.

'Fuck me,' I shouted, my feet almost level with the belay. 'What happened? The gear was right next to me.'

Ian didn't say anything.

Angry, I grabbed the eight-millimetre rope and began pulling myself back up to my highpoint. When I was almost there I shouted down: 'Take me tight on the eight.'

'Eight?' came the reply 'I thought you were climbing on the ten?' That would explain it. Ian had not been holding both ropes.

'Lower us down,' I said, suddenly not keen to push on into the dark. 'I think we've got to finish this in the daylight.'

Down I went, and nothing was said about the ropes. It was an easy mistake to make. Instead we began trying to make the best of a bad deal, to make a home for the night.

With much chopping we cut out two poor bunks into the ice that spanned the chimney, one above the other, both too narrow to lie on properly, or wide enough to relax. My bed seemed to have half a dozen rocks sticking out of it, so while I chopped away Ian cooked.

I tended to do most of the cooking, being a bit OCD about it, having had some bad experiences of the only food you have getting burned. We'd brought two days' worth, dinner being rice, cheese, olive oil and chilli powder; an odd meal for some, but pretty good on cold climbs.

My bed made, I sat down as Ian passed up the pan.

'Here you go mate, you deserve the first mouthful.'

I was starving, having eaten nothing but a banana energy gel all day, or monkey cum as we affectionately dubbed it. I swallowed a mouthful, the cheese and rice already cooling on the spoon.

Then it hit me, a fire that filled my mouth and burned my throat.

The food, our only food, seemed to be contaminated by rat poison or napalm or something.

'My God Ian, what have you done to this?' I said, panting like a dog.

'Nothing,' he said, looking confused.

'Its bloody burning my teeth,' I replied, grabbing a handful of snow and stuffing it into my mouth.

'I just put all the rest of the stuff we had left into the pan,' he said, looking up sheepishly.

'How much chilli powder did you put in from the film canister?' I asked.

'Erm …all of it?'

It was our total supply, a month's worth in one hit. It was our only food though, so we forced it down.

On the upside, it did warm us up a bit.

Tea over, I pulled out my sleeping bag, which now seemed to be simply a frozen lump, retaining its stuff bag shape even when slid out, the down the consistency of stale candy floss. If that wasn't bad enough, the inside was frozen together, requiring me to peel it apart to get in. With all my clothes on already, all I could do was keep my boots and mitts on as I squirmed in, careful not to tumble off the ledge.

'You okay, Ian?' I asked as Ian moved around beneath me.

'Not bad,' he said. 'You?'

'In one word, good,' I said. 'In two words, not good.'

The best thing about climbing hard late into the night is that you do get tired. Within a few minutes I was sound asleep.

First there were the sounds. I could hear a steam train puffing along, loud and getting louder. I could hear voices, like a million possessed people speaking in tongues, an ominous jibber jabber.

I could hear an Indian sitar playing.

Each sound overlaid the next until all I could hear was a formless din that ran through my brain.

Someone once told me that you can't die of hypothermia in your sleep, that your body will wake you first as some physiological alarm is triggered. I was aware that I was cold – beyond cold. I was a lump of meat left for too long in a freezer, a body trapped beneath the ice, sinking down into the dark.

I was freezing to death.

I fought, fought to come round, to move, to stay alive.

The sound of the sitar drifted away.

The voices stopped.

All that remained was the train chugging on, pistons driving air in and out. The sound came from me, from my lungs. I was hyperventilating, the cowl of my bivy bag over my face like a shroud.

The author high on the unexpected crux of the Lafaille route (Lafaille went up the left side of the pillar).
Photo: Ian Parnell

1 The sun brings no warmth on the Lafaille. *Photo: Ian Parnell*

2 Looking down the final belay on the Lafaille, the glacier 800 metres below. *Photo Ian Parnell*

3 Jean-Christophe Lafaille – the little big man of mountaineering. *Photo: Ian Parnell*

4 Ian Parnell: a man for all seasons, but mainly winter. *Photo: Andy Kirkpatrick*

5 The best part of a great climb - when it's over. *Photo: Ian Parnell*

6 The author moving through crevasses on the way to the Dru for the third time. *Photo: Ian Parnell*

7 An easy pitch on the Lafaille, but still dangerous, with loose rocks almost hitting Ian a few minutes later. *Photo: Ian Parnell*

8 The art of suffering – a cold belay on the Lafaille. *Photo: Ian Parnell*

9 Tough times on the Lafaille as storms lash the face for a week. *Photo: Andy Kirkpatrick*

1 Ian tries to fit our route map together. *Photo Andy Kirkpatrick*
2 Like a pig in shit on the Dru. *Photo Andy Kirkpatrick*
3 The author trying to find a way up the Lafaille. *Photo: Ian Parnell*
4 Ian Parnell enjoying the luxury of our portaledge on the Lafaille. *Photo Andy Kirkpatrick*

The art of climbing is to be colour co-ordinated – the author on the Lafaille. *Photo: Ian Parnell*

1 The author making home in a crevasse, Patagonia. *Photo: Ian Parnell*

2 Coming up for air after a night in a crevasse. *Photo: Ian Parnell*

3 When you're on the top you're only halfway there – Ian Parnell setting up rap anchors on Mermoz.
   Photo: Andy Kirkpatrick

4 Approaching the Devil's Dihedral at dawn, Patagonia. *Photo Andy Kirkpatrick*

5 The author settling down for a very cold bivy on Mermoz. *Photo: Ian Parnell*

6 Nearer the dangerous snow mushroom on Sylchris. *Photo: Ian Parnell*

7 Ian at the base of the hard climbing on the Devil's Dihedral. *Photo: Andy Kirkpatrick*

Ian leading on difficult ground on the Devil's Dihedral. *Photo: Andy Kirkpatrick*

With all my will I pushed it away, feeling the cold, as sharp as the Arctic ocean, rush in, waking me, making me aware not how cold I was, but of how little warmth remained. I lay there stunned, visualising the heat drifting off me to be swallowed by the black night. In my mind, solid and real, I could see a gauge measuring my life. It read sixteen percent – its dial in the red.

I felt each and every particle of energy leaving my body.

Numbed beyond numb I fumbled for my headtorch; still attached to my helmet, and switched it on.

There was no light.

For a moment I thought I'd gone blind, only to realise I'd forgotten I'd put my balaclava on backwards to stop my face freezing. I unclipped my helmet and twisted it round.

I was beyond shivering, but knew I had to escape. But there was no escape; I was stuck. The only option was to go into Alcatraz position, so called because this is how prisoners, denied enough blankets, slept on that cold island. I turned over and made myself into a ball, lifting my knees to my chest, hugging my legs, trying to expose as little of my body as possible. From below I heard a movement, the shift of another body moving with its sleeping bag. I wondered if Ian was suffering like me?

'Ian, are you alright?' I whispered, my words warm against my lips. I thought: perhaps if we shared how we felt then things would seem much better, or at least less lonely.

I heard a zip slipping and a groan.

'Ian, are you okay?' I said again.

'I'm so hot!' he muttered. I felt his warmth drift past as it escaped from his bag.

'What time is it?' I asked, hoping we could get moving soon.

'One-thirty,' said Ian.

It was late the following day, as we moved up a large tilted sheet of rock-hard ice, that we knew we were at last close to the top, thinking it could be only a pitch or two higher.

As I took over the lead I was certain that there would be no more bivys for me. We had to finish it now, or else retreat. I wouldn't make it through another night.

What's more, as the sun began to set somewhere out of sight we could see red clouds gathering up for a storm. Our time left could be measured in a few hours. We were a long way up, a long way out, a long way from home.

Every metre we climbed would have to be abseiled, which in a storm would be hell. All we had to do was hold our nerve a little longer, inch our necks a little further onto the block.

Just one more pitch.

It grew dark and cold. The wind, still only a whisper, was turning me to stone as I stood paying out the rope, Ian grunting above out of sight of my headtorch.

'Only one more pitch,' I told myself.

This time, like the last, we knew there could only be one more pitch left to do, and then we could go down.

Ian spoke, but I knew he was talking to himself. He was at the end of his tether.

'Ten more minutes.' I thought, 'that's all I've got left.'

I jigged on the spot, trying to spark up some heat, but it was no use. I stood feeling utterly naked, the cold cutting through eight layers.

I froze.

The rope stopped moving up but jerked around instead, a snake in its death throes, no longer slithering through the night.

I think I was sleeping.

'Ian must be at the top,' I said out loud, the words coming out like glue, my lips slow and awkward.

I looked down and saw I was no longer holding the rope, my hands just hanging by my side.

I knew whoever was above, tied to me by this rope, wouldn't fall. Not now.

Who was above?

What was above?

Where was above?

I heard a noise, a tiny noise, too quiet to write.

'He's there,' I said, grabbing the rope.

I followed, up past marks of Ian: nosebleed blood, fractured ice, the odd piece of gear. And there he was, smiling, sat astride that midnight ridge, greeting me with a tired pat on the back – not too hard, it was a place easy to fall from. All those metres of hard climbing, and two tough nights, but we'd done it.

'Right,' I said, standing up, my axes dangling from my wrists, the wind blowing harder through the gap. 'Lets get the fuck out of here.'

All the way down I focused on not making any mistakes, Doug Scott's voice in my head: 'Be careful on the descent youth.' Every rap was perfect, and

I gave no thought to the cost of leaving valuable gear behind, only the price of not leaving enough. Being the most experienced in going down, and the most paranoid, I went first each time, hitting the bottom slope shattered in all senses.

It was 4am.

Almost at the rope ends I made one last leap across the bergschrund, then unclipped my belay plate from the rope.

'DOWN!'

At last I could relax.

Safe.

I stepped back, only to feel myself falling, down into a second hidden bergschrund. Instinctively I dove downhill, falling past the hole, tumbling head over heels to the glacier. Ian just thought I was being selfish, seeing my headtorch slide away and leaving him to sort the ropes. I waited where I'd come to a stop. It seemed so warm down here, the comfort of the snow hole only half an hour away. Tomorrow we could be back in El Chaltén eating steak and chips, drinking cold cans of coke.

Ian stumbled down to join me, dragging the ropes behind him through the snow, smiling a big daft grin of victory, not victory over the mountains, but the victory of the living. He started to sort out the gear, then sat down, only to stand up again, neither of us knowing what to do now we were down, intoxicated, exhausted, no longer needing to watch over each other, or ourselves.

'Well done,' I said, giving him a pat on the back.

'Well done yourself.'

For once my mind was free of climbing thoughts.

Empty.

Empty of everything.

I wondered if it was worth climbing such things, to go through it all, just to reach such a place as this, a mind for once empty of absolutely anything, a moment belonging only to me.

Six

Park

The slide was high and *very* long, built into the side of the park's wooded slope and obviously constructed long before society's obsession with health and safety. A flight of concrete steps led up to its dizzying summit, from where you could look down at the stainless steel chute kept mirror-smooth by generations of children.

The rest of the park was down-at-heel: broken swings with twisted chains; roundabouts that no longer went round; blank spots with empty foundations, and just the scuff marks of feet, like fossils, left to show what might once have been there. It reminded me of the parks of my youth, dangerous and exciting, worn out through a strange combination of love and neglect. Before computer games and kids' television channels, the only place to be when not at school was in the park, an arena for crazy kids and their stunts, gladiators among the welded tubing and battered wooden boards.

I brought Ella and Ewen here most weekends, walking up the valley of parks that snaked out from Sheffield's centre, a long trail through woods and fields, crossing roads, rising towards the first hills of the Peak District, each step a step away from the city, the valley closing in on us as we climbed.

The parks not far from the centre were well managed, with statues of kings and queens, rockeries and a nice cafe. Its rides were still in one piece, a place for middle-class parents to fuss over their kids. Up here, where the valley began to pinch, things always seemed a little darker and danker, the Wild West end. It was further to walk and there was more to worry about.

Whenever I was away climbing, I often wished I were back in that park with Ella and Ewen.

My uncle Doug used to take us to a big wood outside of Hull and tell us to be quiet as there were cannibals living there, which scared me to death, and I carried on the tradition, telling Ella and Ewen about the wolves that roamed among the trees. You knew – like I did when my uncle told me stories – it was make believe. Yet like magic, UFOs and God, although it scared you, you wanted it to be true.

My kids never wanted to go, but once there, they always enjoyed it, ticking off what they always did in order: feeding the ducks; jumping over the stepping stones; having an ice cream, every trip a pilgrimage to the last.

Getting to the park was always the highlight, both because it meant it would soon be time to turn back, and because there was another cafe, a place to get penny sweets – most usually red strings of sugar – like alien seaweed that made them hyper. Because what's wrong with being hyper once in a while?

The cafe was like the park, well past its best. It needed a new roof, but again this had its own charm. The menu was the roadside cafe variety, everything coming with chips, the man behind the counter looking like an ex-steelworker, only with a pinny on. The other cafe down the hill – the posh one – had once been like this, all chips and tea and eggs and bacon. Then it had been taken over by a young guy with big ideas, something that jarred with the regulars, who just wanted chips and tea and eggs and bacon. I remember being in there the day it reopened and listening to a gruff old man ask for a 'chip butty,' something you knew he had bought countless times from this counter, perhaps since he was a kid; something cheap, filling and decadent in a working-class way. The nice man behind the counter, who looked like he'd used the profits from playing in an Indie band to buy the place, scribbled down his order on his pad, then looking back up he asked: 'Do you want that on ciabatta?'

'Chu-bloody-what?' the old man said.

A few weeks before I'd brought Ella and Ewen and a friend's two kids, Phoebe and Harry, for a long walk through the woods that ringed the city, ending at the park and our favourite rundown cafe. There was a great deal of bribery and distraction involved to get them to keep walking. The highlight was finding we were cornered in a field of cows, the children's whine of complaint cut short as they contemplated being trampled to death.

I'd taken these two kids out a few times, probably because their mother was separated from their dad and I could remember how little trips away were so important when I was young, even though most of these trips were a disaster.

I'd taken the four of them camping in Scarborough that summer, turning up at a family campsite where everyone else had tents bigger than my house complete with generators and satellite TV. I wondered why people even bothered going camping like that. Why would they bring all their crap with them when camping was about leaving it all behind?

Unfortunately, I was further outclassed when I realised I'd forgotten to bring the outer for the tiny tent I'd hoped to squeeze us into. I'd also forgotten the tent pegs – and the stove. Discovering this they all looked crestfallen, and I was glad Mandy or their mum wasn't there to tell me how useless I was.

It was the kind of mistake my dad made, the kind of thing I thought he did on purpose to test us. Now I knew it wasn't a test.

Standing looking at these four kids, I just thought: 'What would my dad do?'

'Look kids we can either go home again, or we can make do, but I promise you if we make do you'll never forget it,' an observation that could be taken either way since the best and worst memories are equally memorable.

'Let's go home,' they all said, screwing up their faces.

'Let's stay, it'll be great.'

'No let's go home.'

'No let's stay,' I said 'I've lost the car keys.'

At last they agreed to stay, tricked by my confidence that things would work out, then watched as I failed to make a flysheet out of bin bags and gaffer tape, then use our cutlery as tent pegs. I cooked on a barbecue improvised from a baking tray I found in my car, last used as a snow shovel, and some scrounged charcoal.

I'd also forgotten to bring a torch – the list of forgotten items was now longer than the gear I'd remembered – but having some candles I made lanterns out of beer cans, peeling a window in the side and tying some string to the ring pulls, before sending them off to explore in the dark, like mini-miners.

'Cool. Where did you buy that from?' asked a child from the next tent over.

'My dad made it,' said Ella. 'He climbs mountains.'

Very soon the campsite was full of kids pestering parents sat watching television in deluxe nylon palaces for lanterns just like those belonging to the kids from the bin-bag tent.

That night, with no tent to sleep in, we all just slept in a line under the stars in our sleeping bags, watching real satellites cross the sky beneath a flysheet of stars. It was a night they never forgot.

On our trip to the cafe things also went wrong. As they stood outside salivating at the menu, I realised I'd dropped the ten-pound note I'd brought to pay for it all. In the end we managed to scrape together enough money to buy a bag of stale bread meant for ducks, not children, and fed them that instead, telling them that 'a chip butty would be nice, but at least you've got a story you can tell the rest of your lives, kids.'

In the park, Ella and Ewen liked to be pushed on the swings, going higher and higher, higher than the other kids, beyond the boundary that neurotic parents feared to cross. I always wondered if I was a bad father, and I suppose it's the curse of the modern parent to fear such things. I'm sure my parents didn't even think about it; life was for getting through, without worry about such things. As long as you were healthy that's what mattered – even if you had a few broken arms.

I usually felt surrounded by parents feeding their kids carrot sticks and rice cakes, their children dressed immaculately, while mine always looked well used. I have to admit I didn't care about such things, feeding my kids what I ate and assuming that scruffy hair or muddy trousers were no bad things.

Flying high on the swings they were always safe. They knew the danger, and the closer they got to the limits, the tighter they hung on. Centrifugal force did the rest. I'd always believed, like my dad, that exposure to some danger is the best way to stay safe. I avoided stair gates and leashes to rein in my children, knowing that one day the stair gate would disappear and the pull of the leash would be gone. Falling down stairs is a right of passage, and anyway, kids are much more bendy and bouncy than we give them credit for.

After the swings came the roundabout, where the aim was to spin it at dizzying, death-defying speed. I always felt a stab of guilt when pushing the roundabout. I'd once ganged up on my school friend Surjit Singh, tying him to a roundabout then started making it go faster and faster. Unable to get off he was forced to hang on for dear life. Unfortunately this wasn't enough for me, and I grabbed his foot as he sped past and he fell off. With his hands tied to the bars, his body dragging on the ground finally brought the roundabout to a standstill, his trousers ripped and knees bloody.

You'd be forgiven for thinking me a sadistic racist, but most kids have similar tales of torture hidden in their past, moments when they stepped over a boundary and took things too far. Twenty years later, having not seen Surgit since leaving school, I bumped into him in a supermarket while visiting my mum in Hull. There aren't many Sikhs in Hull, so he was easy to spot, and we swapped the embarrassed pleasantries most people do when faced with their past, seeing in the other's eyes how much they themselves have changed. Before we said our goodbyes I said sheepishly: 'Do you remember that thing on the roundabout?' He replied without a moment's hesitation: 'Yes.' He'd never forgotten it. All I could say was sorry.

With the roundabout's appeal exhausted, we went over to the slide, standing like an Olympic ski jump, swooping down the hill, its curve flattening out into a long silver runway that ran into the centre of the playground. In the past Ewen had always been down sat on my knee, but it seemed fine for him to go down on his own this time.

The slide cut through deep bushes, giving a real sense of exposure and excitement at the top, the chute dropping away. Even as an adult I'd sometimes grip the sides to slow myself down. Ella went first, with clear instructions to catch Ewen at the bottom. She slid off with a whoop, rocketing down to the end. Now it was Ewen's turn. He climbed up the final few steps and shuffled to the edge. That day he was dressed in a shiny one-piece waterproof suit, which allowed me to carry him by the scruff of his neck when crossing the road, the way a dog carries a pup, and also allowed him to get dirty with impunity.

Unfortunately I failed to take into account the lack of friction such a suit would offer until it was too late.

The second he went over the edge, I knew he was going too fast. He shot down like a red bullet, hitting the final straight where he was meant to slow with no apparent change in velocity, barrelling towards Ella, who stood ready to field him. Instead of stopping he rocketed off the end, hitting Ella in the stomach with his feet and knocking her over like a skittle. Ewen flew across the rubber matting and rolled dramatically to a stop.

The whole playground went quiet, all eyes on the two bodies lying on the floor. Mums rose from seats, kids froze on their rides, swings slowed, their grown-up attendants distracted.

Then there was a giggle, followed by a second one, as Ella and Ewen began to laugh. Ewen stood up, performing a drunken wobble. Ella was now laughing hysterically.

'Who are those children with?' said a voice below in a clipped and concerned tone, the park seemingly suddenly full of mothers with stern expressions.

'Come on kids,' I said, sliding down myself, feeling the disapproving eyes of perfect parents boring into me. 'Lets go and have some chips.'

SEVEN

Fear

January 2003

East Midlands was busy in a regional airport kind of way. Ian and I were doing the usual hustle to get our heavy bags through check-in without paying an excess baggage charge. Neither of us was as skint as we had been a year ago, so this was now more about pride than necessity.

Mandy had given us a lift that morning for our flight to Geneva at the start of a two-week winter trip to the Alps. Ian wedged in the back between Ella and Ewen's child seats. Now she and the kids hung around me as I stood in the queue, Ella pulling my rucksack across the floor as we inched forward.

'I'll stick it on the trolley, Ella,' I said, seeing her struggle.

'It's okay Dad, I want to help you,' she said, stubbornly pulling at the shoulder straps.

We sat in the cafe watching the departure times, waiting for the moment to go through, drinking tea and talking, the kids sat on both knees. I'd have preferred to have just gone through and got this over with, only it seemed rude to cut and run after being given a lift. In the past I had wanted to get on with it, partly to begin something I had spent so long thinking about, but also to escape Mandy and the kids, to leave real life behind, put on my Superman costume and fly away.

Now it was different. Leaving the kids made me feel physically sick, as though the moment of leaving was toxic, and the only antidote to stay or to go. It had never been like this before.

Mandy chatted to Ian about his love life, listing her friends to see if she had any she could set him up with, her love matches often working out well. Ian wasn't interested. I kept introducing him with the words: 'This is Ian. He's a bachelor, but he's not gay,' which I don't think he really appreciated.

Mandy liked Ian because he wasn't the same as 'most climbers', by which

I assumed she meant he wasn't judgmental that she wasn't a climber herself. Climbers, like any mildly obsessed clique, can be dismissive of anyone not part of their group. The same happens with Christians, golfers, and real ale drinkers, even people with kids, all dismissing ever so slightly anyone who isn't following the one true path.

Ella gave me an unexpectedly fierce hug.

'What is this for?' I said, looking down at her hair, face pressed against my chest.

'Wanted you to know I love you, Dad.'

'I know you do daft head,' I said, hugging her back.

'Dad, how long will you be?' she asked.

'Erm,' I said, trying to work it out, 'about twenty-two sleeps.'

'That's too long,' she gasped. 'Why do you have to be away so long?'

'It takes a long time to climb up a big mountain. It'll go quickly, don't you worry.'

I thought back to when I was a kid waiting for my dad, and how long a single day could seem when you knew he would be coming, even a single hour. I would stand on a chair and look out the kitchen window of the flats we lived in, willing his car to appear around the corner, every one that wasn't his a provocation for disappointment, wanting him with every part of my little being, until I felt ill with want. When I heard people singing songs about being lovesick I knew what it meant – to not have the thing you want more than anything else, heart and soul.

'I have to go climbing, it's my job,' I said looking down at her sad upturned face. She nodded to show she understood. 'I don't have a normal job Ella, but that means I'm around much more than a normal dad.'

'But why do you have to go away so much?' she said.

I felt irritated, it was like talking to bloody Mandy, and I wondered what she said to the kids when I was away.

'I don't go away that much,' I said, knowing that each trip away was probably remembered like a wound. 'I'll get you a nice present when I come back,' I added, feeling guilty for the offer, imagining that a child could be bought off so easily.

I told myself that kids were easily distracted arch-manipulators, and that as soon as I was gone they'd forget me. I looked up at the TV screen, now wanting to be away, to escape from the grip this child had on my heart.

'I think we should go through,' I said, the words awkward and uncomfortable, tickling Ella to get her to let go, only for her to slip down and hug my leg. Ewen copied her.

We walked down the corridor to the security desk and I kissed everyone goodbye, lifting Ella up and giving her a hug. She smelt of shampoo and fabric softener. Of home. I didn't want to be home, I wanted to be in the mountains. I'd been home too long. And yet it would be so easy to stay, to live a life like that smell.

'Be good for your mum,' I said, putting her down and lifting up my rucksack. 'I'll ring,' I said, kissing Mandy, who formed up with the kids, Ewen balanced on her arm, Ella holding her hand, everyone waving, Ewen with wild abandon, Mandy with a forced sense of duty, Ella with sadness.

Passing the desk, I began zigzagging through the maze of tapes funnelling passengers towards the x-ray machines, smiling and waving back, eager to pass beyond the screens so they couldn't see me anymore, wanting to run, seeing Ella still waving when I ducked behind the screen, free of them at last.

It was time to focus on climbing.

'Dad!' Ella screamed. 'Daddy.' Her voice was full of tears.

I ran back, zigzagging through the tape again, past confused passengers, until I saw her, straining against Mandy, her face red, crying. I lifted her up and hugged her tight, feeling her little damp cheeks pressing hard against my neck.

'Don't go dad,' she said, her face pressed hard into my chest.

'I'll be back soon, I promise.'

'Don't go dad,' she said again.

'I have to,' I said.

As the plane lifted off I had the usual feeling of roller coaster weightlessness in my belly, only this time it stayed there the whole flight. All my thoughts were about Ella and if she was okay. I told Ian that she'd be fine five minutes later, and that going to the airport had been a bad idea, wondering if sprinting out of the front door was in fact any better.

'How does that make you feel?' asked Ian, no doubt intrigued by what it's like to be a father.

'It makes me think that my time is nearly up,' I said.

We arrived in Chamonix in early January, the valley locked down with serious cold, the wind blowing from the north. No one was climbing, but with both of us unable to ski, the only way for us was up.

We found some floor space in a flat rented by Kenton Cool and his New Zealand girlfriend. I had known Kenton for a long time without ever feeling comfortable around him, but he'd climbed a lot with Ian and they got on well, which made me think how I felt about Kenton was no fault of his. He, like almost every good climber I knew, was training to become an alpine guide and therefore skiing every day in order to get up to scratch. He was living the dream. I was on holiday. Maybe that's why I felt the way I did.

I envied Kenton more than Ian, because while Ian's climbing life was a
success, everything else about him always seemed a little chaotic. Kenton
seemed to be better at juggling, always having an attractive girlfriend, going
on trips, working and having money, and generally enjoying a well-balanced
life. He could come across as brash and a little arrogant, but I guessed that
was show, and underneath he was as unsure of himself as most other good
climbers, a characteristic that fuelled his ambition just as it did mine.
He had something to prove, maybe as much to himself as anyone else, and
no doubt it was this that helped propel him to the super-guide status he
achieved in the years that followed, taking clients up Everest more than half
a dozen times. Whatever made Kenton tick it seemed to be working out.

Kenton could always wind me up, pushing my buttons, forever on the
attack, probing for any weakness. I guessed it was because he knew he was
better than me, and it irked him that I still climbed hard routes and got
some credit. People like me are annoying, but our flaws are always visible so
it's easy to shoot us down and restore the balance.

A few winters before we'd gone into the Northern Corries in the
Cairngorms, climbing with different partners. Dick Turnbull and I had
done White Magic, a much sought-after grade VII mixed route, and one
I'd heard Kenton had failed on. We got up it quickly and so had time for a
second route, The Message, a classic grade V. Walking down we met Kenton
and his partner and told him what we'd been up to. You could hear in his
voice that he didn't believe it was possible for us to have pulled off two hard
routes in such a short space of time. It was still daylight. He was silently
enraged. Despite being the best climber there that day, he hadn't climbed
the hardest route. Back then we hadn't been that far apart. Now he was
pulling away and because of that I resented him his brash confidence.

'Right lads, what are you two going to climb this year?' asked Kenton,
as Ian and I sat on his settee drinking tea. Straightaway, I was on my guard,
anxious he would shoot down any plans we had with his clear, alpine-god
rationality.

'Not sure,' said Ian, looking at me. 'Don't really have any plans, do we?'

'Well, I hope you're going to be a bit faster this time, and not drop all
your gear,' said Kenton, laughing.

'We'll try not to,' I said.

'Also, try and do a proper winter route, not a bleeding rock climb,'
he went on. 'Anyway, conditions are rubbish at the moment.' he said. It was
the same tale I heard every year.

'If this was Scotland you'd think it was amazing,' I replied. 'Just because
it's the Alps everyone sits around waiting for the conditions of the century.'

'Well mate, this isn't Scotland.'

'We might try Omega on the Petites Jorasses,' Ian interrupted, always the peacemaker.

'Cartwright won't be happy if you two rock up and climb his route. He's had his eye on that for a long time.'

We knew Jules Cartwright was interested in this ephemeral route, a slender ribbon of ice firing up the barrel-shaped buttress of the Petites Jorasess, and that it was still awaiting a second ascent.

'He'll have to pull his finger out then, stop skiing and go climbing. Everyone's going soft with this skiing lark, it'll be the death of British alpinism,' I said, sounding pompous.

'You should try it mate,' said Kenton.

'I don't have time for fun' I replied grumpily. And it was true.

The following morning we slowly made our way up to the West Face of the Aiguille du Plan, towards a route called Sylchris, a seldom climbed line up a deep gully first done in 1985. It was meant to be a warm-up for Omega, but that was the only thing warm about it, the temperature plunging off the scale as cold winds blew down from Siberia.

The face was complex, seamed with spurs and couloirs and seven hundred metres high. We were hoping to bivy at the bottom and climb it in two days, or less, since the bitter temperatures weren't conducive to a good night's sleep.

'What an awesome spot,' said Ian as he broke trail, the face opening up in front of us, able to look over at the vast North Face of the Aiguille du Midi to our right, looking across at the Frendo Spur, a steep ridge, dark and towering, over a kilometre high, the place where it had begun for me. It was my first alpine route, climbed in the winter of 1996, a grim battle where everything went wrong. Yet we got up it, although my partner Aaron quit alpine climbing on reaching the top. Not me. That battle, both physical and psychological, had got me hooked. I guess it was a traumatic birth for an alpinist, and it soon became the norm, each route chasing that feeling of being on the edge between success and failure, life and death. There is no beauty or pleasure or fun, just struggle and fear and anxiety. I was addicted to cold war.

Looking up at the Frendo as we climbed I wondered where I would be now if I'd failed up there. I'd been lucky. Most of my trips had been fruitful, if only due to sheer force of will and desperation. How long could you go on if every trip was a failure? How long till you cut your losses and took up golf?

We reached the bergschrund, climbed down into it and fashioned a place to sleep, the temperature too cold to sleep outside its shelter.

Just above us I could see the route Le Fil à Plomb, a ribbon of ice with the crux up high, a vertical smear about forty metres high. I'd soloed it in 1997 and looking up at its exposed vertical crux, I wondered just what I'd been thinking to do such a thing. What had my mental state been like? I knew the answer. Someone had asked me the day before, after I'd failed on yet another climb, 'Why don't you do easier routes?' Those words, his lack of faith, got me up the route. Gazing up, linking those thin veins of ice, remembering hooking up ice only an inch thick, I envied that carelessness of youth. Soloing that route had been an advance in my self-belief, making me feel for the first time like I really could be a good alpine climber, that I had the guts, and not just the ambition, that I was able to risk it all. In that route I saw my potential. I had tested my courage. Two days later I soloed the thousand-metre high North Face of Les Droites in six hours, a premier league solo. I know now that I didn't really care if I'd died up there. I guess not caring is what it's all about.

'Coming in?' asked Ian, crawling into the hole we'd dug.

I crawled after him, dragging my rucksack, and we made ourselves at home, putting on the stove for a brew, pulling out our sleeping bags and mats.

'Sleeping in snow holes seems to becoming a regular thing,' I said as I scraped off any lumps and bumps in the roof, knowing that they would create drip points once the temperature rose.

'I think I've gone off sleeping outside in the cold,' replied Ian. 'I think maybe I'm getting old.'

'No, I think we're just going soft,' I said, having also noticed both of us had much heavier sleeping bags, and lots more warm clothes than in the past.

'Do you think we're the only people daft enough to be climbing right now?' I asked.

'Yes,' he said.

'Then I guess we're not totally sensible yet.'

The alarm beeped at six, quite a late wake-up call, but then we were on our holidays, and the route started pretty much at our door. Ian put on a huge down jacket, and I wore every stitch I had as we picked our way up a series of short technical steps, gaining height until at dawn we reached a deep wide chimney, the crux of the route.

Ian led up a corner with just enough ice in it, carefully planting his front points and hooking with his axes for balance, finding a peg halfway up.

I followed then led on up to the crux of the route, a kind of open elevator shaft that soared up between granite buttresses. Jules Cartwright seemed to keep reappearing on this trip. He'd soloed Sylchris a few years before but the route had come at a cost, his toes suffering frostbite. I could imagine Jules not paying any heed to his poor toes as they froze, always a climber who made no compromises, showed no weakness.

I'd met him on the day he reached the summit, slowly hobbling up towards the Aiguille du Midi cable car at the top of the face, looking exhausted and obviously glad to be in one piece with the end in sight. It was the one and only time I'd seen him struggling. Now, at the base of the crux, I could see it was a tough solo, and recognised his boldness.

Climbing up the chimney, my way was blocked by a car-sized blob of hard-packed snow, formed by the wind and probably weighing a ton or more. I moved up until I was below it, banging my helmet against its mass to check it was solid. It was. There was no way round, so I'd have to go through it.

'Ian,' I shouted, 'there's a bloody massive snow mushroom up here. I'll try to dig through it'.

'Be careful,' he called back, both of us aware that although appearing harmless, these blobs of snow had killed many climbers when they fell. Ian had several ribs broken by one several years before in Alaska.

I took off my sack and hung it from a nut, then started digging, chopping away lumps until I made a space and inched, snow showering down on me, sticking to my face. I soon became chilled in the mushroom's shadow.

Hack hack hack.

Inch up.

Hack hack hack.

The snow was dense, like ice cream, hard and heavy, a block only as big as a football enough to brain you. This blob was vast and if it fell would crush me, squeeze the life out of me.

Hack hack hack.

Inch up.

Hack hack hack.

The more I chopped the more I sensed how dangerous it was, that something this unstable would be more unstable when I hit it with an ice axe. It felt like defusing an atom bomb with a hammer.

Hack hack hack.

I heard Ella crying.

I knew it was all in my mind and tried to ignore her, sensing the hallucination was triggered by fear, and that it was irrational.

Hack hack.

I could still hear her but I kept on digging, knowing the sound and how it made me feel was simply an expression of weakness, some part of me trying to gain leverage to force me to back off.

'Daddy.' It was Ella at the airport, repeated over and over again. I swung my axe less energetically. 'Daddy!'

I remembered my promise: 'I'll be back soon.'

I stopped digging.

I focused hard, forcing the memory away, until there was just the muffled sound of my breathing within this tomb of snow.

I lifted up my axe to hit the snow again but couldn't.

'Fuck, fuck, fuck,' I whispered to myself, banging my head against the snow.

I climbed down a little way, still in the firing line, looking for something else, something safer. To the left there was a faint, hairline crack. Perhaps I could aid around the mushroom? Climbing up I placed a birdbeak, one of the tiny bits of aid gear I carried as a kind of 'get out of that' rack – two beaks, two hooks and two copperheads. I tapped it in with my axe. It seemed good. I could see that half a dozen placements would see me on top of the mushroom.

It would be thin.

I hesitated.

'I don't think I can do this,' I shouted. But only once the words were said did I realise just what it was I couldn't do. I knew I could do the climbing.

I knew I wanted too. Sort of.

I just couldn't.

'Okay,' said Ian, down below and out of sight.

'Maybe you want to have a go?' I asked, thinking a man less attached to this world might do better.

'It's okay, I'm not that bothered,' came the reply, a response no doubt inspired by standing around too long in the cold.

And so down we went, telling ourselves it was just a warm-up after all.

It snowed a few days later, and we hung around town, letting our psyche build again, drop by drop. I tried ringing home but couldn't get through. I was almost glad I didn't have to hear Ella's voice.

One night we went out for a pizza with a group of superstar alpinists from Britain and the United States, the talk mostly about climbing and skiing, but mainly skiing. I ended up sat beside an American climber called Sue Nott, an up-and-coming star of world alpinism.

She had that look most good American climbers have, tanned, perfect, a proper athlete, serious and ambitious. She told me about future trips, each one booked in her calendar – Alaska, India, Yosemite, Canada – the list long and exciting, and no doubt never ending. She was a rock star, with a world climbing tour all planned out. Like Ian she was working to a plan, working towards some far-off goal, some alpine gold medal. She seemed well sponsored and supported, and much of the talk with the other sponsored climbers was about who was doing what, and how much 'what' was worth to their sponsors.

The big thing was to do a photo shoot for your sponsor's catalogue and website. That made you harder to ignore. The climbers round the table needed cash to live the life of a full-time climber; its pursuit was as important as the climbing itself, just as it is for any top performer. If you wanted to be a pro, you had to act like one. I could see that even without money or the limelight these people would climb just the same, only on a shoestring like climbers of old, stealing, scrounging and pushing their luck in the valley just as they did in the hills. They'd do anything to keep climbing.

Sue's eyes sparkled as she talked about Alaska, and as she talked I tried to imagine what it would be like to have a climbing girlfriend, to not have to worry about climbing as an issue. Maybe, like most things, it would be the other side of the same coin. Who could live with someone as bad as me? To know that fundamentally, and no matter how much they denied it, you were never really first in their thoughts, the person to come back to, to fill the times in between.

'What are you up to next?' she asked, her face bright and smiley, realising the conversation had all been about her.

'Not sure,' I said, feeling like a troll beside her. 'I've got two kids, and it's becoming hard to be away from them.' She nodded as if she understood, but I knew she must have no idea, that I just sounded weak, my sentiment as good as a death sentence, something like: 'I've got cancer, I don't have long to live.' I knew because I used to feel the same.

'Would you like kids?' I asked, the question unexpected, deviating as it did from climbing and training and skiing, a question that only a grown-up would ask.

'One day,' she said as she lifted her beer to her lips, her eyes moving away from mine, the conversation over.

Jules Cartwright came in, short and stocky, holding a large jug of beer, sitting down next to me. The beer was all for him. He eyed me up and down.

'Why are you wasting your time on easy routes Kirkpatrick, you should be up on the Jorasses.'

I made some lame excuses, probably that we were warming up, thinking he must not know we were after Omega. Jules could be an intimidating character, with that public-school directness comprehensive kids like me lacked. 'You need to pull your finger out and get to the proper mountains and stop fucking around, you'd do well in the Himalayas.'

I tried to tell him why not, that six weeks away was too much for my marriage to bear, but knew he'd just laugh at my feebleness.

'Why are you married? It obviously makes you miserable. You should be like Ian,' he said. Ian turned and smiled at both of us, as if to say he knew he was the topic of conversation.

'I don't think so,' I said, laughing off his directness, but knowing he was right. I was miserable. 'I don't let go easily,' I said. 'That's why I get up hard routes sometimes. That's why I'm still married'.

Jules didn't reply, just lifted up his glass and waited for me to do the same. Then he made a toast: 'To never letting go.'

It was a late night, but my heart wasn't in it, all the talk of other people's trips only making me feel down. I felt they all knew I was losing my edge, getting weak, but I'd show them all. They had no idea. If I was them – free of responsibility – I'd be the best climber in the world. I couldn't know that within a few years half the people round the table would be dead.

The following morning we shuffled up to the Leschaux hut on borrowed skis, our minds set on climbing Omega on the Petites Jorasses, the frozen wall left of the Grandes Jorasses.

The hut was still a few hours from the base of the route, perched on a buttress of rock, and so we left our skis on the glacier and climbed up to it, a simple wooden box with a door at one end and filled with bunk beds.

Once inside, we found we were not alone. Two young eastern European climbers were already installed, sharpening their axes and looking focused and serious.

'Hello,' I said, stepping through the door.

They nodded, but remained silent.

'Hi,' said Ian, following behind me.

The same nods.

We put the kettle on the stove and asked if they fancied a cup of tea, miming drinking from a cup. They shook their heads and continued sorting their gear.

'What route you climb?' asked one.

'Omega maybe, on the Petites Jorasses,' I replied, both of their faces relaxing a little, no doubt finding we were not in competition for the same route, '- and you?'

'We climb the Croz,' he said, a classic route on the Grandes Jorasess. His tone – deep-voiced and matter-of-fact – made it sound like a one-way mission during wartime. 'We leave at two in morning.'

'That sounds nice,' said Ian.

The tension was high in the little hut that night, but not with Ian and me. Watching the two young climbers, who turned out to be Slovenian, sort and resort their gear, reminded me of so many pre-climb nights of my own, that feeling of excitement and terror, the constant fussing and repacking the only way to take your mind off the climb. Getting up early had nothing to do with an early start. What else could you do when you know there is no way to sleep?

This was no longer true for us. Our gear stayed in the sacks, and we flicked through old magazines and the visitors book, looking through it to find our own entries, and those of friends.

'Fancy another brew before bed?' asked Ian.

'Not sure. I'll be pissing like a Chinaman.'

Going outside just before bed to have a piss and check the weather, I noticed that it was getting warmer, and that the wind had got up, blowing snow around outside the hut, making me shiver at the thought that tomorrow we'd be sleeping on the face.

'I am getting too old for this,' I said out loud as I pissed over the edge into the darkness, then went back inside, making sure the big solid wooden door was pulled tight before going to bed.

I switched off the hut light and got into bed next to Ian, the two of us looking like Morecambe and Wise. It was still early so we lay in the dark talking.

'Have you got any good hut stories?' asked Ian, knowing I tended to have some stupid tale to tell about most things.

'Paul Ramsden once told me a story about being in a hut one night, its bunks full to bursting, so quiet you could hear a pin drop, and how he'd heard a woman whisper in the quietest voice to her boyfriend, "Do you fancy a blowjob?"'

Ian giggled, and so did one of the Slovenians.

'What happened?' asked Ian.

'Paul couldn't help himself and whispered "Me next", and then someone else said the same, and then the whole place erupted with laughter.'

There is no such thing as a lie-in when in a hut. When someone's alarm goes off, everyone wakes up. You think it would be annoying, but instead there is the comfort of knowing that although awake you don't have to get out of bed. And that makes you ungrumpy. So I lay in my bunk and listened to their whispers, the clunk of their boots, the stove being lit, water boiling, eating, drinking, until at last I heard them gearing up to go, the clink of gear on their harnesses, and the click of buckles being snapped together.

But then there seemed to be a problem.

The metal latch lifted on the door but there was no blast of icy cold blowing through the hut. In fact, there was nothing at all.

I heard the Slovenians speak quietly to each other, then the sound of pushing, a little grunting, and a soft thud, as though one of them was bouncing off the door.

I opened my eyes. In the dark the sound grew louder and more urgent.

'Ian, are you awake?' I whispered.

'Erm, yes.'

The Slovenian voices sounded more panicked and one of them started kicking the door as I flicked on my headtorch and shone it at them.

The door seemed to be jammed shut.

Both of them were now taking turns kicking at it, one of them looking quite worried and claustrophobic.

'The stupid door opens outwards,' I said. 'Maybe it snowed in the night, or the wind has blown snow over the door.' They had probably guessed this already.

Ian and I got up and stood beside them as they kicked and shoved at the door, like workmen watching someone dig a hole. A tiny gap appeared, snow trickling through. It became apparent that the door was blocked from top to bottom in packed snow. We seemed to have somehow become entombed in the hut.

Only the shoddiest of French hut builders would build a hut with a door that opened outwards. Perhaps it was simply a joke.

It took over an hour to get the door to open enough to allow one of the Slovenians to squeeze out and dig the entrance clear, at which point we decided that it was better to leave at the same time, rather than risk being trapped in here again, gearing up and following them out into the night.

It was pitch black and cold as we skinned up towards the Petites Jorasses, watching the headtorches of the Slovenians turn to pinpricks as they skinned up to their own objective, all four of us wrapped up in our own worlds, the night-time glacier like some twilight alien world.

We knew very little about Omega, only that it had yet to have a second ascent, and Jules Cartwright had his eye on it, which was good enough for us. I guessed he'd probably tried it before and kept it a secret, as for every hard route climbed there are generally dozens of failures and near misses. A few years ago I'd failed on the Lesueur route on the Petit Dru, and two years later Jules climbed it with Matt Dickinson. So often when you climb a hard route it's on the shoulders of all those who've tried before, even if it's simply to prove you're better than them.

The slope steepened and we zigzagged left and right, left and right, up to the bergschrund, arriving while it was still dark, the cold really biting at our sweaty bodies once we stopped. We stood panting, then unclipped our skis and began walking up the last bit, towards the start of the route. The wall above us a big black space before a black sky.

As soon as our head torches reached the wall we both looked up.

Right from the off it looked improbable: hard, overhung, devoid of ice.

Maybe Kenton had been right about conditions.

Maybe he was being helpful.

'Maybe we could aid up the side?' I suggested, shining my torch up a line of grubby looking flakes.

'Mmmm,' hummed Ian. 'I'm not convinced'. When Ian was unconvinced it was time to call it a day.

We stood there getting cold, neither of us saying anything, just shining our headtorches at this small bit of a mountain.

'I think I've lost my hunger Andy,' said Ian, taking off his pack and sitting on it. 'I just can't be arsed.'

'I know what you mean,' I said, taking off my rucksack and sitting down beside him. 'I can't get Ella crying out of my head. Every time I do anything I keep thinking that I have to get home to her, that she means more to me than this.'

I switched on my phone, to see if I had any messages. It beeped.

'DAD HOPE UR ENJOYING CLIMBING THOES MOUNTAINS LOVE ELLA'

I showed it to Ian.

'Maybe you're falling out of love with climbing,' said Ian, switching off his headtorch to save the battery as the sky towards Chamonix turned red, and the rising sun lit up the spires of the Aiguilles, one by one.

'I really hope so,' I said.

EIGHT

Xmas

On Boxing Day we drove over to Hull. It was damp and grey, one of those journeys when everyone else seems to have stayed at home. I wished I had too, my belly stuffed and the top of my trousers still unbuttoned.

We passed the same old signposts, apparently unchanged from the journeys I took as a kid up and down this same stretch of road. Even the distances were familiar: Hull 57, Hull 23, Hull 16. The world back then seemed impossibly huge, a journey of one hour almost too much to bear. Driving from Hull to Scarborough in my mum's boyfriend's car felt transatlantic. You forget this when you grow up, when driving eight hours to Scotland is nothing. You forget it's more than boredom, being trapped in a car. When a child says, 'Are we there yet?' it's the desperation of someone wanting to surface for air.

Doncaster. Scunthorpe. Goole. Drifting along the motorway towards the slow Humber. Then I see it up ahead – the bridge. It's a sign we're almost there, but also a welcome in its own right, the mightiest bridge in the kingdom of Humberside, if not the world, highlight of any journey down the poor end of the M62 and as beautiful as the Golden Gate, only joining two places no one wants to go.

The bridge opened on my tenth birthday, in 1981, a rarity in 1980s northern England as something to be proud of. The whole city turned out when the Queen came for the official opening that summer. I know my memory of that day – all flags and bunting – is false, more newsreel than reality, but I still remember with total clarity the feeling of awe at seeing the bridge's massive span held by the two giant towers on either side of the estuary, like two colossal tuning forks, setting the tone for a future that never quite materialised.

When people ask why I climb big walls, I know that part of the answer is held in that ten-year-old child's mind, warped by the bridge's scale and beauty.

I still feel it – every time – as I pass under the bridge, seeing its towers tilting up and over me, and then just for a second, glimpsing the span, end to end, across the river, seeing its vanishing point before it's gone.

Encountering such a structure, you'd be forgiven for thinking you were entering a modern city of glass and concrete, but architecturally things pretty much start and end at the bridge. The Luftwaffe destroyed almost everything that would now be deemed historic, and Hull's town planners destroyed anything that might have been deemed classically modern, going instead for classically grim. Still, it was home. I pulled off the main road and threaded my way through the back streets, the only signs of life being kids playing out on new Christmas bikes.

I hate Christmas. I'm not sure why, but I rank it close to the top of my events hate list, just behind weddings and funerals, the latter slightly more tolerable for their generally shorter length. Being told at six that Father Christmas wasn't real may be the reason why I went off the festive season. I was put straight by my mum, after I bluffed that I didn't believe in Santa, when I did. We all want to believe in things we know can't exist, that defy our growing rationality, to keep the magic alive. But I've never quite worked out why I was told that Santa didn't exist when God did, along with ghosts, UFOs and sea monsters.

The tooth fairy did turn out to be a construct of adults, as I discovered after stealing tooth money from under my brother's pillow, a crime I guessed would be undetectable. I assumed the absence of cash would be blamed on a sloppy 1970s fairy, no doubt on strike like everyone else at the time. Of course my mum knew better, and although I was gullible enough to believe in fairies, it didn't stretch so far as to believe one would grass me up. I often wonder if my lack of faith is due to having my childish illusions dispelled so early.

I drove down the familiar streets, past parks where I'd played, corners where I'd hung out, and walls that I'd fallen from.

'Dad, where's your old house?' Ella would ask on these trips home.

'Knocked down,' I would reply. It was like a ritual.

'Dad, where's your old school?' she would ask.

'Do you mean my primary or secondary school?'

'Either,' she'd reply.

'My primary school got knocked down, and I went to two secondary schools. The first got knocked down while I was there, and the second got knocked down after I left.'

'Do they like knocking things down in Hull dad?'

I once had a dream where I was back in my old school Villa Place, a pre-war building surrounded by post-war flats, the latter looking older than the former, a social experiment done on the cheap. In the dream I was being taken around the school by a teacher, through the hall, into the library, to my old classroom, the teacher so proud at how well I'd done. I felt proud too, a self-made man returning, perhaps not as a millionaire, but aware of what that child had done, how far he had travelled. And then I woke up, and remembered it was now only dust and landfill.

The pace of life is even slower in Hull than Sheffield, and you could feel it as we drew nearer to my mum's house, set on a small council estate bolted on to a nice part of the city. The people weren't rushing as if they knew the world turned without their help. It seems the further north you go, the calmer things become, the nation's lifeblood growing thicker the further from the centre it is pumped. Someone once told me that the 1960s didn't arrive in Hull until the 1990s but even in this new century I wasn't so sure things had moved on that much yet.

I turned the corner, just past the bus stop, and was home, my brother Robin emptying his car as we pulled up, his kids running around excited at the start of a rare family reunion.

'Right kids, we're here. Everyone out,' I said.

Robin's kids are called Kyle and Kiely, which sometimes makes people laugh, seeming funny in a rhyming sort of way. But then so are Ella and Ewen, names that are short and easy to spell, handy when you're not good at spelling. Robin's two were the same age as mine, his kids blonde and well turned out, looking newly bathed, while mine were dark and always well worn in. Although cousins they hardly ever saw each other, Robin being based down in the south of England.

'Hello, Rob,' I said, getting out of the car and shaking his hand, like a real man, never quite sure what to do in such circumstances, knowing that our meeting really warranted a hug. Robin, although two years younger than me, had always been more like 'a real man', whereas I was just pretending. He had the sensible gene I was missing, always had proper jobs, listened to sensible music, dressed in clothes you had to iron and had worked hard to get into the RAF.

'Your two have grown,' he said, as both sets of kids shyly hid behind our legs.

'Say hello to your cousins,' I said, trying to force them out front. 'Have a good Christmas Rob?'

'I wasn't in Iraq or Pakistan, so yes, it was great.'

'I guess instead of a war on terror, it's a war on terrors,' I said, grabbing Ella and Ewen by their arms and giving them a little shake.'

'Don't get me started.'

Standing there in the street he looked much older than last time I'd seen him, much older than me, a little harried, a little strung out, overworked and red-eyed. He had the look of a man under pressure.

I often felt uncomfortable around Robin, partly because he was sensible, a proper man, and partly because I felt a little guilty for being so horrible to him when we were young. I inflicted a million little tortures on him, starting by pushing an aquarium on to him when he was four years old, and working on from there. If I told you that he'd tried to stab me with a knife twice, and that I would have deserved it if he had, that would sum up our relationship. Decades later he still refused to accept my apologies for what I assumed were minor events in our childhood: me pushing him into the docks; locking him in a burning building; dropping him from the roof of an aircraft hangar. The normal stuff I assume most brothers do to each other.

One of my favourite stories, where I didn't technically inflict any pain, involved chopping Robin's head off. We were in woods just outside Hull, on a day trip with Mum and her boyfriend. Robin and I slipped away, and finding a big pile of leaves next to a busy road, I hit upon a clever plan. I admit I was a morbid child, no doubt due to living in a house where the last occupant had hung himself on the stairs. My ruse was to bury Robin in the leaves so just his head poked out, while I would bury my head a short distance away, so just my body stuck out. The overall impression, to a mother who would soon be anxiously searching for her missing children, was obvious.

The problem was Robin took his role as decapitated head too far, and began screaming like a girl. This alarmed our mum and her maternal instincts went out of control. Blind with panic, she and her boyfriend rushed through the woods towards the sound, running headlong through nettles and brambles, only to step into a scene of total horror, her son's severed head laying beside his body and still screaming. Cars sped past, their drivers peering at us open-mouthed.

My mum almost fainted.

Needless – or headless – to say, Robin got the blame on account of his screaming, and got a whack around the head just to check it was in fact still well attached.

How we laughed – twenty years later.

'I'm dying for a cup of tea,' said Robin.

My mum was stood in the kitchen, caught off-guard by our arrival, her small terraced house going from silent to chaotic as everyone rushed in. She worked as a care worker, one of the toughest jobs you could have, both physically and mentally. But although over fifty, she had the build of a woman strong enough to cope with most things.

Coping is what she was best at.

I gave her a hug, and grabbed her shoulders. 'Oh, Mum, you're so strong. You should get yourself a job as a builder.'

She laughed. 'Oh you daft 'a'peth. Get off me.'

I never understood what an 'a'peth was.

'Come here my little darlings,' she said, the kids coming up for a hug.

'Can we open our presents, Grandma?' asked Ella.

She always told us that she'd hate being called grandma, but hearing it from a loving grandchild there was no word sweeter.

'I'll put the kettle on while the kids open their presents,' she said.

After lunch we went to Little Switzerland, an old chalk quarry beside the Humber Bridge that had been turned into a wooded park. Robin and I had climbed there as kids, abseiling down the steep – and loose – quarry walls in homemade harnesses constructed from webbing, the rope tied to the safety railings at the top. The thought of it now made me shudder. We once brought a friend of mine to the quarry to teach him how to climb. He was a refugee from Lebanon, and after we set up a top rope, just by passing the rope around a tree at the top, I said, 'Okay, off you go.'

He was a strong lad, but instead of climbing up the rock, he just grabbed the rope and went up it hand over hand. At first we shouted for him to let go and then shouted for him to hang on when he got so high that he'd kill himself if he fell. Unable to take in the rope, we shouted at him to keep going. He made it though. Like I said, he was a strong lad.

'Remember climbing up there when we were kids?' I said to Robin, looking up at a gully that would have made Silvo Karo shudder. 'How did we ever survive childhood?'

'How did I ever survive being your brother?' he replied.

We walked along talking as the kids played.

'I'm off to Pakistan again next week,' said Robin, 'flying missions into Afghanistan.'

'Is it dangerous?' I asked, already knowing the answer.

'Between the Pakistani military and the Taliban? Yes, it's pretty dicey. Surface-to-air missiles, rockets and mortars when you land, suicide bombers when you're not in the aircraft, and that's not to mention people shitting in your water supply in the hotel'.

'Nice.'

'Can you give Tammy a ring every now and then to check she is okay? I don't know if I'll be able to contact her while I'm away. Not to sound melodramatic but my will is at work. Whatever there is goes to her and the kids.'

'Oh, you'll be okay, you're only an air stewardess in a green uniform,' I said. There didn't seem much else to say.

We walked on a bit further.

'But really Rob, what are your chances of getting killed?'

'At the moment? Moderate to good. What about about you?'

'I'm pretty safe,' I said, the tables turned, 'I don't take any risks'. Robin raised his eyebrows. 'I hardly ever go climbing these days anyway, so maybe I'm saving up my luck.'

'Do you ever think about giving it up?' he asked.

'All the time,' I said. 'Do you?'

'All the time.'

Ella and Kyle found a swing hanging from a tree, both taking turns to push.

'The boss called a squadron briefing the other day,' said Robin, as we took turns. 'He told us we were going to replace some of the 47 and 70 Squadron crews as they need some rest. He stood in front of this big roll of honour, a big wooden plaque that goes from floor to ceiling showing all the 30 Squadron personnel that have lost their lives. I started reading the names again, hoping no one would get added. It was a rousing speech, telling us what a marvellous opportunity it was for us to use the skills we've gained through our training and go into a hostile environment in the footsteps of our sister squadrons and in the best tradition of 30 Squadron and the Royal Air Force. I asked the boss if he was coming with us. He looked me in the eyes and said, "Fuck that," smiled and walked off.'

'It can't be that dangerous, can it?' I asked, thinking what threat could there be when you're in a Hercules transport plane, the Taliban having no aircraft, not even kites.

'The C47 is very slow, and a big target taking off and landing, and the Taliban have a lot of machine guns, rockets and missiles, so pretty dangerous. They can shoot us in the air, landing or taking off'.

'They haven't shot any down yet,' I said.

'They've shot down a lot of our helicopters, and they shot down a lot of Russian planes when they were there. We trained them to do it. So I guess it's not if, it's when.'

'Are you scared?' I asked, imagining what it must be like when you have to go, not like a climb, where the only machine in motion is you, and you can just stop.

'It's my job... but yes I'm shitting myself.'

'What if we go into Iraq?' I said.

'I just hope we're not stupid enough to have more than one war at a time. We're stretched as it is.'

We drove back home for Boxing Day tea, my sister Joanne joining us, a teacher at a local school, our little sister.

'How's work,' she asked Robin after having a hug.

'Fine.'

'You're not off to any wars are you?'

'Oh, I doubt it' he said.

Gathering the kids and their presents together, I bundled the lot into the car, Robin and my mum coming out to say goodbye.

'Lets not leave it so long,' I said to Rob, shaking his hand, knowing we would, and I probably wouldn't see him again for a long time.

I gave mum a hug and kiss, turned to get in the car, but instead spun around and gave Robin a hug too, probably the first one ever, lifting him off his feet.

'Steady on,' he said, as I put him down. He felt light, not like a man, but like a brother.

'Be careful Rob,' I said quietly, so mum wouldn't hear.

'You too.'

NINE

Troll

February 2003

The trip out to Norway was long, driving from Sheffield to North Shields, the Northeast's answer to the port of Hull, only without the charm. There we would board the ferry for the overnight trip across the North Sea, our destination the Troll Wall, the highest in Europe.

'The Troll Wall is mighty,' I had told Paul Ramsden over the phone, seeing if he was interested in trying a new route, and in winter, on one of the most serious challenges around. 'Mighty big, mighty loose, mighty dangerous and we mighty die.'

I'd been climbing with Paul off and on since we went to Patagonia in 1999. He had a reputation as the quiet man of hard alpine climbing, his hangdog expression making him look older than he was. Until Patagonia, I'd never heard of him, but he had ticked off more hard routes than many of the more famous climbers of his generation. He was only a year older than me, but felt like my dad, perhaps because he'd lived several lifetimes' worth of hard climbing and adventure.

Paul was from Bradford, a typical northerner, and worked as one of the country's top health-and-safety men, helping to draft legislation to protect the public, then breaking all the rules in the mountains.

I often say that when going on an adventure it's best not to go with professional climbers, as all they can talk about is climbing, which gets stale quickly. People with proper jobs are always much better, as you can learn stuff from them. Stuck in a tent or snow hole with Paul I learned about many things, like Britain's regulations on asbestos, the manufacture of incontinence pants and how they polish the cockpit of the Eurofighter.

Just before getting on the ferry, we stopped at a North Shields branch of Netto, wary of how much higher the cost of living was in Norway.

Throwing in bags of pasta, tea bags and soup, we racked our brains for all the things we thought might make life tolerable for two weeks on a huge wall in winter.

Pushing the trolley around the aisles it was impossible to ignore the state of the other shoppers, who, by and large, looked as though they were in transit from prison or the grave, either coming or going. When I'd been on the dole in Hull and London I'd shopped in places like this, the bottom of the food-store chain, the next step looking in bins. I realised I'd avoided them ever since.

'Bit grim in here, isn't it?' said Paul, nodding at a man with no teeth, shuffling along holding up his trousers and wearing dirty pink slippers.

'If they attack remember to go for the brain,' I said.

'How come they don't have baskets in these shops?' said Paul.

'I guess people pinch them,' I replied.

'What could you do with a basket?' Paul asked.

'Use it to fry chips?'

I watched a harried mother holding a can of lager with two grubby kids, their fat faces a sign that at least they were fed with something. I wondered how you got in such a state, and how my mum, a single a parent in the days before the state looked after such people, had managed to bring up three kids without recourse to drugs or alcohol.

I knew the answer: she fought for life, for hers and her kids, never compromising, never letting the weight of poverty crush us. Here you saw people who were squashed flat, their lives, the lives of their children, as low as the prices.

We sat in the car, waiting to go on to the ferry, the car's suspension loaded down with a ton of gear: haul-bags, a portaledge, big-wall gear as well as alpine kit. This climb would test everything we'd learned as climbers, the wall requiring a unique set of skills: aid climbing to a high standard as well as hard mixed climbing in axes and crampons. With the wall close to the sea, we'd have to survive every kind of atrocious weather, from Arctic cold to Scottish conditions of freezing rain and snow. The biggest challenge was mental – we'd have to be mental enough to imagine we could do it.

I hated silence, something I put down to having a television as a kid which required fifty-pence pieces to work. Silence in the house meant we didn't even have fifty pence to our name. With Paul there were often silences, he being a man who didn't waste words. That meaning I was always finding something to talk about to fill the void.

'How come you don't have any tapes in your car, Paul?' I asked, opening the glove compartment and knowing he spent a lot of time driving.

'Not really into music,' he said.

'Do you listen to Radio Four?' I asked, twiddling with the knob.

'Too posh,' he said.

'If you did listen to music what would it be?' I went on.

'The Beatles?' he said, sounding unsure.

'What album?' I asked, now searching in the door pocket.

'The Best of The Beatles?' he said.

I looked at him, his expression that of a man waiting to go in for a major operation.

'Excited?' I asked.

'Oh yeah,' he said, his face as deadpan as ever.

'Are you an optimist, Paul?' I asked, wondering how such a man could climb so many hard routes.

He looked at me, his face looking like it always did, as if he was about to cry. 'I hope so.'

The lights of the cars in front came to life. A man in a yellow high-visibility vest waved us on to the boat.

I love that moment of driving down the ramp onto a ferry, and being directed where to park. There's the ritual of switching off the car, sticking it in gear, grabbing your kit and heading up the steep staircases to the fancy part of the ship, everyone excited, doing the same little tour, checking out the bar, the restaurant, the soft-play area and the aisles and aisles of seats. Even on a routine ferry ride, there's a sense of embarking on an adventure.

A night ferry was another matter. Instead of trying to sleep in the play area's ball pool, which generally smelt of wee, the balls all sticky with kid glue, we had a cabin, raising my excitement to new levels.

'We'll never get out of here if the ferry rolls,' said Paul as we lay in the cabin, feeling the boat rock as we moved offshore.

'Best keep morbid thoughts for the wall,' I said.

Paul gave a dirty chuckle.

I thought about the route, how we had loads of time, loads of gear, and loads of experience, and that it must be in the bag.

It wasn't about doing a new route. This was about the next step. It would also put a ghost to rest, having tried to solo the wall a few years before.

The wall – and its trolls – was no match for us.

We rolled off the ferry in bright, cold sunshine, Kristiansand's harbour edged with ice, and began the long drive along the coast to Oslo, then north to Romsdal.

The temperature dropped as we drove, sun turning to icy clag, passing through Oslo and up to Lillehammer, the heater unable to cope. It would have been nice to have some tapes, as the Norwegian radio was worse than silence.

I got Paul to tell me the story of climbing the Eiger when he was still really only a kid with his uncle Peter, a tale of climbing up waterfalls and a night at Death Bivouac, all told with typical Yorkshire understatement.

'Pretty easy really,' he concluded.

Paul operated under the radar of climbing magazines because he had no reason to seek fame, having a good job and no need to make money from his climbs. I was different, and felt a bit like a whore next to Paul. What was my motivation? Was I making money from climbing, or climbing to make money?

'Tell us a story about an industrial incident,' I said, knowing Paul had a wealth of these, having been involved in investigating many a horrible death.

'There was this industrial oven…' and so he began.

I liked Paul a lot, both for his skill as a climber, but also his skill at being normal: married, with a good job, balanced and uncomplicated – at least on the surface.

It was dark by the time we arrived in the Romsdal valley, snow banked up beside the road, the tarmac grey and bloodless with cold. We parked up at the viewing point for the Troll Wall, where the coaches and sightseers stopped in the summer to gawp.

We got out and looked up into the darkness.

We couldn't see it. But we felt it.

Paul had climbed the wall by the Rimmon route several years before, while I had my own memories.

Such a wall never leaves you.

Looking up, both of us were thinking the same things, imagining ourselves up there, a chunk of our bravado leaving us in the cold, feeling the huge weight of space hanging unseen above us – a space we would have to cross.

We drove into town and found it empty, the inhabitants locked away inside for the winter. The only place open was the petrol station, where we hung around eating a hot dog for tea, Norway being the world capital of hot dogs. They were also about the only hot food we could afford.

There are many ways to read a culture, but one of the best is to check out its magazine stands. There you will see a slice of its people's interests, obsessions and peccadilloes. A news stand in Geneva is very different to one in Milan, the glossy, high-brow magazines on business and culture replaced by gossip rags, their paper as thin as their content.

The magazine stand showed a healthy society, with a good mix of middle of the range titles, without much gossip, but lots of healthy outdoor covers – pictures of rifles, fishing rods and dirty boots. The one thing out of the ordinary was the bottom shelf, which contained a section of children's magazines on one half, brightly coloured, complete with attached toys that would be forgotten the instant they were ripped from the cover, while the other half held porno magazines and adult novels.

Maybe this showed a healthy Scandinavian approach to sex.

I explained my magazine stand world theory to Paul and pointed out the bottom shelf, but he just looked at me like I was a bit mad as he popped the last of his hot dog in mouth.

'Maybe Norwegian pervs tend to be on the short side?' he said.

In the morning we drove back to the wall and pulled in between giant mounds of bulldozed snow, finding it just as vast and daunting as we'd remembered – a mile-high span of rotten and loose rock topped by troll-like spires, giving the whole edifice the appearance of some warped dark fantasy castle, the lair of something horrible. The nature of the wall defied any logic for it to be climbed apart from that very reason itself. It was a horrible cliff, ugly, terrifying, and so it had to be scaled.

'Looks good,' said Paul, with his hands in his pockets. 'Let's start.'

The crux of the climb would probably be getting all our kit to the bottom of our proposed new route, which was several hundred metres up the huge approach slope of steep scree, and would involve ice climbing and a great deal of toil.

I couldn't wait.

A wide river full of ice and slush ran between the car and the wall, meaning we had to do a big detour across a railway bridge in order to start our approach to the wall, repeating the trip again and again, bent double from heavy loads.

We had enough hardware to tackle anything we might find, from wide cracks to ice and snow, plus two weeks' food, stretchable to three, learning lessons from the Lafaille Route on the Dru. Each carry into the base of the wall felt like a step towards success, the greater the pain in our shoulders the better our cards when it came to climbing, like stockpiling ammunition before a battle.

Nevertheless, the slog up the slope, the snow deep and unhelpful, was exhausting, each flex and straightening of my legs under such a heavy load making my thighs scream.

After three days of work, we were hauling our bags in the dark up to our first proper portaledge bivy, set up under an overhang at the base of the wall, a mile above the river, snow slopes and ice cliffs below us. From here we'd push up our ropes for several pitches then move our camp, hauling our bags with all our gear and supplies after us, before repeating the whole process, climbing capsule style, a tactic Ian and I had also learned on the Lafaille.

With the slope dropping away below us we felt a long way up before we'd even started, and the first pitch, which began with crampons and axes, felt like cloud walking.

True to form, once the ice dried up the rock became pretty poor, split with cracks and some sections loose, others okay, everything stuffed with mud and moss and grass. It was about the most unappealing rock you could climb, but we weren't there to be appealed to, and as long as we were moving upwards then that was fine.

It took most of the day to climb two pitches, crossing a small roof, the rock always unpleasant. I led all day while Paul belayed, jumaring up after each pitch, happy to take it easy the first day, huddled below me in a huge duvet jacket.

The section ended at a good ledge, our next home, and it was a delight to simply abseil down the ropes back to our portaledge, rather than haul in the dark and face the usual struggle with the ledge, always undertaken when most exhausted.

'Cup of tea?' asked Paul as I lay down, happy that we'd begun.

'Oh yes, love,' I replied, as he lit the hanging stove and stuck on a pan of snow, the flame warming up the tiny space within the flysheet of the ledge in a few minutes.

'This is the life,' I said, laying back in my sleeping bag, warm and cosy, tea and biscuits in hand, as dinner bubbled away in the pan.

'It sure beats alpine climbing,' agreed Paul. 'Sat on some ledge with too thin a sleeping bag, not enough food, and not enough gear.'

'I doubt we could have any more food or gear,' I said, half congratulating myself, and then stopping: 'Maybe that's not a good thing? Maybe it's not meant to be like this? Maybe this is cheating?'

'Aye,' said Paul, laying back. 'Maybe it's not meant to be a foregone conclusion?'

We climbed for a few more days, pushing our ropes up the wall, the climbing never hard, but potentially dangerous. We were always careful about what we pulled up on, or pounded pegs into. Reaching a sloping ledge, the spot for our next camp, Paul led the pitch above before it got dark.

'Good fun this,' said Paul as he carefully eased onto a skyhook.

'Good for married men,' I shouted up.

'I think I might need a birdbeak for this bit. Any tips?' he asked, fiddling for some beaks on his harness.

'Stick one in, hammer it until it doesn't come out. That usually works.'

'Right, okay,' he said, tapping the beak in.

'You know what they say about Yorkshiremen, Paul?' I shouted.

'What do they say?' he asked.

'You can always tell a Yorkshire man, but you can't tell him much.'

The pitch half finished, Paul made an anchor and tied off the green lead rope, before we rappelled back to the portaledge.

Next morning, we started early, packing up all our kit into the two huge haul-bags to begin the gruelling process of hauling. I went up first and taking in the slack on the haul line, which fed through a locking pulley, Paul lowered the bags out into space. The weight of the bags was tremendous, and we could only haul them with both of us weighting the haul line, dragging the rope through inches at a time as the bags slowly rose up the wall.

It was knackering work, the same process repeated at each belay until we'd reached the ledge. Putting in a big effort I hauled up the bags alone, while Paul gave them a push from below, helping them avoid catching on loose rock.

It was a great feeling to be working as a team, to be climbing carefully and with a big margin of safety, this style of climbing perhaps the antidote for my growing unease about the risks in pushing the limits.

Pulling up the bags, and attaching each one to the belay, I looked up at the next pitch, thinking we had enough time to push another rope length up the wall, then scanning around to check there was enough snow on the ledge to live here for a while.

The climbing above looked very hard and the rock compact, requiring skyhooks and birdbeaks. I was ready for it, my first new route and on the Troll Wall in winter. Paul took a while to arrive, and as soon as I saw his face, pale and strained, I knew something was wrong, his movements awkwardly mechanical.

'It's my back,' he said, as he stepped onto the ledge and leaned like an old man against the rock.

'My back's gone.'

I'd heard all about Paul's back, and the damage he'd done to his spine having landed straight-legged from a boulder problem. As a result of his injury, he'd spent months laid out on the living-room floor, totally incapacitated. He'd seen every back doctor he could, unable to sit for more than fifteen minutes. Clutching at straws, he'd seen an acupuncturist, whose treatment had allowed him to walk and sit again. Since then it had flared up again from time to time, but not like it did in the middle of the Troll Wall.

'How bad is it?' I asked, suddenly panicked at the idea that maybe we'd have to go down, then worried if he could actually make it down under his own steam. Rescue helicopters would not fly close to the wall due to rock fall, so we were on our own.

'It's bad. Last time it was like this, I had to lay on the floor for a few months,' said Paul, his face now grey and crossed with shocks of pain each time he tested the limits of his diminishing flexibility.

'Sorry Andy, we'll have to go down.'

I couldn't stand it, to fail just as we'd started, after such a mammoth journey here, all that money and effort wasted. My mind looked for a solution, but I knew he was right. Our climb was over.

'Do you think I could carry on by myself?' I asked, looking for an answer from me just as much as Paul, thinking he could just abseil off and leave me to carry on, with no thought for his pain, only my own.

'I need to get back to Britain,' said Paul. 'And you'll have to drive.'

That was it. It was over.

'Okay,' I said, my mind switching to how we'd get all our stuff down, especially with me having to do it alone.

Then I had another idea, but I only had a moment to work out if it was a good one.

'Right, this might sound a bit mad, but – ' I began, trying to sound authoritative and considered, '– I'll leave a haul-bag with all my gear in it here, with all the food and the portaledge and stuff on this ledge, chuck off the rest, then tie all the ropes together to reach the base of the climb, and leave them fixed.'

Paul just looked at me.

'I'll drive you home,' I continued, 'then I'll come back, climb my ropes and try to solo it.'

It was a monumentally stupid idea, monumentally stupid on so many levels, to imagine that my ropes and gear would not have been smashed to bits or cut by rock fall by the time I returned, that I could just 'come back.'

But I was clinging tight to my dream. I wouldn't let go.

'Okay,' said Paul. His answer was a sign of how much pain he was in. Any other time he'd have told me not to be stupid and I'd have agreed.

Half an hour later I tossed off one haul-bag containing all Paul's gear, and the gear I'd need to get home and back, and watched it spin down the wall until it disappeared below our feet, hitting the snow out of sight, shooting down several hundred metres to the trees and the river below.

I didn't care if we couldn't find it.

'Were the passports in that one?' asked Paul.

We abseiled down the ropes, my plan permitting a fast descent, down our fire escape of rope. I adjusted each belay as we went, placing more gear and attaching the rope to it with an alpine butterfly knot, so that on my return I wouldn't have to trust just a single strand of rope running unhindered over many sharp edges.

Eventually we reached the bottom of the wall, and the top of the snow slope, and Paul began to climb down, while I tied off the rope, not wanting it to swing free in the wind and get hung up on a flake higher up.

With the rope secured, I looked up at it, spidering up the wall, a string that held all that was left of my collapsing dream. I was leaving every bit of climbing gear I owned. If I lost it I could never replace it. I thought back to the Lafaille, to that broken haul-bag. We had been faced with a choice, to go down with all we had, or leave all we had, forcing us to return.

We had made the right choice then. But there had been two of us. And it hadn't been a new route.

It hadn't been the Troll Wall. And it hadn't been me, not the person I was now. It had been someone else.

But it was done.

Live with it.

I followed Paul down, who wasn't far ahead, knowing he had to wait as I had the spare rope we needed to abseil down the band of cliffs two hundred metres below us.

The snow was dangerous, a slip deadly. I focused on this as I climbed down carefully, the snow thick and sticky.

Focus. Focus. Focus.

I looked down to check on Paul's progress.

He was gone.

I knew he must have slipped.

My heart dropped.

I moved down carefully, shouting Paul's name, knowing he could well have fallen all the way down the slopes, following the track of the haul-bag. That he'd probably be dead if he had.

I imagined having to tell his wife Mary that he was dead, thought about having to ring her from here. Tonight.

'Do I have her number?' I thought.

'I'm okay.' Paul's voice was weak, his head visible far below, just above the big drop.

'I'm okay,' he repeated, and I wondered if he was talking to me, or to himself. 'I slipped,' he shouted. 'Watch it, it's dead icy just below you.'

I climbed down carefully to where the belay was for the abseil.

'I bloody slipped. I thought I was a goner, but just managed to stop myself before I went over the edge.'

I didn't say anything.

An hour later, after staggering, wallowing and bum sliding, we made it to the trees.

'I'm going to try crossing the river,' said Paul. 'It's only a few hundred metres if we go direct. I don't think I can go all the way round.'

I followed him to the edge of the river, knowing crossing it was very risky, but that he was in serious pain. The river was only a hundred metres across, and low because it was winter, but how would he cope with the temperature of the slushy water, choked with blocks of ice that had broken off the bank and were floating downstream?

Paul set off, the water soon over his knees, then up to his waist, inching up to his armpits. It occurred to me that I should have tied the rope to him, but it was too late now.

Slowly the water inched down his body as he reached the shallows on the other side.

'It's fine,' he said, 'but cold,' and waved me on, then moved into the trees, heading for the car.

I followed him, the water moving up my gaiters until it spilled over the top, the water, ice cold, filtering into my boots and under my clothing. It was painful. I inched forward, knowing I had to ignore the cold and cross quickly, the thick slushy water forming up around me, trying to suck me down river.

I thought about getting stuck, of freezing to death, sticking out of the ice, caught by the trolls in some wicked spell. I tried not to panic.

Caught by the trolls? Wasn't I already caught?

The water was over my waist.

Nipples.

Breathless.

I felt the haul-bag begin to drag me back. I wanted to run, but knew its weight might tip me backwards, into the water.

The level began to drop.

I stopped for some reason, and pulled out my camera to take a picture of my half-submerged legs, to take stock of this moment. It came to me, a realisation that was profoundly worrying, that here, standing in this almost frozen river, was the most fun I'd had in a long time.

I heard Paul start the engine.

TEN

Hard

36:01
36:00
35:59

My eyes are fixed on a digital readout, black on grey, a clock slowly counting down, the moment between each second a small torture, the change a tiny relief. As I row back and forth on the rowing machine, back and forth, it feels like I'm chasing down time itself.

35:01
35:00
29:59

The gym is almost empty in the midmorning. It's just me, the usual gang of off-duty bouncers pumping iron in the corner and sometimes the odd pensioner keeping fit. Dance music thumps away but I barely hear it as I pull hard, slide back, pull hard, slide back, the display my only focus.

30:01
30:00
29:99

I hear the bouncers laughing, dropping the dumbbells onto the mat so they ring out, breaking the rules but knowing no one will dare make a point of it. One of them shouts at his mate: 'Tough times don't last. Tough people do.' I've been rowing for a little over ten minutes and already I feel as if I'm going to die.

27:01
27:00
26:59

Sweat stings my eyes and I want to scratch my nose. I want a drink. I want to be sick. But I also know that if I do anything but row, and row hard, I'll miss my target: ten kilometres in under forty minutes. I know I can do it

physically. I've done it every day for two weeks straight. My body is dumb, easily bossed around. It's my mind that's the weakest link, making excuses why I should stop, one after another: you need a rest day, you're overtraining, you're damaging yourself. And yet some part of me overrides it and we go on once more altogether.

25:01

25:00

24:59

You'd be forgiven for thinking this was a typical day for a professional climber, pushing the body, honing yourself. But it wasn't. It was the desperate act of a man trying to get fit quickly. I knew I was unfit, unready for my next climb, too lazy to put in half the effort over twice the time. That meant I now had to beast myself into shape, perhaps not physical shape, but mental, to remind myself how to push the limits of failure.

23:01

23:00

22:59

I used to have a pair of trousers that dried super-fast. In fact, that was their main selling point, the adverts and swing-tags making a big thing about how no matter how wet they became, they would dry in a flash. What the adverts didn't explain was the flipside – that while they dried fast, they also got wet quickly. The trousers had all the water-repelling qualities of kitchen roll.

My fitness was like those trousers. I could get fit very quickly, very often while actually on the climb, but once home I would do nothing, and so my fitness would go back to zero. Zero to hero and back again. Being fit is a full-time job, and like most real work, I tended to avoid it.

To make matters worse, I learned that you didn't actually have to be that fit, and the psychological commitment to climb was more important than pull-ups and ten-kilometre runs. This was my greatest asset, and my biggest downfall.

While some trained every day, I trained a few times a year. Also, my lifestyle was not conducive to fitness, being a binger in all things: work, food and climbing. This meant I usually went away as unfit as I could be, and came back in good shape, having often lost a lot of weight. It was the most extreme diet you could imagine, with the added benefit of involuntary colonic irrigation if it got really scary.

I did aspire to be fit, and this was part of my addiction to climbing. Coming home thin and fit meant that climbing created the person I wanted to be but was too lazy to do on my own.

The reason I could get away with this lack of preparation was the climbing

I did tended to be slow and technical, meaning you didn't have to be an Olympic athlete, just a plodder, even if you were plodding up vertical granite. Knowing this truth – that you didn't need to be a superman – was probably my biggest asset.

Ian, as well as most climbers better than us, spent all their time training, each extra pull-up or personal best reached bringing them mentally closer to being the superman they believed they had to be. Many people train all their lives for a race they'll never feel ready to run. I'm just ignorant – or arrogant – enough to set off anyway, confident that I'll wing it.

21:01

21:00

20:59

I try not to look at the counter. The faster my heart beats, the longer the pause between each second seems to grow, stretching the laws of physics. It is like rowing away from a black hole.

Eyes closed, I picture myself zipping across the water in the Olympics, or trying to outrun a tanker during an Atlantic crossing – anything but sat in the gym, the space between now and the end unimaginably vast, only tempered by the tiny joy of the distance readout changing, the relief of passing each kilometre mark, knowing that eventually it will go from thousands to hundreds to tens and then single digits.

20:01

20:00

19:59

People have told me I must have good muscle memory, but I have no idea what that really means, and it seems to go against the three things all alpinists need: fortitude, a bad memory and – I forget the third. The point is if you could remember how scared, miserable and frustrated you were during a climb you'd never go back. I didn't think of myself as being strong or fit, but I did have strong legs and thick bones, which seemed hard to break.

Truth be told, I did have a resting heart rate below forty beats per minute, which some might argue puts me in the bracket of super-athlete. I put this down to being a sloth, a languid kind of chap, easygoing to the point of not going at all. I lived by the Iranian proverb: 'When the river is in flood you should swim, and when the river is empty you should rest.' I did almost nothing at all between big climbing trips: no rock climbing, no running, no going to the gym, my biggest exertion climbing the stairs, my heaviest load my kids on my back. Laziness wasn't the only reason for this. I also felt duty bound to be a normal person, to take off my super-climber costume, and just be a dad and a husband.

11:02
11:01
11:00

I push a little harder for the three-quarter mark, fearing if I weaken now I'll not hit my target time. My stomach muscles ache from the bar hitting them, a thousand little punches, as I watch the numbers tick by.

10:35
10:34
10:33

The usual thought comes to me, whispering, rational, convincing: 'Why not stop now? You've done enough.'

Stop.
Stop.
Stop.

There is no need to be persuaded, it's all I want, just to stop – but that is too easy. Where would be the satisfaction of getting to the end? All I would have is the lazy guilt, the lazy guilt I was here trying to wipe away for just a moment. For once I have to shake off this laziness, buckle down and train hard. I am off to the Alps in a week or two.

'The fitter you are, the harder you are to kill,' was how Marc Twight put it, the sentiment that got me down here to train.

10:28
Stop.
10:27
Stop.
10:26

We make a science out of giving in and giving up, offering reasons that excuse our weakness. Failure feels good. Giving in feels good. That moment of relief, showing love and compassion for yourself, being weak.

Weak.
Weak.
Weak.

But it only lasts for a moment, and that joy is soon gone, leaving only the grubby guilt. Whereas to finish, or at least, to be utterly defeated while never giving in, that lasts forever.

10:01
10:00
09:59

I hit the three-quarter mark, my brain almost too fuzzy to work it out, the banging of the bouncers' weights on the gym floor mirroring my pounding heart, my arms stretching out before me on the rack. 'That feeling is weakness leaving your body,' shouts a bouncer at his mate, as he lets out a primal grunt, a set of weights the size of two small cars above his head.

All I have to do is keep going hard for ten more minutes.

08:01

08:00

07:59

At first you try and focus on form, sitting up straight, legs and arms working together, just like the diagram on the rowing machine, breathing in and out smoothly. But this only gets you so far. Soon you begin to lose your shape, leaning back and using your core to give your arms a break, going faster with less power and then slower with more. After that it's survival rowing, chased down by the great white shark of failure. To the finish or death.

05:01

05:00

04:59

Most people would set out with a rigid and comprehensive fitness regime, but I don't. I'm easily bored or sidetracked, wanting expedition fitness, not to be a body builder or a tri-athlete. On an expedition you really go into the red, many times feeling sick with hunger and thirst, pushing your body beyond the boundaries of comfort, deprived of sleep and generally running on empty, breaking most of the rules of athletic performance.

I'd read that the body can only store two thousand calories of easy-to-access energy, and so based my training on that. I would take Ella to nursery and put Ewen in the gym's crèche, just down the bottom of our hill. I'd do two thousand calories of exercise – running, cross training, rowing, anything just as long as the machine showed my calorie output. I didn't have time to do it properly. I had to go for maximum pain.

When Ewen wasn't there a session lasted about two hours, and after it I'd go back up the hill slowly, legs wobbly, feeling a bit sick, and gobble down my lunch. It was an unconventional approach, and one that worked not on the usual male obsession of a six-pack, but rather an expedition sick pack. This regime lasted a month, with six visits a week. I never felt the benefit, never really recovered. But then again, that's what it's like on a trip.

01:01

01:00

00:59

With a growing sense of relief, I try to put on a sprint, realising I'm still on target for a sub-forty-minute finishing time. My whole system shudders with the strain, my heart ready to give out, suddenly not sure I'll make it down the home stretch.

00:56

00:55

00:54

I know I must look and sound a state, really puffing now, trying to draw every last ounce of oxygen into my sore lungs, spit splattering the display, my fingers having to grip the bar harder, hands callused from doing this every day for a month, feeling as if I've gone too soon, that I'm about to black out. I know what will happen when I stop, that I'll let go and slump forward, the bar springing home, my body shaking, as if it is unable to cope with stopping and wants to go on. I'll be gulping air, my lungs scorched, tasting blood, expanding to new dimensions in the depths of my chest.

00:32

The fitter you are the harder you are to kill.

00:31

The fitter you are the harder you are to kill.

00:30

The fitter you are the harder you are to kill.

00:29

I don't want to die of laziness. One day giving up would not be an option. Then it really would be a fight to the death.

00:11

00:10

00:09

I pull HARD. I pull HARD. I pull HARD.

I close my eyes and prepare for the amazing release to come. To just stop. To let go.

00:08

00:07

00:06

I pull HARD. I PULL. PULL. I try to snap the chain. I know I've almost done. In three metres I can stop.

00:03

00:02

00:01

00:00

ELEVEN

Troll II

May 2003

'Where are you going?' the old woman asked. She was the only other soul left on the platform when the train from Oslo pulled away. Her head was wrapped in a scarf and she walked stooped over her stick.

'Åndalsnes,' I said, pointing west beyond the plateau, towards the sea where I guessed the village lay.

'Are you on holiday?' she said, looking me up and down.

'Sort of,' I answered, trying to be polite. Her manner reminded me of Yoda from Star Wars. I imagined that at any moment she would poke me with a long bony finger.

She mumbled something under her breath and I wondered if at her age – she did look very old – there was no time for anything but direct answers.

'What is in that big bag of yours?' she asked, pointing at the huge haul-bag beside me, a bag almost as big as she was, before stabbing it with her walking stick.

The bag contained all the gear I'd taken with me when Paul and I abandoned the Troll Wall, equipment which I'd carried all the way home with Paul, and all the way back on the bus, plane and train, back to the Troll.

'Climbing equipment,' I answered. 'I'm sort of a climber.'

'Climbing? What do you go to climb?' she asked, sounding intrigued rather than irritated now.

'The Trollveggen – maybe,' I said.

She looked up and down the platform.

'Alone?' she said, her face turned up to mine, her bushy eyebrows raised.

'Alone.'

She pulled a sour face, and shook her head. 'I am very, very old, but I know life is very, very short, and it is precious. Don't waste yours on the Trollveggen.'

With that she walked slowly down to the other end of the lonely platform.

And there we stood, waiting for the train.

I didn't need a warning, I knew this already, knew that in a lifetime betting against the odds, this was my most dangerous gamble yet.

To say the Troll Wall had been on my mind was an understatement. Ever since leaving my gear on the wall, I had thought of nothing else. The image of the wall, black and looming out of the mist, had filled my mind. I would wake up at night and lie there imagining my ropes hanging down the rock, gently swaying in the dark, or perhaps frozen solid, or more probably cut to shreds by stone fall. The wall itself, already a dark and mysterious place, became darker still. My dreams were filled with trolls but I would never see them whole, just catch glimpses of them: oily fur, a fang dripping mossy slime, their breath, their smell.

They had been petrified up there for millennia. They could play a long game.

Waiting for me with the patience of stone.

The thought of going back up there terrified me. First, I must trust those ropes, so long exposed to the elements, and then go it alone, up a new line on the most dangerous wall I knew. I searched for others to join me, a new partner, but no one was interested. The wall's reputation preceding it, but then so did my own. People could see through me, could see my madness and wanted no part of it.

It sounded like a one-way trip.

Yet in the mornings, when I woke from another nightmare with the spring sun shining in, it didn't seem so bad. A solo first ascent was not impossible, it was just yet to be done. Someone would have to do it.

I could be the first.

The wall wasn't so loose or blank – or so deadly. No one had ever died on the Troll Wall.

Again, I could be the first.

Whatever I thought, there was no backing out. My gear was up there, worth several thousand pounds, and my flight was booked, the train times sorted. I would leave Britain and be on the wall next day. It would be painful but it would be quick. I reminded myself I had enough experience to pull it off, and climbing it would put my career back on track. That in itself was worth the risk.

Once I was back on the wall, there would be no fear then.

Fear was for real life.

But then night would come again and I would lie there knowing – without doubt – that I was going to die.

The train snaked down the valley towards Åndalsnes, and turning a corner the Troll Wall came into view, a black tombstone a mile high, darker and wetter with the melting of the winter snows. It seemed oppressive. I peered up through the window, the rest of the passengers unaware it was even there, scoping my line, seeing that snow still clung to many of the ledges, the thousand-foot approach slopes covered down to the trees.

I slowly climbed back up the snow slope, the haul-bag digging into my shoulders, the snow deep and old and granular, like sand. Kicking steps, I'd stop for a rest, then kick a bit more, always listening for falling rock, the ground peppered with an acne of stone shards.

At the initial slabs, the band of cliffs blocking access to the upper wall, which Paul had almost fallen down, ice was forming down one side. I pulled out the spare rope I'd brought in case my fixed ropes were damaged, uncoiled it, and tied one end to me and the other to the haul-bag propped in the snow.

I began climbing up with my axes, the exposure below me instantaneous, knowing that, without a belay, if I fell I would slide a thousand feet down to the river. But the ground was only steep for less than a rope length, with little bulges of soft wet ice, and soon I was pulling up the bag, sticking it on my back and climbing up the slope again, eager to see round the corner and discover if my fixed ropes were still there.

In those final few minutes, as I neared the edge of the buttress that hid our line – my line now – I was unsure what I wanted to find, the ropes intact and ready to be climbed, and the route continued, or the ropes gone, just unreachable strands swaying above, the route and all my gear swallowed up by the trolls. If that was the case at least I had come this far, and not bottled it at home. I'd made the effort, but would be safe. In stealing my gear the trolls would have saved me.

Perhaps I could come back next winter with a new partner, freed from my obsession for the summer, and then continue. Perhaps I could live a very long life and stand at train stations with my stick and tell youths not to squander their greatest gift.

Having the roped dashed by stones would be a blessing.

The ropes were still there, trailing down and secured at the bottom with the single cam I'd left behind. I clipped into the cam but added a nut as a backup, aware of the drop below. Then I took off the haul-bag and clipped it in.

The rope looked okay from here. I could see the next thirty metres and the anchor I'd placed on the way down, the rope re-belayed under a roof, before it continued over it unseen.

I tried to envisage where I'd placed the extra anchors, each of them put there in the hope of avoiding abrasion by the wind, allowing me to climb back up them safely, spotting any damage before I was committed. When climbing a rope with jumars, your life really does hang from a thread.

I attached my jumars, the blue one above the yellow as usual, and took in the stretch in the rope, looking up as I did so, knowing if it did break I'd be backed up by the cam and the nut. The rope seemed fine, solid between me and the first anchor.

This was it.

I took out the two pieces of gear at the bottom and tied the haul-bag to the end of the rope, thus allowing me to pull it up once I reached the first belay. Then I let the rope take my weight for a second, stepping back a little so that gravity could take hold of me.

Now it was just me and the rope.

I took a deep breath and tried to stay calm, telling myself that the rope was fine and that I'd done this hundreds of times before as I pushed the blue jumar up, rested on it, moved the yellow one attached to my foot with a sling, stepped up in it, and pushed the blue one a foot higher, making each action as smooth as possible.

Twang.

Falling.

Suddenly weightless.

I hit the snow and tumbled backwards, my hands still holding the jumars attached to the slack rope, sliding towards the cliff band.

'No!' I screamed, knowing it would be impossible to stop with the heavy haul-bag tied to me.

I was going the whole way.

TWANGGGG!!

The rope snapped tight, stopping me dead on the slope twenty feet from where I'd first fallen.

Looking up, I saw the first anchor had ripped out and that I'd fallen onto the next one higher on the wall, somewhere over the roof and out of sight. The fall was caused by the slack between them.

My mind raced ahead. What if the next one rips out? What if the rope's broken above? I crouched on the slope and stared for a long time at the point where the rope disappeared over the roof. Below it was a knot with a nut dangling from it –the blown anchor.

Staring but seeing nothing.

I seemed to be temporally blinded, distracted by the vivid images playing in my head, my body spinning down the slope below me, cart-wheeling over and over, bones smashing, tendons ripped apart, an empty suit of a man.

How far would I go before I blacked out?

The wet snow began to soak into my trousers, but I just couldn't move. I was stunned.

This was what I was scared about. The trolls were playing with me, testing me, drawing me in and then pushing me away.

I wanted to go back down.

I wanted to go home.

How could I find the strength to climb the rope? I'd now have to do a free hanging jumar over the drop with no idea what it was attached to.

I could die doing this. And if I don't then it could be the next thing, or the next, or the one after that.

Water was trickling into my boot.

A rock crashed down the wall opposite the face, echoing back and forth until it ploughed into the snow slope with a dull thud.

If I went down now I'd never be free of the Troll's spell.

I'd leave more than just my gear on this wall.

I must not be weak.

I pushed the blue jumar up, then the yellow, walking up the slope until the rope hung plumb from the overhang, and I could leave the ground.

Push. Push. Step up.

Push. Push. Step up.

The jumars slid slow and steady.

The rope stretched, my weight drawing down the slack until, like a balloon dropping its ballast, my feet left the ground.

I was away.

Committed.

Push. Push. Step up.

Push. Push. Step up.

Tied to the wall, and the wall to me. Neither could escape the other. I'd show it. Whatever happened it would be worth it to be free.

Up the rope I went, concentrating only on the action of jumaring, the sound, the rhythm, blanking out the drop, or the lurch that would come if the next anchor ripped – or the rope snapped.

Push. Push. Step up.

Push. Push. Step up.

I looked up and measured my progress by the distance to the knot of the failed anchor, growing closer and closer, as the drop below me opened up.

Push. Push. Step up.

Push. Push. Step up.

I reached it and just hung for a while and tried to relax. I told myself: 'Either the rope will snap or it won't and going fast will make no difference.'

I absorbed my position, alone on the Troll.

Hardcore.

'Isn't this the climber you've always wanted to be?'

I looked down at the river flowing far below, a red tractor moving down in a farm below the wall, the dots of tourists walking near the viewing platform beside the road.

'Can you see me?'

I looked at the nut hanging from the knot, and guessed it had been wobbled loose by the wind blowing the rope over the past few months, or by the cold. I took off the top jumar and reattached it past the knot, weighting the rope again. Now I was able to untie the knot, racking the nut on my harness.

Shifting my legs I swung out a little, trying to look up at the rope, trying to see if it was still attached to the next belay, but saw instead that the rope was running over what looked like a hanging block on the slab above.

I swung back in without another look.

'Well, you're committed now, son.'

I hung there some more.

It would be getting dark soon.

Moving up to the lip of the roof, I was no longer hanging free, the rock once more to hand. I reached out and touched it.

It felt cold and slimy, troll-like, but still nice after nothing but space, even comforting, me and it.

I could now see the rope was hung up on a block the size of a small television set. If it came loose it could hit me or cut the rope.

'It hasn't so far.'

I moved up, focusing not on the wall, but on a visit I made many years before to the factory in Switzerland where they made my ropes. I recalled trying to break a single hair's breadth strand of nylon, and watching it spun with a hundred more to make a core strand, this strand spun again with several others before it was wrapped in a tough sheath. The process was inspiring. Infallible. The rope was indestructible.

I pushed on and reached the block safely, carefully passing it, wanting to kick it free, but leaving it in case it hit my haul-bag below.

'You'll need to remember to kick this off if you retreat.'

'I won't be retreating.'

Taking out my headtorch, I climbed on, taking the anchors out as I went. The darkness calmed my nerves a little since I could no longer see the ground below me, only the rope, the rock and the jumars in front of my face.

Push. Push. Step up.

Push. Push. Step up.

I reached a steep slab and it felt good to have my toes on the rock, then moved up a final loose corner, part of my stashed haul-bag flashing into view, making the final few metres much easier on the nerves, as though it was waiting to greet me like an old friend, the bag the wall's prisoner, me its rescuer.

I pulled onto the ledge.

I was there.

I was back.

I put my arms around the haul-bag and hugged it. It was still where I'd left it, which you'd expect, since there wasn't much chance of petty thievery on the Troll Wall, just hanging from the anchor on a small sloping snowy ledge.

Inside everything was intact but covered in a thin layer of ice. Water had found its way in. It was cold now, but I warmed up by hauling my rucksack and coiling the ropes as they came up, ready for tomorrow.

With that sorted, I pulled out the portaledge and fly, set it up, crawled in and got a brew on.

It had been a long day.

I had not rested since leaving this ledge months before.

In the food bag there was a big piece of Norwegian almond cake and I had a greedy chunk to celebrate the ropes not snapping.

Lying there drinking my tea, I thought about the anchor pulling out, and why I'd carried on in the face of danger. It made no sense, but I felt glad of my past self's fortitude to push things, and made a note that I mustn't let that version of me down now I was up here, and how it would be a great story once I climbed the route.

How I almost failed but pushed on regardless.

That night I lay in my sleeping bag, nice and warm, comfortable in my double portaledge, and listened in the darkness to the rocks falling. The winter snows were melting out, and as they did so down came a rain of rocks day and night. Most of the time the sounds would be small and distant, like the drip drip drip within a cave, but every quarter of an hour there would be a barrage of stones close by, their sparks lighting up the night and flashing across the fabric of the flysheet. It was a terrible sight, but one I made a point of watching. Afterwards, silence returned, before it was broken as the drip drip drip of the more distant stone fall resumed.

I pulled out my mini-disk player and tried to block the sound with some music, which worked, leaving me with just the nagging doubt about how safe I was, laid here on my back, with only a thin layer of nylon to protect me.

The morning was windy, with wisps of snow blowing round the ledge. I was faced with another rope-climbing exercise to reach Paul's highpoint before pushing on. I ate some more cake and had a brew, then climbed out of bed and began sorting out all my gear, checking it had survived my absence okay. It felt good to clip on cams and nuts and hooks, and all the other gear I might need, making me feel ready to fight, rather than passively suffering the intimidation of the trolls. For the first time in ages I really felt excited about climbing this route. There was no longer the fear of doing, just the doing itself. I was fighting back, not cowering from the fear of being beaten.

Climbing the rope wasn't too bad, even though I had no idea what Paul had anchored it to, but I'd trusted him with my life before, and so trusted him again, finding a couple of small nuts equalized together. I clipped in and sorted myself out for soloing, stacking the rope in a bag, attaching the self-belay device that would hold me if I fell and tying the backup knot in case it didn't.

'This is it Andy, you made it all the way back.'

I began.

The rock was blank and compact, any cracks full of dirt and bits of grit and pebbles, but I made steady progress upwards. It felt great to be climbing, the process of doing the right thing in the correct order replacing darker thoughts and fears.

I became absorbed in the next few feet of rock. The trolls lost their grip on me, and now could only watch as I ate away at their wall.

In many places I could use the narrow tip of my hammer to bash out the grit from the crack in front of me and place tiny wires, while in others I hammered birdbeaks straight into the muck. Like all such climbs, I knew if the wall were to be beaten, the battle would be fought one placement at a time.

The crack closed down and I switched to copperheads, tiny blobs of aluminum that could be hammered to fit any holes or weaknesses in the rock's surface, each one a little time bomb, their holding power only bodyweight. The copperheads ranged in size between the width of a triple-A battery and a Tictac, and were all about a centimetre in length, formed from a hollow tube of soft alloy and crimped to a length of wire, a clip-in loop swaged at the other end. I knew that so far few climbers had used them on the Troll Wall, and I hoped they would open up some of the wall's blanker sections.

To place one I'd find a spot where there was a slight constriction, a corner where the two sides pinched down, but not enough to hold a normal nut, a spot that may one day evolve into a placement, or else be washed away by time and the elements. Eyeing up the shape of the void it would fill, I'd bash the head to fit, shaping it, making a customized nut, a key to fit a lock, which I hammered into place, trying to get every molecule of alloy in contact with the rock. It was like smearing decorator's filler into a crack in your wall, only less forgiving and about as strong.

I moved up on a sequence of copperheads, testing each one with hard tugs, aware that if I was to fall, the gear below me would rip out and I might hit a ledge below.

'Just don't fall then.'

Rescue would be difficult, if not impossible, and would take days not hours, due both to the wall's steep angle and because the face was deemed too dangerous for helicopters, their rotor blades a target for the ever-present rock fall. I thought about Phil Thornhill, a British climber who had attempted a bold winter solo of the wall in the 1980s but had fallen close to the top and broken his femur. He had sat there for days waiting to be saved, the rescue team lowering a climber down from the top. For me there was no real chance of immediate rescue. If anything happened I'd have to rescue myself.

I crept up a corner to what looked liked a good crack, each placement a dose of fear, but found instead the crack was formed by a loose skin of rock overlaying solid rock beneath, the whole lot looking like it was ready to peel off, its edges sharp and toothy, a new booby trap set by the trolls. I didn't want to touch it, but knew I had to get past it.

I lightly tapped it with my hammer.

It sounded like a vase: hollow, fragile, and easy to send crashing to the ground.

I gripped its edge and tried to flex it, and thought I felt it move. I imagined what would happen if I placed a cam between it and the wall, how it could so easily be prised away, sending us both crashing down.

The wind grew, buffeting me as I hung there, flecks of snow sticking to the wall. I shifted in my aiders, feeling exposed and in danger, the trolls waiting for my next move. They had been here forever, and neither the flake nor I could wait. One of us would have to yield, and it could only be me.

To beat the wall I mustn't charge headfirst. I would have to sidestep its traps, and outsmart it. I backed off and moved back down the crack, taking out the gear I'd fought so hard to place as I went.

I guess you'd call it a tactical retreat.

It would soon be dark and I'd made less than a quarter of a rope's progress.

Down I went to the portaledge.

Gathering up snow from the ledge, I cooked some pasta, finding it gritty but welcome. I felt disappointed at my progress, but knew I had my food and Paul's too, meaning I could probably stay up here for a month if need be, which was great logistically, if worrying emotionally.

The wind had increased during the day and I pulled out my mini-disk player to record the flapping of the portaledge.

Being inside the ledge reminded me how as kids Robin and I would spend hours camping out in a duvet cover in our bedroom, imagining that beyond the thin cotton stood a vast wasteland rather than our bedroom. Now it was true, but I was on my own.

I wondered what Robin was doing; flying over the Hindu Kush, perhaps, or camped out on some smashed-up Iraqi runway.

No doubt both of us were in harm's way.

The wind died in the night, and next morning I made my short commute back to the highpoint, having had an idea how to get round the loose section by traversing across the wall to another corner I'd seen from below. This would mean very little height gain, but would get me to more promising new ground. This new corner led up to another area of hanging death, but it looked as though before reaching it I could make another rising traverse to a ledge near the edge of the buttress. What lay beyond that I had no idea, but it seemed the best thing to do at the moment. If in doubt, just keep climbing.

I moved left across the wall using a series of poor cracks, and found the corner itself just as poor, taking birdbeaks, the whole affair horribly marginal. I got as high as I dare and knew I had to move left again, out onto the blank wall, which I hoped would offer some edges for my skyhooks.

The holds were there, and I moved from the bleak crack with its poor gear, to the bleaker wall where there was none, simply trusting that each hook I hung from would hold and the rock wouldn't break. If I fell I was in no doubt I'd be smashed to pieces crashing back across the wall, having no gear that would hold a fall until Paul's old highpoint.

Hook.

Move up.

Hook.

Move up.

The edges ran out.

My only option was to drill tiny holes – called bat hooks – on which I could hang a filed skyhook. The idea was distasteful ethically, but had been used on the Troll before on new routes, and was a way of crossing blank sections without placing a line of bolts.

I wanted to beat the wall so much I was prepared to do anything.

I pulled out the drill, a five-millimetre drill bit attached to a rubber-handled grip. Stepping as high as possible on the hook I was on, I began hammering.

Tap, tap, tap, I went, twisting the bit after each hammer-stroke. The rock – like most rock – was bullet hard, but I only needed a hole a few millimetres deep to take my weight.

I'd never drilled a bat hook before, or placed a bolt on a climb, and it seemed like a hell of a place to learn, but what could be so hard about drilling a hole?

Tap tap tap.

Twist.

Tap tap tap.

Twist.

The hammer blows echoed around the wall, backwards and forwards, overlapping each other over and over again, calling and answering, one dying tap overlaid by another.

I was a medieval siege-miner, digging away with pick and shovel beneath the castle's wall.

I would bring it down.

Tap tap tap.

Twist.

Tap tap tap.

Twist.

The hole was drilled, a hole no deeper then the head of a match. I placed the hook into it, its tip filed to a sharp point, then slowly weighted it, ready to drop on the hook below if it ripped.

It held.

I waited for my heart to settle.

I moved up, creeping up the steps of my aiders one at a time, until my waist was level with the new hook.

I tried not to dwell on how it could hold my weight, or why the rock didn't chip off under such a load. It just did.

Taking off my gloves, I reached up and swept the grimy rock looking for another edge. There was nothing positive, so out came the drill again.

I drilled another hole and hooked on.

In my pocket I had several bolts, brought along because I knew there would be places where I'd find no good anchors for belays, or a good runner on a pitch. I knew placing a bolt mid-pitch would lower the grade of the route, but I couldn't afford to fall, and felt I'd pushed it far enough after hooking high on the wall, telling myself that anyone repeating this pitch would be as glad of it as me. I also needed to have something to safeguard me on the next section.

Out came the drill, only this time the hole was drilled with an eight-millimetre bit, and ten centimetres deep. It was hard going, hammering and twisting, blowing the dust out, all the while trying to remain aware that I was standing on a tiny hook barely touching the rock's edge.

After twenty minutes it looked like the hole was big enough and I fished out a bolt, careful not to drop it. The bolt was a round length of steel bar with a slight kink in it to hold it into the hole. The idea was to slot it through a bolt hanger, slide it into the hole until the kink, then hammer it home, giving me a runner that could hold a car.

I slid the bolt onto the hanger, then pushed it into the hole, but found it was a little too big to fit easily, so tapped it in with my hammer. I felt it trying to resist, but eventually felt it begin to give way. Then, after only a centimetre, it started to bend.

I tried to hammer it out to try another, but it was no use. It was stuck.

I'd blown it.

My first bolt was a dud.

I knew I should start again and drill another hole, but thought it would look a mess, and felt guilty, cursing myself for not practising this at home.

I felt that peculiar male shame of DIY gone wrong.

As punishment I looped the cable of a nut over the stem of the bolt, telling myself it would be strong enough to hold me, and stepped up.

It held.

More hook moves followed, but I now felt in harm's way, my brain screaming for another bolt, the crap one below only amplifying my fear. I hooked again, and then, past caring, pulled out the drill and started hammering.

Tap tap tap.

Twist.

Tap tap tap.

Twist.

This time I took more care, each hammer blow well placed, knowing my life depended it on. With the hole drilled, I spat on the bit and twisted it in the hole to dig out every grain of rock dust, then fished another bolt out and pushed it in.

Tap.

Tap.

Tap.

The bolt bent again.

I screamed in frustration, the sound echoing around me, the wall shouting back. I felt like a bomb-disposal man clumsily cutting all the wrong wires. Hanging there below the bolt I tried to consider what was going wrong. The only answer was that the bolts were an imperial size that did not match my metric drill and were consequently a fraction too big. I'd been given the bolts for free and now I knew why.

Not far above was a ledge I guessed would be the size of an ironing board. If I could reach it perhaps I might find some gear.

On I hooked.

Just below the ledge I looked down at the rope feeding back to the belay, passing a lot of blankness, two crap bolts hanging out like crumpled cigarettes and then, far below, just the birdbeaks. If I fell now that would be it.

I imagined the fall, weightless, dropping, uncaring – my life in flight.

You can never be sure, something might stop me, but the wall was well featured with slabs and ledges, and wherever I stopped my body would be a mess.

I grabbed the lip of the ledge and carefully mantled up, wishing I had my rock boots on, or trousers with more grip than slick Gore-tex, as I rocked on, ending up on my knees and off balance. I needed to sink some gear, but the only thing that was sinking was my heart. There was nothing. Nothing at all.

I knelt there terrified.

A large rock boomed down the wall behind me. It sounded house-sized and hit the slope somewhere below me with the dull impact of a hollow punch.

My heart was beating fast.

This is it.

I thought about Ed Drummond calling this wall 'The Altar', and saying that only those who'd knelt before it would understand.

I understood.

I couldn't go on.

I couldn't go back.

I didn't feel as if I even dare stand, terrified my plastic boots might skate off the greasy rock and pitch me off.

My knees started to hurt.

I felt the trolls watching. I eased the drill out and began my third hole, taking the utmost care. It really had to be perfect.

Tap tap tap.

Twist.

Tap tap tap.

Twist.

My knees began to throb.

Tap tap tap.

Twist.

I adjusted my balance with each hammer swing, never striking too hard in case I toppled off.

Tap tap tap.

Twist.

The hole was deep enough. I spit on the bit and twisted it in the hole to remove the dust. Out came the bolt.

A magic bullet.

I held it up against the hole and tapped it – just a little – striking it as if it was made of glass. Gently. Carefully. With love.

As if my very life depended on it.

The bolt bent.

I couldn't feel my knees.

Unclipping the haul-bag, the bag I'd travelled so far to find again, I gave it a little push and let it fall from the ledge, watching it spin for a second before disappearing beneath me and then listening for its impact. It thudded dully, and I imagined it shooting down the thousand feet of snow to the river. This was the third time I'd thrown it from the Troll Wall.

If it was lost I didn't care.

I'd made it back to the ledge the previous day after abseiling from that single terrible bolt. I knew I was defeated. I told myself that without bolts I couldn't carry on. Without them I would find myself marooned. But the defeat was more than a technical issue.

The trolls had broken me.

I checked the anchor, then set off down with the rest of the gear: two haul-bags and the ledge, the stuff that I couldn't throw off. Getting down was as hard as the way up: rappel without anything, attach the ropes to the next belay, jumar back up, rap down again with all the bags, pull the ropes and repeat.

With much relief I reached the snow slope once again, only now without the fire escape of ropes above me. I couldn't down climb with all the bags, so just cut them loose and watched them tumble away, hoping they'd make it down in one piece, then followed after them, each step taken as if crossing a minefield backwards.

The trolls had beaten me, but I was still alive, and if I could get down that would be my triumph.

Down down down.

One thousand steps.

Down down down.

The snow wet and sucking.

Down down down.

Shards of rock sticking out here and there like sharks' fins.

All the strength left me on the last hundred feet before I hit the forest, my bags sat waiting for me like dogs, always eager for more. I looked at the biggest one, the one I'd left on the wall all those weeks, and saw that its indestructible shell, which had probably been full of ice, was threaded with cracks, vinyl fibres bursting out like white hair, shattered by the impact.

I sat down beside it.

I noticed the sun was shining on me.

I didn't care.

Instead of rock fall and the weight of the wall there was now the chatter of birdsong and the murmur of the river.

I didn't care.

I emptied out the food from my bags onto the floor, a big pile of ambition now become bird food, and torched my rubbish with my remaining fuel.

I felt let down. Let down by myself, for my weakness and lack of forethought; for being so bold and ambitious; for not thinking things through; for thinking too much.

I felt rejected by the wall.

I felt rejected by myself.

All my hardware was piled in front of me, all those little bits and pieces I'd accumulated over the years, bought and scrounged and given, used on El Capitan on a dozen ascents, the Lafaille on the Dru, three trips to Patagonia, all that weight carried on my back, saving my life and the lives of my friends countless times. They were the tools of my trade, but I despised both them and that trade.

I had the urge to throw the lot into the river. To go home unburdened by climbing. To open the door and hug my kids and tell them I'd never risk it all again.

Just throw the lot in the river.

No.

I packed up my haul-bags, creating one giant knee-grinding load, a load too heavy to bear, and resting it on a rock so I could strap myself to it, I staggered all the way back to Åndalsnes.

I didn't look back.

Twelve

Breathing

Someone coughed, waking me instantly. It was a little cough from little lungs, breaking the quiet of the dark house.

I'd been asleep on our shabby red settee under a grotty sleeping bag, forced out of bed, probably due to my snoring, or heavy breathing, or some minor annoyance. You'd think the longer you were married the easier such things would become, but generally it seems the reverse, and so I was sleeping in the living room. Ella was in the room above me in her child-sized bed, Ewen in the room beside hers.

The cough came again.

The settee was old and comfortable, worn by our weight and the brush of hands and feet and backsides, its edges, like those on a badly packed haul-bag, exposed to their woody bone. The kids jumped on it, the family crammed together on it, and drinks were spilled on it. A friend had handed it on. I think we did him a favour taking it off his hands. Still, we weren't proud. Our house was usually a tip anyway, and so it fitted in well. I loved that settee, and I seemed to spend more and more time on it, especially at night, bivvying out in my own house.

I didn't really mind, imagining myself on some mountain instead, a small adventure, the smell of a well used sleeping bag pulled around me, cushions like soft heather, car headlights passing the window like distant lightning. It reminded me of camping out under my bed as a kid, something my mother thought worrying, but under the mattress, with a ceiling of interlocking wire, I would imagine I was in a cave, a snow hole, or stowed away in the hold of a starship. I guess even as I kid I was never happy to simply be where I was.

A third cough.

It was Ewen. Only they weren't normal coughs. The sound was different. It was only a half-tone from normal, but it was undoubtedly wrong. Ewen's cough had brought me from deep sleep to total consciousness, as if I'd heard a bear prowling through the house. I opened my eyes and lay there, wondering if I'd dreamt it, one part of me saying go back to sleep, the other that I must investigate, the part of you that asks if the gas is off or the candle blown out. The neurotic part that is nearly always wrong. Nearly always.

I sat up and listened, but it seemed as if the house had turned over and gone back to sleep. A memory drifted by, of my primary school teacher Mr Peterson, a man who had looked grey – grey hair, grey cords, grey cardigan – but with a face that had looked out at the sun and the stars for many years, telling the class about fighting the Japanese in some jungle far from our Hull classroom. They would know when the Japanese were close because the jungle would become, like now, in the house, deathly quiet. Why had I thought of that? The memory had lain hidden for decades without ever being referenced before? Why now? Something was wrong.

Tip-toeing upstairs I entered Ewen's room, opening the door quietly, expecting to turn immediately away when I saw him safe and sound, but happy that I'd checked, feeling that thrill of jumping back into bed – or at least, the settee – knowing everything was as it should be.

Deep down all parents fear that their kids won't wake, which is strange because when they're babies all you want them to do is fall asleep and stay asleep for as long as possible through the night, a desire that always seems, quite literally, beyond your wildest dreams. Until that morning comes, you wake and find that you have been dreaming, and that the baby has slept all night. Instead of relief all you feel is panic, sending you running to their room to check they're still alive.

A child's breathing is so quiet, their sleep so deep and peaceful, that they can easily trick you into believing that they aren't breathing at all as you creep in to check on them. It's only by holding your fingers close to their nostrils, feeling the hairs on the back of your finger moved by their soft breath, that you know how stupid you were for thinking the worst.

I knew I was just being paranoid, as I pushed open the door, but instead of a peaceful, silent child, I found Ewen laid on his back, his breathing laboured. Something was wrong. I stood over him for a minute, feeling my body cooling, waiting for the sound to die, for life to return to how it was so I could rush back to bed. Instead it continued, a rhythmic heavy sound, like an old man labouring for his last breaths.

I lifted him up out of his bed and held him in my arms, trying to wake him up, calling his name. Instead of waking, he seemed oddly dozy. 'Stay calm,' I thought, knowing I had to do something.

'Mandy, wake up!' I called up into the loft. 'Don't panic but I think there's something wrong with Ewen.'

In less than a minute the house went from tranquility to subdued panic, Mandy running down the stairs in her dressing gown and taking him from my arms, visibly worried, stroking his hair and looking at his face.

'Don't worry, I'm sure he's okay,' I said, having no basis to make such a diagnosis, but trying to be positive. I looked at my watch. It was two in the morning.

We went downstairs and sat on the settee and looked at him in the light, giving him some water. Now his breathing seemed worse than before. He'd gone to bed perfectly healthy but now he looked as if he could slip away in front of our eyes.

'What should we do?' said Mandy, looking really worried, saying his name to see what his response was.

I thought about ringing the doctor, but knew it was urgent and didn't want to be fobbed off. So my usual urge not to bother anyone was superseded by the need for decisive action. For the first time in my life I dialled 999.

'Emergency services, what service do you require?' said the male voice that answered in a stern, authoritative voice.

'Hello, my son, who's three, has woken up with laboured breathing and we're not sure what to do.'

'What's your address?' said the man, his strong and positive tone making me feel better straightaway. I gave him our house and street number. 'Okay, we'll send an ambulance straightaway.'

'Thank you,' I said, feeling relieved.

'They're sending an ambulance,' I said, putting down the phone, Mandy now rubbing her hands up and down Ewen's back.

'Thank you,' she said.

'What for?'

'For being so calm.'

'Don't worry, Mandy,' I said. 'Kirkpatricks are never ill.' And I went to put the kettle on, not because I wanted a cup of tea, but because that was what people usually did in such situations, like boiling water and getting towels when a baby is due.

I came back in and saw Mandy was deeply upset, so I sat next to her and stroked her back to comfort her, while she did the same to Ewen, and both of us sat and wished for the best while considering the worst.

'You'd better get some clothes on in case you have to go to hospital,' I said, and I took Ewen from her as she ran upstairs to change.

He seemed more alert now, but his breathing still didn't sound good. I put on a DVD of Barney the annoying American dinosaur, with his annoying American kids, all ham and cheese and teeth with braces. The DVD drove me round the bend. Years later I heard it had been used to break down prisoners in Iraqi jails, played at full volume twenty-four hours a day. But on that night it seemed to tilt the balance back towards normality, and for the first and only time I was glad to hear him sing.

I stood and walked round the living room, Ewen in my arms, his head on my shoulder, feeling the warmth and weight of his body, his chest against mine, his soft breath brushing my neck. We stood just as we had the day after he'd been born, as I watched the twin towers falling, fearful for his future.

A light flashed by outside and I walked to the window as a taxi passed, no doubt taking some clubber home, slumped in the back, a pizza on their knees. I thought about how we move through the world, our own world, unaware of all the miracles and tragedies around us. Untouched. We all have our own stuff to deal with, things we need to get done. That's how I seemed to live my life, avoiding anything that involved me emotionally with other people's lives, complications that may impede me in my own desires. I was married but I could easily not be, both of us having insulated ourselves – with the depth of time we'd been together – from the fact that we were broken. The only strong emotional connection, the thing that was inescapable, was Ella and Ewen.

The lights of the cab disappeared leaving the street still and empty.

A fox padded over the road and disappeared into a garden.

Being up so early reminded me of waking up too soon on Christmas Day, and being told to get back to bed, only this time we were waiting for an ambulance and its gifts, not Father Christmas. How many times had I still been awake at two in the morning on a climb, battling on, searching for a place to sleep, or even waking up and setting off, trying to hold all the cards daylight would offer. Climbing seemed far away right then, utterly irrelevant.

A blue flash flashed around the walls of the houses at the end of the street and then the ambulance appeared, pulling up in the middle of the road outside the front of our house.

'Okay love,' said the paramedic, dressed in a shade of green no doubt designed to calm, looking like a retrained ex-steelworker, his big hands on Ewen's chest: 'I think we'll give him some oxygen in the ambulance and take him to hospital.'

Mandy looked both relieved that we'd done something and Ewen would be as safe as he could be, but disappointed that we hadn't been told off for wasting their time and being fussy parents.

'You go, I'll stay here and look after Ella,' I said, and wrapping Ewen in a blanket she was led to the ambulance by the paramedic and I watched as the doors were shut and they drove away into the night.

I walked back up stairs and went into Ella's room, and sat at the end of her bed, as she lay oblivious to what was going on.

For me the night always brought fear and clarity about my life, and waking in the dark I would lie there dwelling on my future plans and see them as being dangerous and foolhardy, that I was playing an endgame, and that on waking I should remember how I felt and pack it in. But come morning things always seemed bright.

Tonight I considered the lives of my children, not mine, and how it would feel to lose a child. How would you ever get over it? Someone had told me about interviewing the mother of Alex MacIntyre, one of the greats of Himalayan alpine-style climbing, who had been killed by a single falling stone on the South Face of Annapurna in 1982. Even though to climbers his life and death were in the distant past, his loss was still raw for her, a wound that would never heal, her living room full of his pictures. How would my mother and father feel? My brother and sister? It's easy to make excuses for a climbing death, make fancy eulogies, talk about freedom and choice and a life lived to the full. But what about those who are left behind, their lives hollowed out forever?

The phone rang.

'Hi, he's okay,' Mandy said, laughing with relief. 'The doctor saw him straightaway and he said he's just got croup. Sometimes it can just come on in the night, but he said he'll be fine.'

'Are you okay?' I asked.

'Oh yeah, I'm fine. I think he enjoyed going in an ambulance. The ambulance man was really nice. Anyway I'll get a taxi back, I won't be long.'

'Okay, see you soon, and well done,' I said and listened as the line went dead.

I walked back to the settee and slumped down into its soft cushions feeling relieved – life restored, no change – and watched Barney sing as I waited for Mandy and Ewen to come home.

THIRTEEN

Lesueur

December 2003

I sit on a rock and cry my eyes out. I bury my face in my knees, feeling the dirty fabric against my wet face, still gritty with rock dust and musty with days of ice melting in and drying out, the smell of a week on the wall.

I try not to cry, try to focus on the smell of the fabric, its components, part me and part mountain. It smells of action and adventure, of being alive.

It reminds me of my dad, of him teaching me to climb.

The tears come again.

The Dru stands above me.

Again.

Climbed for the third time. It feels like the last.

On its dark side for too long now, I sit in the sun, in an alpine garden of fine grass, delicate moss and lichen and tiny flowers, the peaks and glaciers set out before me – a perfect place to be. And yet I sit here crying, not quite sure why.

I rub my eyes, and try to hold it together, watching as he slowly walks away.

His pack looked ridiculously heavy as we dropped down from the Montenvers railway, zigzagging down to the steel ladders that led onto the glacier, the Dru standing watch over us all the while, grey in the December light.

The night before we'd argued over how much food to take, me pushing for less, while he pushed for more. I'd told him Andy Parkin's line about food: 'Why take any, you'll only run out.' But he remained unconvinced with my lightweight philosophy.

I wanted a packet of noodles a day, some tea bags and muesli bars for breakfast. He wanted an alpine banquet: cake, croissant, sausage and a whole array of foodstuffs that I thought more appropriate for a hamper than a rucksack.

The reality was I didn't feel strong enough to climb with such a big load. I was overweight and unfit, gambling on being able to climb hard by the fact that's what I always do.

We worked out a compromise, that we would take all the food, but he would have to carry it to the route. The plan ignored the fact the load would still have to be shared on the climb, the leader climbing with a light sack, the second toiling behind with this hamper on his back.

I'd never climbed with him before, but he had come recommended through a friend of a friend. I was told he was a guide, was 'up for climbing' and lived near Chamonix. With no one else to climb with, I dropped him an email, wondering if, during the autumn, he fancied trying the Guides' Route on the Dru, one of the North Face's hardest routes with only a handful of previous ascents. The autumn is a strange time to climb in the Alps, being neither winter nor summer, but with no one around – either climbing or skiing – it offers remoteness to any climb. He seemed keen, and offered to pick me up at the airport, which was a good start.

Emails tell you little about a partner, and the man who met me at Arrivals was a quiet Scotsman with sandy hair. He had a gentleness about him, and a melancholy, but he looked strong, with a rugby player's physique, a man you would struggle to provoke, but who'd beat you to a pulp if you did. I'm generally a bad judge of character, no doubt due to always being overly optimistic about most things, but I felt at once he would be a good climbing partner. He had an easy manner, and promised to be good company on some gnarly epic.

The truth was I didn't care who or what he was as long as we got up a route.

Driving back to Chamonix I did most of the talking. He seemed reticent about his experience, which I put down to being Scottish. The only worrying comment was that he'd only ever bivied once on a route, which I took to mean he was very fast.

The sky was grey as we descended to the glacier, and no doubt the staff in the train station thought us foolish to be setting out on such a day, but then perhaps after a season or two you cease to care when you work in such places, and anyone who leaves the sanctuary of the gift shop or cafe is a fool. I joked to him that by setting out in bad weather we could guarantee good weather would arrive, rather than the reverse.

The route we hoped to climb worked its way up the North Face of the Dru, a cold hole that had a mysterious air, without the razzmatazz of the West face, and known for being very steep and loose, with a preponderance of wide cracks, which at this time of year would be full of ice. There would be no big wall climbing like on the Lafaille, this would be down and dirty mixed climbing and alpine jiggery pokery.

The glacier was devoid of snow, leaving only a muscled ice rink, something I'd never seen before, having only crossed it in winter. No longer buried under snow, you could see its surface embedded with a sharpness of stones, pieces of old rope and shards of rusted metal, giving the impression we were crossing a disused factory floor.

Careful not to trip on the detritus, man and mountain-made, we crept across.

The winter snow could only be a week or so away, and I hoped it would hold off until we got down again. The summer had been one of the hottest on record and the glacier showed signs of major change. Universities had opened up new departments in glacial archaeology as ice melted away to reveal what the mountains had once swallowed. Planes had been found, some almost intact but lost for decades, as well as soldiers from World War Two, gunned down by bullets, avalanches and rock fall.

The hard work began as we climbed off the glacier, up a hazardous mess of mud, rubble and fridge-sized blocks, blocks that had once been part of the Dru. He pointed out a spot where a young girl had been crushed, and all the while you felt as if you were in acute danger, the ground always moving, shifting and uncertain, scraped by the remorseless and lugubrious glacier.

Speed was crucial, but unacclimatised – and unfit – I found my legs and lungs unable to keep up with his and he powered on, finding the way, his big rucksack obviously proving no impediment. Even at the back his occasional halting was welcome.

I was glad I'd found such an able partner.

Higher up, the glacier offered easier-angled progress, but was also buried in snow, so again I was grateful as he ploughed on in front. The sky grew dark, night coming early. Short days would mean a lot of climbing in the dark, or if that wasn't possible, long bivys. Without a portaledge I had already braced myself for some bum-numbing nights sat out on the wall.

We stopped at the boulders where Ian and I had camped before climbing the Lafaille. I looked for the cave we'd spent a few days in, but found instead it had been filled with rubble and boulders, a sign of the continuing disintegration of the wall above. Looking in, and thinking of us lying there, mates and climbing partners, I felt a sudden and surprising sense of loss, and rejection. Why wasn't I here with him, instead of this stranger?

With nowhere else to sleep we trampled down the snow in the lee of an overhanging boulder. I pulled out my down sleeping bag and mat and got into bed before growing too cold, taking off my inner boots and using them as a pillow, making sure everything was at hand. Winter was still a calendar month away, but although the snow had yet to arrive, the cold had, and the short days only added to the sharpness.

He fiddled around, taking a long time to empty out all the food from his sack, piling it up neatly beside him. I watched from the comfort of my sleeping bag, wondering when his sleeping bag might appear, or if he'd simply forgotten it, as the rucksack grew emptier and emptier. I'd seen he had a huge green down sleeping bag on his bed, but couldn't fathom how he'd managed to fit this in the space he had left once he'd emptied out a shopping trolley's worth of fodder.

The answer was he hadn't.

Instead of his big winter bag, out came a small grey tatty stuff sack from which he pulled out the kind of sleeping bag a boy scout might use for a summer camp, its faded fabric and slim synthetic lining ironed flat by years of use. 'Bloody hell, you're going to freeze in that,' I said, sitting up. 'Why didn't you bring your big down bag?'

'It was too heavy,' he replied, looking as though he'd suddenly become aware of an earlier overconfidence in how warm it would be up here. I thought back to Mermoz, and my own frigid night-time agonies and shivered on his behalf.

'If you need a big thick sleeping bag in your house, didn't you think you'd need a big thick sleeping bag up here?' I asked. 'Also, where's your sleeping mat?' I added, looking round.

'I'm just going to use this one that's folded into the back of the rucksack,' he said, pulling out a slim concertinaed flap of closed cell foam, something that was little more than a nod in the direction of usefulness.

'No one actually uses those things to sleep on,' I said. 'They're just there to help sell a rucksack to unsuspecting punters.'

'It'll be okay,' he said, as he lay down and pulled the sheet-like bag over himself, manoeuvering his body so his arse and shoulders rested on the small pad of foam.

I'd brought along a red Gore-tex portaledge flysheet to use on the route as a tent, which could be hung above us to keep off the spindrift. I pulled this out and flung it over us for some extra protection, more for his benefit than mine.

Then we lay there in silence, waiting for sleep, feeling the cold nibbling our noses, aware of the Dru staring down at us. I knew he was in for a bad night, but he wasn't me, so I didn't really care. But I did wonder if this was why he'd bivied so little.

The night was calm but cold, and he soon began shifting around, seeking some warmth, a fruitless task made even more torturous when you know there is someone beside you who's cosy and warm.

By three in the morning I could hear and feel him shivering beside me, rubbing himself to keep warm, in obvious bivy hell. If we'd been friends longer we'd have spooned together for warmth, but being Scottish I guessed he'd have preferred death.

All I knew was there was no way we'd be climbing tomorrow. Instead of feeling frustration, all I felt was a sense of reprieve, that familiar paradox, doing anything to climb, only to find any excuse not to.

We woke at five and began to pack, with no tea or breakfast, silently accepting the way things were, that we were going down. Somehow he fitted all the food back in and snapped the lid of his rucksack shut, forcing a large triangle of dense cake in on top, then shouldered it. Then he began not to walk back down our tracks, but up, continuing our trail to the Dru as a purple dawn began to build.

I stood and watched him, amazed at his toughness, realising the climb was on, at least for another day. I followed, happy for him to keep on chugging.

'I think this is the wrong way,' he shouted, axe scratching at the blankness blocking his way up the first pitches on the North Face, a steep gully capped by overlapping slabs with the appearance of an upside down staircase.

'No, that's the way,' I shouted up, 'I've done it before. It shouldn't be too hard.'

'Are you sure?' he said, looking down at me as if to check it wasn't a wind-up.

'Honestly,' I said, holding his ropes, wondering why he couldn't do it as he turned and half heartedly gave it another go, convinced already that it was beyond him.

The minutes ticked by without any progress, until feeling impatient I shouted for him to come down, so I could give it a go.

Swapping rope ends I climbed up grumpily, and without too much stress, jammed my axe into a crack, twisted it, and pulled over a small roof onto a slab, climbing up to easier ground and a solid belay.

'The rope's fixed. Jug up,' I said coldly.

Crouched there waiting as he started up the rope, the big rucksack pulling at his shoulders, I began second-guessing what we were doing. I thought about his sleeping bag, his skinny mat, that if he had trouble on the first easy pitch, how would he fare on the hard climbing to come? My initial acceptance of retreat had passed, and now I'd sunk my teeth in, I was in no mood to let go.

I began making some calculations.

We had very few choices. Either we could push on up the Guides' Route and see what happened, switch to the moderate classic North Face route, or try the legendary and mysterious Lesueur route, a climb with only a handful of ascents. If he was struggling on the first pitch then the Guides' Route was out of the question, since I needed an equal partner to even consider it. The route was beyond me on my own.

The North Face was a rock route, and the easiest route on the face, and thus unappealing. I wanted to struggle on something really hard.

All that was left was the Lesueur, a spiral stair of vertical corners that worked its way across the North Face until it intersected with the Dru Couloir close to the summit. It would be hard, something attested to by the few people who'd climbed it. The route was also notorious for its lack of bivy spots, something worth considering with such short days.

'I'm thinking maybe we should switch to the Lesueur,' I said as he jugged up, the rucksack on his back looking painfully burdensome.

'Okay' he said, his positive expression hiding any embarrassment at not climbing the pitch.

I thought back to climbing the Northeast spur of Les Droites with Rich Cross, my second alpine route. I recalled how I'd backed off a pitch early on the first day, unsure of myself, and how Rich had led it instead. I'd stood there and cursed myself for not being brave enough to just push on, to go for it like he had. I promised myself then I'd never fold again and take my share, whatever that share might bring.

'It was harder than it looked down there,' I lied. 'Give me the rucksack and keep leading, you're fitter than me, so I might as well let you use some energy up.'

He led on up the gully, and onto the snow terrace that curved around to the North Face proper. I reckoned that being out in front would exorcise any negative thoughts he had, and avoid the dangerous flip into a mental position of weakness. And with him leading, I could be carried somewhat by his strength, as we moved up past the Guides' Route, and on up to the Lesueur.

At first sight the route looked forbidding: vertical corners and chimneys laced with ice, one leading up to another, moving out in steps across a vertical wall. Once we began there would be no easy way off, the route traversing across the face. I could also see no obvious places to sleep.

As we stood looking up snow began to fall, light at first, then heavier, spindrift tumbling down in showers.

'Being so steep we won't have to worry about avalanches,' I said, trying to sound positive, knowing that it was daft to carry on.

But we did.

As he moved up a red rescue helicopter appeared out of nowhere and hovered above us for a moment, the crew – pilot, co-pilot and winch man – clearly wondering what the hell we were doing out on such a day. Unsure what to do I held up a fist to signal 'N' for 'No, we don't need rescuing,' instead of two arms raised above my head for 'Y.' Convinced we were okay, and not just lost, they swooped away, heading home for tea.

'Not sure seeing a rescue helicopter so early on a route is a good or bad omen,' I said as he punched his feet on up to the first icy grooves.

'Maybe they were just checking out some future customers,' he replied.

'Eat some more donkey dick,' I said, digging out a huge salami from the second rucksack and jabbing it at him. Snow pelted the flysheet covering us, as we sat side by side on a narrow cone of snow. 'We've got to get the weight of this bloody pack down. It weighs an absolute ton,' I said, raking around inside it, looking for the heaviest items for him to eat first.

He sat in his sleeping bag beside me, the stove purring between us, hanging by a wire from the roof of the fly, as I went on with my lucky dip, unable to eat myself, feeling sick with the altitude.

The bivy was uncomfortable, but better for the flysheet, as snow fell outside and poured down the walls above us. Its constant hiss and the roar of the stove made it hard to hear each other.

The minor storm had blown in during the afternoon, often obliterating all sign of him as he front-pointed upwards, showing no sign of weakness even as the weather turned grim. This time it had been my turn to struggle, jumaring with the rucksack, its shoulder straps threatening to cut off the blood supply to my arms. I was glad I was jumaring and not climbing under such a weight.

'Might be worth filling a water bottle with hot water and sticking it between your thighs,' I said, imagining this would be our highpoint after a second night for him in his featherweight bag.

He'd climbed so well, and reached this tiny perch just after dark, seemingly unfazed by the prospect of a night sitting on a ledge no bigger than a toilet seat, looking cheerful as we hacked away at the ice, only stopping to hide our faces in torrents of spindrift. For me the whole thing was a reminder of what I hated about alpine climbing, the romance and machismo of it long worn thin.

'Okay, if you think it'll help,' he said, passing me his water bottle, his mouth full of stale croissant.

I poured in the boiling water, knowing we could use it in the morning to make tea and breakfast.

'Don't confuse it with your piss bottle in the night,' I said, passing it back, a strong plastic smell filling the tent as the bottle heated up. 'Having to be rescued for a burnt todger would be very embarrassing.'

Dinner over, we packed everything away, switched off our torches and sat slumped, listening to the hiss, urging ourselves to sleep.

It was another very long night, and by three he was shaking beside me once more, obviously gripped by cold. There seemed nothing to say, phrases like 'Are you cold?' or 'Did you sleep?' as useless as his sleeping bag.

But once again, when the alarm went off at five and I switched on my headtorch, his face appeared in its beam with a smile, the cold brushed off with a few shudders as the stove warmed our little red world once more.

And so up we went, climbing, belaying, seconding with the god-awful pack, the day seeming to finish almost as soon as it had begun. Then would come the start of another awful sitting bivy.

We chose to climb two pitches in succession and then swap, meaning the poor soul who'd jugged with the rucksack had a rest. At one point he almost folded again, beneath a nasty looking crack, the face dropping away far below us now, but this time I firmly pointed out it was *his* lead, not mine. This was nothing to do with me insisting we stick to our system, but because the pitch looked desperate, and I didn't want to lead it.

Unable to back out, he led the pitch perfectly and by the time he'd reached its end, he knew he'd never back off again.

As we climbed I began to see that he was in fact the better man: stronger, faster and more positive, climbing with style and never complaining. His only shortcoming was that he didn't know this yet. He soon would. With each pitch his confidence grew. He was eating the climb up, instead of being eaten.

On the third night – another sitting affair – I complimented him on how well he was climbing.

'It's bloody amazing,' he said. 'It's so hard and sustained. I've never climbed anything like this before.'

'You must have done stuff like this when you were training to be a guide,' I said, imagining that all guides, even fast ones like him who'd only bivied once, must have had to tackle their fair share of hard routes.

'What do you mean?' he said, looking puzzled.

'You know, you must have done some hard north faces?' He looked blank. 'I thought you had to do loads of grand courses to become a guide?'

There was a pause. 'I'm not a guide.'

'But I was told...'

'I'm not a climbing guide... I'm a walking guide,' he said. 'That's why I moved to the Alps. I want to become a guide, to build up my experience, but I've never done anything like this. This is amazing.'

The penny dropped. The sleeping bag, backing off hard pitches, the weight of food – this route was a quantum leap for him. He was a novice. On paper it was way out of his league. On paper he was going to die. In reality he had found his calling.

We climbed on the following day, myself with a new found respect for him as the pitches got steeper and trickier, the ropes more threadbare with heavy jumaring, the second's rucksack never getting any lighter.

Late in the afternoon I'd climbed up a steep crack and reached the end of the rope in a near vertical gully, the night not far off, but with nowhere to stand, let alone sleep.

'I hope you find somewhere to bivy at the top of your pitch,' I shouted as he jumared up, the belay that held us both just a slung spike the size of a yoghurt pot. 'If not, we're screwed.' I was glad it was his lead, and desperately hoped he'd find some glorious sanctuary just round the corner.

He took the rack and we swapped rucksacks. Up he went, tapping and stabbing his way, resting his calves every couple of metres by stepping onto rock spikes that sprouted from the ice. As usual he was steady and methodical.

Night fell and I hung there feeling a deeper and deeper sense of dread about what fate would bring. Standing all night would not only be hellish but also dangerous, and our only option lay above. I willed him on.

'I can't see anything,' he shouted. His voice seemed closer in the dark, the hiss of spindrift yet to start. 'It's too dark. I can't see anywhere to bivy. It gets steeper above me.'

'There must be something?' I shouted.

'It's overhanging. We have to find something down there,' he shouted back.

'There's nothing down here' I replied in bullying desperation. 'Keep going.'

'I can't. I'm coming down.' This sounded final.

'Don't fucking come down here,' I shouted back angrily, and then switched to a more desperate tone. 'There's *nothing* here.'

...?

'I'm coming back.' His words were final this time.

Down he slid until we both hung from the belay, the ropes fixed out of sight above, both of us now desperate to find comfort. 'Maybe we can abseil down a bit and see if we can find something,' I suggested, trying to peer into the black below, knowing the face dropped vertically for a thousand feet at the limit of our weakening headtorch beams.

All I wanted was to stop – to just sit down and have a nice cup of tea. It didn't seem too much to ask.

I slid down the rope feeling I was on a fool's errand, finding a just off vertical vein of snow wide enough for one and a half arses.

It was all we had.

Hacking at the ice, I reckoned we could cut out a slim step to sit on and so called him down to join me. We worked together, chopping at the ice with our axes, but to our dismay hit rock after only a few inches, our ledge no bigger than a folded newspaper.

Trying not to panic, we made a go of it, using our rucksacks to fashion a makeshift extension to the ledge, pulling the trusty flysheet over us as the spindrift began to fall again.

Inside it was a battle of slings and rucksacks and ropes, searching for a nugget of comfort, adjusting our daisy chains and knots, shifting our mats, the whole time scared that we might drop something vital. One second of inattention, and it would be gone for good. We couldn't get into our sleeping bags until we'd cooked, so just had to live with the cold, half-standing, our crampons still on, but at least we could relax a little bit.

'Erm. I need a crap,' he said.

'Now? Really?'

The main problem with the prodigious amount of food he ate was the number of times he needed to have a crap: twice a day, every day. I had yet to go once, my food intake still minimal.

'Can't you wait till morning?' I said, not wanting to upset our hard-won scrap of comfort.

'No.' With that he dug out the toilet roll, climbed out from under the fly and jumared down ten feet to the edge of the ice, the blackness below. He hung there, his pants down, and went.

I took a photo to remind myself of this moment then ducked back inside.

'Finished!' he shouted. 'I don't think my digestive system is taking this well.'

'I know. I can smell it from here,' I replied, my head buried in the fly, not wanting to impinge on his privacy – beyond taking a photo – for either of our sakes.

He jumared back up, and again we shuffled around trying to regain the hint of comfort we'd had earlier.

'What's that smell?' I said, as a horrible stench filled the flysheet.

'I've got an upset stomach,' he repeated.

'No… it's in here with us,' I said, trying to stay calm.

'I don't think it is,' he replied, looking around.

'Yes it is,' I countered, the smell growing worse by the second. 'Check your boots,' I added, pointing at his feet, only to see, to my utter horror, that my arm was smeared in shit. 'Oh my God!' I shouted, wanting to get as far away as I could from my arm. He looked just as shocked as me, no doubt trying to find some way to explain that what we were seeing – and smelling – had nothing to do with him. 'Fuck, fuck, FUCK!' I shouted, totally at a loss what to do.

Trying to find an explanation, he noticed that he'd somehow managed to crap on his boots and it was now smeared all over his crampons, and me.

A few minutes earlier I'd have been hard pressed to imagine a more desperate situation, but now that had been trumped. A moment later it was trumped once more, when, thanks to all my squirming around in horror, my bum ledge gave up the ghost and collapsed, leaving me hanging in my harness, my feet scrabbling, desperate to hold on, while trying to avoid getting in an even worse mess.

'I'm going,' I said, rather illogically, as he tried to clear up the mess with a spare pair of gloves and a carrier bag.

'I'm going,' I repeated, flashing my torch into the night, spotting a spike of rock that looked like my only option.

'I'm sorry, I'm going,' I said once more, and with that slid out from under the fly and jumared down, my sleeping bag clipped to me. I swung towards the spike, jammed myself onto it and wrapped the bag around my shoulders.

'I'm sorry,' he called down in his sad voice, now muffled behind the flysheet. I sat feeling sorry for myself, rubbing my arm on the ice, spindrift pouring down in buckets, my arse soon feeling as if I was sleeping on top of a gnome.

It's fair to say this was the climb's low point.

The night stretched on, snow hissing down over me, around me, into me, the only other sound the soft rattle of fabric as he shivered above.

I felt as if I'd been on this route a month.

Sleep came and went unnoticed. When I was awake I dreamed of being asleep, and vice versa, that familiar bivy limbo. But my anger passed. I wanted to shout up, give a friendly sign, a few words that showed I was over it, even if *it* was still all over me: 'It's great here,' or some other oblique English shorthand for sorry. I doubted I'd ever had such a strong partner, wondered if my anger was due more to my own inadequacy and frustration than anything else. Maybe it wasn't that he was so good, but that I was so crap.

Then again, being smeared in someone else's shit probably does warrant an overreaction.

Instead of shouting up, I sat silently waiting for a crumb of sleep, not wanting to wake him, or break the spell of any half-sleep he may be enjoying.

Dawn unlocked us, and stretching out my stiff legs, I climbed back up to the bivy. He apologised as we stood under our red canopy and melted some water.

'Shit happens,' I said.

He climbed back up to his highpoint and unlocked the hardest pitches of the route, an overhanging crack, followed by a steep corner, showing persistence and stamina. The rucksack was finally beginning to feel lighter as I jugged up behind him, glad I didn't have to second, let alone lead, arriving at my pitches, then climbing them slowly and with much less style.

Night, as usual, came on quickly as we traversed across the face on insecure snow-covered ledges, the steepness nearly over, the summit close. I was unsure how to finish the route, as we'd simply followed our noses so far, but now I needed some better idea. I seemed to remember something about crossing the Dru Couloir and climbing up the steep rock on the other side, but simply finishing up the couloir would be faster, getting us to the top in no time, getting this torment over with. The problem was we only had a single ice screw, meaning only a single runner per pitch, ignoring the fact it may be required for belays as well, of which there tends to be two.

The second problem was the state of my axes and crampons, whose tips had been embarrassingly blunt before setting off, and were now almost non existent, the mono-points on my crampons looking more like nono-points after eight hundred metres of rock climbing.

Route finding could wait again, as we came to the end of our traverse at the edge of the Dru Couloir and set about digging yet another pair of bivy bucket seats.

My appetite had now returned with a vengeance, but searching through the food bag he found mainly empty packets and wrappers. Only a few scraps of food remained. We had banked on climbing the route in four days and this was our fifth night. We had to make do with some muesli bars and tea.

At least we had tea.

Tonight I was determined to get some comfort, and rigged up my rucksack so I could lean against it and sleep like a baby – although I've noticed babies can sleep anywhere. As I lay there, I thought about how the body adapts to such discomfort, how a sore arse and stiff limbs that scream to be stretched out become commonplace, along with the cold, the climbing and the drop. Up here, once adapted, life was really simple. Was it any wonder that people love it so much? True suffering was down there.

'Got any brothers or sisters?' I asked as he also shuffled around seeking comfort.

'I had a twin brother,' he said. 'He died.'

I left it there, and thought instead of my own brother, wondering where in the world he was right now.

Grey dawn became blue morning. Abseiling from our bivy into the chasm of the Dru Couloir, I hung from a sling while he joined me. Today we would reach the top.

As I waited, the route above began to light up. My memories of easy-angled ice into which axe blade and crampon spikes stuck like glue faded. The reality was grey, impenetrable ice as old as the dinosaurs. He slid down beside me and looked up, still hanging from the ropes.

He didn't say a thing.

It was my lead first.

The dull steel of my tools made little impression on the ice, and it took several blows to get a crampon point or pick to stick in by a few millimetres. I climbed slowly up, my arms growing weaker by the minute, my calves screaming, no doubt wondering what they had done to deserve such treatment, everything crying out for the screw to be placed. 'Not yet,' I told myself, inching up and up, until I couldn't take it any longer. I felt I might come off at any moment.

Unclipping the screw, more careful than ever not to drop it, I tried forcing it into the hard ice. It was like driving a wood screw into dense timber, requiring every last bit of energy I had.

I clipped the rope into the screw and felt safe again. But the feeling was lost the minute my feet kicked past it.

I was sure I was going to fall off.

Long before I'd run out of rope, I stuffed a cam in a crack beside the ice, telling myself I couldn't risk climbing higher.

He jumared up and took over, leading his pitches. He seemed to be just as insecure as me, feet wobbling, axes just in, yet he climbed with far more confidence, as if he didn't realize how close to the edge we were. I couldn't watch, but hung there anticipating the toboggan rush as he fell back down again.

The walls closed in on us, and the route seemed to stretch further than I remembered, or hoped.

Soon it was my turn again.

I looked at him, safe at the belay, and hesitated, signalling that I didn't want to do it, that I wasn't able.

He just sat waiting under a little overhang.

I wasn't too proud to ask. 'My axes are too blunt, I think you should keep leading,' I said.

'Take mine,' he replied, unclipping them from his harness and passing them over.

I started traversing away from the belay, heading to where the ice zoomed up around a corner, pitiless and unrelenting. I flayed away, making movements like a man who was climbing, yet remaining rooted to the spot. I had to do it, it was my turn, my lead, this was how it was. We took turns at the sharp end. It was only fair.

But I just couldn't.

I knew if I did I was going to fall.

'I'm knackered,' I said, stopping only a few feet away.

He said nothing.

I leaned in against the ice, rested my head against it and let out a long sigh.

I really wanted a drink.

He said nothing.

'I can't do it,' I said, looking back at him. 'I can't do it. Please will you lead it?'

I felt shame saying those words but they came easily enough. I'd have given everything I had not to lead that pitch.

He nodded.

I climbed back to him.

We swapped axes.

He led for the rest of the day and nothing was said about it.

The notch between the summits of the Grand and Petit Dru, where the couloir terminated, came into view just before the sun set, him boldly leading up, now the master. Out of the gathering gloom the rescue helicopter appeared again, hovering towards us, slipping sideways, the crew looking out at us once again.

The smell of aviation fuel filled the air, as well as the wump-wump-wump of the rotors, the noise echoing back and forth across the walls so that it overlapped. I felt its warmth, knew that someone cared, that someone was worried about us. We were overdue. We waved, one hand up in the air to signal 'N'. We were okay. With that they turned once more, reassured, and swept away, dropping back to the valley, the flashing tail light fading into the night.

We scrambled up towards the summit, speeding over broken rocks, until not far below it we found what we'd been dreaming of for so long: a slab of rock the size of a table, somewhere flat we could at last lay down and sleep. We pulled the fly over us for a final time and rested, our bellies empty, but our bones grateful to be laid out like the dead.

'Well done,' I said in the dark, the wind whipping up.

'Thanks Andy,' he said.

The descent the following day was hell. We got off route on unfamiliar abseils, and the easy way down took all of the day, and much of the night. All the way down I was gripped about not making a mistake, that we had to get down safely, and it was only when we couldn't find any anchors that we realised we'd missed the traverse half way down the South face, and instead had to press on to the terrifyingly jumbled Couvercle glacier below.

We made a long, free-hanging abseil onto the ice at midnight, passing two fixed and frozen ropes no doubt left by someone else who'd made the same mistake, to discover we were in a labyrinth of tottering seracs and a maze of giant bottomless trenches waiting to swallow us, all of which we had to cross.

I looked across at what we had to do, and knew I should be gripped but instead felt a calmness return for the first time in a long while.

'Let's have a brew,' I said as I pulled down the ropes. 'Then we'll go across.'

All I could do was let go of my fear and do my best, and cross the glacier to the other side. Or not.

Our tea over, we started. I led us through a surreal landscape, jumbled and out of kilter, sometimes under wilting seracs the size of houses, sometimes jumping from one to another, from roof to roof.

It was exhilarating.

And we made it, but even then it wasn't over, our way down blocked by a big rock wall, the glacier sitting in a wide canyon.

Now I felt anger.

'I've climbed A5,' I shouted, raging at the mountain's unrelenting stubbornness and unwillingness to let us go. 'I'll get up this fucker.'

Then in that instant the night took pity and a ray of moonlight shone from the cliff face, and following it, we found a tunnel, jammed with chockstones, that led us up to the hut.

The last few yards were through deep snow, but by now struggle was as unnoticed as breathing. We finally reached the wooden hut and fell through its door.

A bird had somehow got in and the interior was full of its feathers.

We stood like Arctic explorers having found their way back to civilization, blinking at the end, eyes only held open by the fizz of adrenaline.

The following morning we woke when we woke, no alarms for us now. Wrapped in thick woollen blankets, I watched the sun streaming in through cracked windows, feeling that familiar mountain hangover.

It felt strange to walk around without boots or crampons on, no harness or ropes tying us to the Dru. Without the bulk of mountain beneath me, I felt suddenly adrift.

We sat at the wooden table, like normal people, with grubby knives and forks drinking tea and eating leftovers scavenged from the shelves of the hut. We hardly spoke. Not like enemies, but like friends. This was the beginning for him. For me it felt like the end, but then it always did.

We walked down through the high alpine meadows, soon to be buried in winter snow metres deep, but so colourful now after the greyness of the Dru. I'd only been here in the winter, and had no idea it was so beautiful.

No idea.

I wondered why it had taken me so long to notice.

We stopped for a moment, because we could.

'I wonder what my brother's up to?' I said out loud, hoping that he too was heading away from danger.

He remained silent.

'How did your brother die?' I asked, without thinking.

'He died climbing.' he said. 'He died climbing with me.'

He stood up and set off down.

I began to cry.

Fourteen

Sheep

I searched through my computer for the number, knowing it must be there somewhere. Not being one I rang very often, it was missing from my phone, but after a long hunt I eventually found it at the end of an email.

'Hi Dad. It's Andy.'

'Hello,' he said. It sounded as though he was outside, the wind blowing against his phone. He was either up a mountain, or on a golf course. I preferred to imagine it was a mountain, slightly ashamed at the idea of a golfing dad.

'I'm doing a talk in your neck of the woods next week, can I stay at your house? You can come if you want?'

It was rare for me to visit my dad, or even call. Our paths only ever crossed through chance or work. It wasn't that we didn't get on, or avoided each other. It was simply the way we were, the way all Kirkpatricks were, the way most families are these days. Nuclear. In meltdown.

I'd been booked to do a talk in the Welsh village of Llanrwst for the Ministry of Defence, talking to the Joint Service Mountain Training Centre. Dad had worked there while he was in the RAF and had settled in the same village, meaning I could see him and get a bed for the night.

'That would be great. I'll look forward to it,' he said.

As a kid, whenever the topic came up of how bad the family was at keeping in touch, Grandma Kirkpatrick would always say, 'We've got our own lives to live.' This seemed to be born out, since decades could pass between visits by cousins and uncles. I'd neglected my mum, and my sister and brother too. Wrapped up in my own life, I reckoned they could wait, that relationships were a given – that they would always be there.

I'd once sat with Uncle Eddie at a wedding, a rare chance to meet cousins who had gone from children to adulthood unseen, even though they lived only a mile from my house in Sheffield. It was the sort of occasion when, at the end, half drunk, the dance floor emptying, you say, 'Why haven't we

stayed in touch?' Suddenly, you feel that little hint of genetic magic meeting others who share your DNA. 'We must stay in touch.'

Of course you don't.

You wake up the next day and carry on as before.

My uncle Eddie was a great bloke, even if he looked like a roughish pirate, a long scar splitting his face. He'd made his fortune diving for salvage, as dangerous a job as climbing any mountain. He'd lost mates and had some very close calls, starting out illegally diving alone on crumbling World War Two U-boats using Army Surplus diving gear, until he was arrested. The authorities let him off as long as he worked for the Admiralty.

Eddie had an endless supply of true Kirkpatrick tales of over-optimism and resulting near-disasters. Like the time he bought his first secondhand salvage boat. Sailing it from Scotland to Hull in a Force Eleven storm, the boat was hit beam on by a huge wave that almost tipped her over.

Like most Kirkpatricks, Eddie attracted disaster and crazy stories, but always somehow won through. He got into scrapes not only with the dangers of the deep, like getting snagged inside a U-boat on the bottom of the ocean and watching his oxygen run out as he fought to escape, but also encounters involving London gangsters, the IRA and anti-terror police.

'We're self contained Andy,' he told me. 'We can be dead social, with loads of mates, but we don't need it. That's just the way we are. Maybe it's why we do daft stuff. I'm like that, your dad's like that, you're probably like that.'

'I wonder if we know how to love, to love other people, love ourselves even?' I said, my mind seeing things afresh, listening to Eddie speak about things I thought only I felt. 'If we did we'd take more care.'

'If you don't feel a strong bond with other people then it's easy to not be there, do you know what I mean? You just don't think they'll miss you.'

'Do you think that's why it was easy for my dad not to see us much when we were kids, that he didn't know how much we loved him?' I asked.

'I don't know. You're better asking him maybe?'

I drove over to Wales early in the morning, arriving to find him eating curry for breakfast, having just returned from working for a month with a charity that helped street children in India. He was supposed to be retired, but had just as much energy as ever. In India he'd been setting up an outdoor centre that would be used to fund work with street children, a model based on Brathay Hall in the Lake District, using corporate cash to solve social problems.

The whole thing seemed quite random as Dad told me what he'd been doing there. Only one of the eight Indian kayak instructors was able to swim, the climbing wall sat beneath a Buddhist shrine, its statues used as belay points, until the locals got pissed off and dumped a dead cow at the bottom of the wall.

I imagined my dad thriving on the chaos of it all, and assumed going to India was part of his ongoing thirty-year midlife crisis, the trip sounding like a good remedy, leaving him obviously thankful for what he had and reflective about his life.

'I'm giving up golf,' he told me as we drank tea in the kitchen. This was a surprise, even though golf had been out of character for a Kirkpatrick.

'Why are you giving it up?' I asked.

'I've been playing for twenty years and I'm still crap. It's time to move on.'

That night we walked down to town for the talk, which was for a bunch of physical training instructors, whose job was to beast Army, RAF and Royal Navy personnel in the Welsh hills. I had been told to do something motivational, and had been racking my brains about how to do a classic corporate talk, all that leadership, team building and goal-oriented rubbish climbers make up after the fact, when in reality it's all about glorious greed, ambition, selfishness and getting one up on your mates. So I decided to tell a few stories and let them reach their own conclusions.

The organiser, who I assumed must be an officer, met us at the local British Legion where I was due to talk, the room looking perfect for bingo, discos and family weddings, the bar full of the usual types you find in such places: toothless, smoking and in a contented stasis of drunkenness. He was dressed in smart chinos, a nicely ironed shirt, polished shoes, looked very fit and offered a knuckle-cracking handshake.

We talked over the evening, how it was a chance for people to let their hair down – not that they'd have any.

'I hope you don't mind,' he said in his clipped accent, 'but there will also be some people from Hereford coming tonight.'

I guessed he meant the Special Air Service, since they were based in Hereford, but chose to act ignorant. 'What, like some farmers?'

'No,' he said. 'I mean people from – *the regiment.*'

'I thought you were all in regiments?' I said, continuing to play dumb, looking baffled, turning to my dad for some clarity, instead seeing only a smirk.

'I mean,' said the officer, leaning forward to whisper even though the room was empty apart from us, 'the SAS.'

'Scandinavia Airlines?'

Sometimes you can take a joke too far.

The room filled up with fit blokes with short hair holding pints, and the odd fit-looking woman, also with a pint and also fit, but with shoulder length hair. The chairs were set up as if for a séance, which is often a bad omen, but you felt these poor guys were just happy to sit down without being shouted out for an hour. I tried to spot anyone from Hereford as the instructors marched in, but guessed they must have been lying in the back among the stacked chairs for the last week anyway, their rifles trained on the door.

Then I spotted them at the back, a scruffy bunch, dressed like climbers rather than soldiers.

The officer jumped up onto the small stage and introduced me like he was my headmaster and I followed him up to well mannered applause, feeling like a magician in a talent contest, standing between the bingo machine and the bakelite mixing desk complete with eight-track cassette slot.

In the dimly lit room they looked like by far the scariest audience I'd ever had, trained killers and sadists every one, except their sadism was meant for their own side, dressed in well ironed jeans and ordered to come and listen to a scruffy northern bloke talk about his holidays.

'Right, is there anyone here from Hereford tonight?' I said, my voice echoing around the room via the cheap speakers.

Silence.

I felt like Gerry Adams.

'Now, anyone can be good if they're successful, but how many people are good when they fail?'

As the final slide faded I slipped off the stage for a sly drink of water, glad it was over. The room was full of laughter, with the usual look – 'What the hell is he on?' – on a few of the smiling faces. We shared the same language, all of us interested in pushing physical and mental boundaries, them being physical, me being mental.

As a civilian, I'd tried to make some connections, with my dad being an ex-PTI and my brother serving in the RAF, suggesting I knew a bit about how they ticked, which seemed to help.

A few people came up and asked if I wanted a drink and shook my hand, then I saw something large coming towards me from the shadows at the back of the room, a guy so big and scary I had the urge to run, but knew that like being faced with a bear, there was no point. He looked fierce, like a fist on two legs, and no doubt boasted a Hereford post code.

I braced myself for his attack.

He shot his hand out, but not to rip out my heart.

'Great talk mate,' he said, shaking me by the hand. 'You're bloody nuts aren't you, I don't know how you do it.'

I laughed off his compliment, which I guessed it was, coming from someone with perhaps the riskiest job in the world.

'What does your brother do?' he went on.

'He's a loadmaster on the Hercules transports,' I said. 'He's probably chucked you out of a plane.'

'We don't get chucked,' he said quietly and I believed him. 'They're good blokes those loadies, we do a lot of stuff with them. Is he over in Afghanistan?'

'Yes, and Iraq. He's never on the ground long.'

'Not a bad idea when you're a big target. What's his name?'

'Rob.'

'I'll keep an eye out for him,' he said.

I suddenly had the urge to make a joke about how I thought his eyes would be blacked out, but thought better of it.

'Do you do much climbing yourself?' I asked, guessing these guys must be from the SAS mountain troop.

'Yeah,' he said. 'I like climbing in Scotland mainly.'

Hanging on to something we had in common I asked if he'd done anything that winter, with conditions that year being so good.

'No,' he said. 'I've been over in Iraq.'

'Oh,' I said.

Before I left the CO grabbed me. For a moment I thought he was going to shout at me for being so scruffy, or about making a joke about how a PTI motivates people – the answer being to 'hit them harder.'

'Andy, we're running a symposium on combat training for the Royal Marines, and I'd like you to tell them what you told us tonight,' he said.

Life is so strange sometimes.

The following day, with no kids to wake me, I woke up late to the smell of curry, went down to the kitchen, and found my dad eating.

'Sleep well?' he said smiling.

'Dreamed I was being buggered by Andy McNab, so not too bad.'

Over breakfast he showed me some photos from his India trip, lots of desperately smiling kids, each clinging on to life. He'd told some of them that they had to wear seat belts in the centre's minibus. They'd found that hysterical. Later he found out they'd spent parts of their lives sitting on top of moving trains.

I had a few hours to kill and suggested we could go climbing. When I was younger my dad always wanted to go climbing, dragging me along to hold his ropes, then dragging me up after him. I suppose holding your dad on his first leader fall is a sort of rite of passage. Dad climbed E2s and E3s when I was a kid and to me he was the best climber in the world. Like fathers and sons who share a love of football, we shared climbing.

I idolised him. I wonder if he ever knew? I wonder if my kids idolise me?

As I got more into climbing the roles reversed, and it was Dad holding my falls. I could tell he was losing his hunger when one day after doing Pincushion and the Fang at Tremadog he suggested we go for a cup of tea when I asked him 'What next?' Even though we had hours of daylight left.

At the time I couldn't believe that he didn't want to just climb and climb and climb. Now I could see that it's easier to sit and talk to friends over a cup of tea, rather than shout distant commands from a belay ledge. There may be some kind of partnership of the rope, but really you're on your own.

We had a lot of time to make up.

Maybe it was too late.

'Why don't we go for a walk instead?' he said. 'I've got something to show you.'

We left the house and walked up the lane behind his house, bordered by steep hedges, the kind of road where you expect to meet nothing but a tractor, the tarmac caked in animal crap and mud. We climbed steeply until we passed through an old gate and into the fields: rough and patchy, only good for sheep.

We talked about work, and future plans, but my dad was more of a listener than a talker, so I just blabbed on about my ambitions. We talked about Robin, and how my dad rarely saw him, but when he did he thought he looked knackered and stressed, the war stretching his unit to breaking point.

There weren't enough aircraft to do the job and my brother was caught between the enemy and a government overreaching its capabilities. Last time they'd met, Robin had told him about landing in the middle of nowhere in Afghanistan to re-supply some special forces, and how they were late. Local villagers had surrounded the aircraft, so Robin had stood there with a rifle at the back of the plane praying for some proper soldiers to arrive before the Taliban showed up. I thought about asking him how it felt to have two sons in harm's way, but couldn't get the words out.

What was there to say?

Eventually we arrived at an avenue of wonderfully tall trees, huge, like giant redwoods, their trunks thicker than any tree I'd seen before in Britain. They must have been centuries old, ostentatious in a tree sort of way, their bark like an old giant's skin.

They were set in two parallel lines, as if they were intended as the entrance to a stately home that was never built, totally out of place among the native Welsh trees that dotted the hillside.

We looked at the trees and I had the urge to ask him why he'd left my mother. Had wanderlust consumed him? I needed to discover if the things I felt he felt too. Then it struck me that he had not simply left my mother. It wasn't just a matter of my parents splitting up. It was his kids he'd left.

It was me.

He'd ran away from us. He'd fucked me up, that was plain to see. But how could I hold it against him?

I knew how he felt. I wanted to escape as well.

The words died inside me, words I was too scared to say, words I felt would bring worlds to an end. I wanted to say:

'Do you regret it?'

'Was it worth it?'

'I love you, but you're a stranger to me.'

'I love coming up here,' said Dad. 'I look at these trees and wonder who planted them, and why. They must have known they would never see them like we do, and yet they planted them anyway.'

We walked down the hill, back towards the house, past fields full of sheep with their lambs, fingers of wool blowing through the fences as we passed by.

'Let's look at the lambs for a minute,' Dad said, stopping.

I watched them jumping around, giddy in the green grass.

'When they're born, they jump and play all day long, only stopping to drink their mothers' milk. We like them because they seem so carefree and happy, they remind us of children, of our own childhood. Then one day, overnight, they stop playing and running about. They just stand there, chewing for the rest of their lives, turning from lambs to sheep.'

I looked at the sheep and their lambs and saw what he was talking about. I'd never really thought about it before.

'You know what it is that changes in them?' he asked, looking out at the field. 'Their mothers stop feeding them and they have to stop playing. They have to eat to survive.'

Watching the sheep, I could see he was right and wondered if my dad was making a point. Perhaps he was, or perhaps he was just talking about sheep.

With my dad you could never tell.

We walked slowly back down the hill, not speaking, leaving the sheep to drift into the shadows of the amazing trees.

Approaching the Diamond in winter – a cold place to spend your holidays. *Photo: Andy Kirkpatrick*

1   Best not to look down. Alone on the Troll Wall. *Photo: Andy Kirkpatrick*

2   New routing on the fearsome Troll Wall. *Photo: Paul Ramsden*

3   Paul Ramsden having just told me our Troll Wall new route was at an end. *Photo: Andy Kirkpatrick*

4 Big wall fingers on the Troll Wall, alone. *Photo: Andy Kirkpatrick*k
5 Looking for a place to bivy on the Lesueur (the foothold being the biggest option at hand). *Photo: Andy Kirkpatrick*
6 Great climbing on the second day of the Lesueur route, the bad weather now clearing. *Photo: Andy Kirkpatrick*
7 Ian Parnell on thick ice for once, below the Diamond. *Photo: Andy Kirkpatrick*

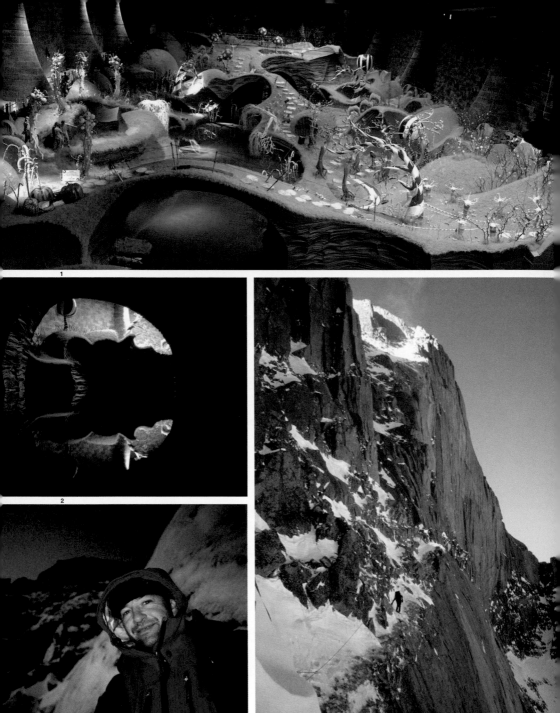

1 I imagine this is what the world might look like if you take LSD. The set of Charlie (see figures on left for scale).
  Photo Andy Kirkpatrick
2 Another day in the office – coming out of the chocolate tunnel on a chocolate river. *Photo: Andy Kirkpatrick*
3 Paul Ramsden on the North Face of Les Droites. *Photo: Andy Kirkpatrick*
4 Ian Parnell treading carefully as we wind our way up to the summit of Longs Peak. *Photo: Andy Kirkpatrick*

Ian Parnell getting scrappy on the Diamond. *Photo Andy Kirkpatrick*

1 Ella. *Photo: Andy Kirkpatrick*

2 Paul suffering from a bad back and virus on our uncomfortable chimney bivy on Les Droites.
Photo: Andy Kirkpatrick

3 Paul Ramsden traversing across to the Lagarde Couloir. *Photo: Andy Kirkpatrick*

4 Ella having secretly skied down from the top of Les Houches. *Photo: Andy Kirkpatrick*

5

6   7

5 Ewen. *Photo: Andy Kirkpatrick*

6 Robert Steiner – a man for hard times. *Photo: Andy Kirkpatrick*

7 Always on my mind: the Dru. *Photo: Andy Kirkpatrick*

Ella and Ewen. *Photo: Andy Kirkpatrick*

FIFTEEN

Diamond

February 2004

Buried in a thick down sleeping bag, I woke slowly in the winter dawn, lashes sticky with frost as my eyes flickered open in the bitter Colorado cold.

I blinked away the frost, unsure where I was for a moment, having woken on so many beds and floors and backs of trucks over the past few weeks. I seemed to have slept next to a wall, which loomed over me black against a white sky, the white fading to a cold blue as my eyes came back to life, the wall turning dark grey, like concrete.

'Where am I?'

My brain was getting up but my body seemed not to want to move, didn't care where I was, only that it was warm in a cocoon of feathers, its comfort so finely balanced between cold and not cold that even the slightest movement would upset it. When you travel to cold places you learn that heat is not a given, but a finite resource, something that should never be wasted. A body, especially a body in a sleeping bag, only has so much heat it can give, and when it's gone it will not return. If I moved my heat would spill out and be gone.

All I wanted to do was lay perfectly still, yet for some unspecified reason my mind was urging me to move.

Then I remembered where I was. The wall was not made of concrete. It was granite, a huge sweep of it five hundred metres high. I was under the Diamond, the wall we were meant to be climbing.

My heart sank.

We'd missed the alarm.

'Ian?'

This single word conveyed an acceptance that the day was over before it had even begun, and that our frigid open bivy had been for nothing.

'Did your alarm go off?'

'No,' he replied, obviously as awake as I was.

Actually, he just hadn't heard the alarm. He'd been wearing earplugs to block out my heavy breathing. So I supposed it was really my fault. Plus, it was hard to blame him as I'd forgotten even to bring a watch. His sleeping bag was so thick – necessary since we were sleeping out at three thousand metres in Colorado in January – that the beeps of the alarm had been swallowed whole by the bag's loft.

I'd also forgotten the bivy food the day before, but this turned out to be useful, since it was only our rumbling stomachs that finally woke us.

I sat up, pulling my duvet jacket out of my sleeping bag, which I'd used to boost its warmth, and put it on quickly against the savage cold. I'd slept in all my clothes.

The Diamond stretched above our heads, the most famous alpine rock wall in North America. It was a summer climbing venue rarely visited in the winter, the cold enough to put off all but the most masochistic. The wall swept up from Chasm Lake, now frozen solid, and at its top stood the summit of Longs Peak, four thousand metres above sea level. It was a hell of a spot.

I gave a shiver and pulled my bag up to my chin, like a man with a towel caught naked getting out of the bath.

Ian remained flat out, so I lay back again, all warmth now gone from my sleeping bag, the feathers dead.

We lay looking up, knowing we'd blown it yet again on our second attempt; the trip was one screw-up after another. We should be cursing each other, shouting about bad luck and fate, thinking of excuses, of why it was his fault and not mine. Instead we just lay there, while knowing we'd have to try anyway.

'Oh, not to be so possessed by this obsession with struggle,' I said in a mock Shakespearian voice. 'To be happy. To live and want no more. Simply to… stop.'

Ian said nothing.

The invitation to talk at the *Alpinist* magazine party in Boulder Colorado had come out of the blue, a dream gig to a new audience in an exotic location, and the chance to mix business with pleasure. *Alpinist* was the *Vogue* of serious climbing journalism, and Boulder one of the main centres of American alpinism. Ian was quick to reply when I asked if he wanted to come out with me and do some climbing at the same time. He was writing a big piece for the magazine about his successful Annapurna trip with Kenton and John Varco, and said he fancied a holiday.

We arrived in Denver without a place to stay, but skimming through the yellow pages we tracked down the legendary Rolando Garibotti – alpinism's answer to Julio Iglesias – who lived in Boulder. He hardly knew us, but I had met him once in Yosemite in 1997 for about fifteen minutes, when he'd taught me how to place a copperhead.

'Hi Rolo,' I began, when he picked up the phone. 'You might not remember me, but this is Andy Kirkpatrick. I don't suppose me and Ian Parnell could stay at yours for a bit?'

Being a climbing bum himself, he said yes.

We arrived by taxi in a snowy suburban street. Rolo shared his tiny wooden house with Beth Wald, a brilliant climbing and wilderness travel photographer. Rolo was a striking guy, half Italian, half Argentinian, lean and smart, with a shyness that kept his achievements obscured.

He was perhaps climbing's darkest horse, very often trumping the big stars and setting new and undreamt of standards in speed and difficulty, yet all the while remaining under the radar of magazines and free of the bullshit press relations departments spread around. He was the Carlos the Jackal of world alpinism, appearing from nowhere, climbing a hard line, then disappearing again, the only word of what he'd done coming from partners or witnesses. He lived by a moral code that few others could emulate.

Among the few ascents to have reached the outside world was a fast ascent of the Infinite Spur on Mount Foraker, a nine thousand foot Alaskan monster of a route. Rolo and his partner knocked ten days off the time taken by the first-ascent team, climbing it in twenty-five hours. He also set a record for the Grand Traverse of the Tetons in Wyoming, a ridge with a combined altitude gain of twelve thousand feet over fourteen miles. Most fast parties took two days, but Rolo soloed the whole thing in just six hours.

We went inside and shared some food and wine. Beth was reserved like Rolo and just as reticent about what she'd been up too. It was only after much digging that it turned out she'd been in Afghanistan for several months on assignment for National Geographic. Beth had been a great climber in her time, but photography, once just a way to help pay for trips, had become her passion.

Listening to her talk about her trips, trips without summits, I felt envious of her, of finding a life outside of climbing, to have a skill that couldn't leave you, or one that demanded so much of others. I often wondered if climbing was just an outlet for my creativity, as many good climbers are very creative people. Perhaps for some climbing is simply a performance.

As the wine flowed I found I kept digging holes with my questions. I am obsessed about knowing what makes climbers tick, about the stories and gossip surrounding them. Having an exceptional memory for pictures in magazines, and who had taken them, I kept asking Beth about climbers I knew she had photographed.

'Did you know Anatoli Boukreev?' I asked, remembering a picture of the late Kazakh climber taken by Beth, a striking shot of Anatoli standing at a train station with a bunch of red flowers. Beth blushed and Rolo coughed, which I took to mean: 'Let's move on.' I changed tack. 'What's Todd Skinner like?' remembering Beth's pictures of the famous free climber on Half Dome. Beth blushed again. Rolo rolled his eyes.

The following day we walked into the centre of town to meet Christian Beckwith, editor of *Alpinist*, to run through the show, which was being put on in the famous Boulder theatre, a piece of Americana, my name emblazoned on its awning in lights. I felt I'd made the big time, for a day at least.

Ian took a picture of me stooping uncomfortably under the sign, thinking how strange life could be.

I'd met Christian a few times before, a climbing media heavy hitter, but still young and good looking. No doubt me telling some yarn at a previous meeting had got me this gig, although we were both a bit perturbed by the fact that no one seemed to understand anything I was saying, which I put down to a combination of my northern accent, speed of delivery and general overexcitement.

Every time I began to tell him a story a confused expression would fall slowly across his face until he'd look at Ian and say: 'I have no idea what he's on about.'

All we could hope was that the audience would.

I was sharing the stage with Michael Kennedy, yet another legend of the old school and someone I'd always wanted to meet, and Jimmy Chin, a young poster boy of alpinism, working as a photojournalist for *Outside* magazine and *National Geographic*. Michael would go first, me second and Jimmy last. I didn't want to bring it up at the time, but past experience had suggested I'm a hard act to follow. Not because I'm good, but because my delivery is sort of Jerry Lee Lewis on speed. Being from out of town, I kept my trap shut.

Christian asked us what we fancied climbing while in the US, and I said we'd been eyeing up the Grand Traverse of the Teton, which, amazingly, had never had a winter ascent, even though it was one of the most famous routes in the United States. Living in the shadow of the Grand, Christian said he'd look into conditions for us, which I thought was nice of him.

The big night came around and it seemed like every climber within a hundred-mile radius turned out, the theatre humming with climbing talk. The one thing I love about Americans is their enthusiasm and lack of pretence. People dressed up, some in what I took to be fancy dress, but may well have just been flamboyance. Everyone seemed to be grateful for a fun night full of climbing. The great and the good were there, many climbers I'd only seen in magazines.

Being surrounded by climbers always made me feel uncomfortable. It was as if I was scared they would find me out, see I was a fraud, say something like, 'Do us a one-arm pull-up Andy.' I knew that as a well-known climber I would always be a disappointment. One problem was that the more I tried to convince everyone of my inadequacy, the more people believed I was simply bluffing.

The people in the theatre seemed so perfect – perfect bodies, perfect tans, perfect teeth – and ready to crank their way up anything anywhere, it was hard not to feel out of place. I was overweight, shortsighted, wonky-toothed. If they'd lined us all up that night, and someone had been asked to pick out the two people who weren't climbers, Ian and I would have got picked.

I assume the Yanks like us Brits for our character. And for making them look good.

Michael took the stage, but the theatre had been constructed with a bar at the back, and because of his quiet style of speaking he didn't engage immediately with the audience. The initial hush rapidly turned into a trickle of background noise of climbing chatter, then a torrent, until ten minutes in no one could hear him at all. Instead of speaking up, or just walking off, he carried in the dogged fashion that had made him a climbing legend.

Unfortunately, most people had soon forgotten he was even on the stage, the theatre just a din of chatter and laugher.

Soon it was my turn, and I walked up onto the stage feeling nervous at getting the same reception, which would be a shame seeing as I'd come so far.

'Hi everyone,' I said, at the same volume as Michael, unclipping the mic from its stand. 'My name's Andy,' I went on, sounding as if I was about to take part in a spelling bee, my voice already almost drowned out by the festivities. 'Before I start I'd just like to say – WILL YOU SHUT THE FUCK UP!'

If someone had dropped a pin we'd all have heard it.

Off I went at breakneck speed, my topic climbing Mermoz and about how crap British climbers are, mocking Americans along the way, with their new age, hippy ways: slack lining, yoga, being 'at one' with everything.

I think people were a bit stunned at first, no doubt having never heard this kind of tirade. But slowly the laughs built, as people began to work out it was all a joke, and it was okay to laugh, and that I didn't have special needs or anything. They were all at one with me.

When my bit was over, Jimmy said he was too intimidated to go on, probably because I'd used up all the expletives he knew, and so he showed some slides over reggae music instead. The wimp.

The evening finished with lots of drinking and not being a big drinker I drank too much and made a fool of myself. Standing in a group someone asked me what I'd thought about the other speakers and I'd said that Michael Kennedy was a bit rubbish.

'It wasn't that bad,' said the guy, who looked familiar.

'Did you hear him?' I asked, surprised that someone had thought he was any good.

'Yes,' he said, 'but then I would. Being Michael Kennedy.'

Ian went home and I went to a party. People generally don't bring alcohol to American parties, preferring quiche and a guitar. A tall male model introduced himself – by this point I began wondering if there were any ugly people living in Colorado – and asked if I remembered him. I looked him up and down and tried to place him, knowing he was too old to be my illegitimate son.

'Sorry I have no idea.'

'When you soloed El Cap in 1999 I was soloing the route next to you,' he said.

Being only a tiny speck half a kilometre below me I guess he could excuse my poor memory for faces, but it did occur to me that I had probably pissed on the guy several times.

I stood in the kitchen and looked around at all these people talking and having fun, mostly couples, their arms around each others waists. I had no idea why I was there.

Slipping out of the party, I made my way back to Rolo's, the streets almost empty, just the odd student walking home, yellow taxis and squad cars cruising by. I looked in through windows and saw people sat in their living rooms drinking, scenes plucked from the television shows of my youth. I felt a familiar pang of loneliness and isolation, the sensation of being an outsider. I tried not to dwell on it, knowing self-analysis only makes things worse. It was best to put this stuff in a box and file it with the others.

All I knew was I wanted to be normal, to sit and drink and make life a party, to fit in. But I couldn't. I could never be still enough to exist in other people's lives: Mandy's, my children's, those of my friends. It was easy to

think it was all part of being a self-made man, and that I was always moving
– moving up. Now I felt I was falling. Perhaps climbing hard climbs was the
only way I could become fixed for a while, in one place, and with a single mind.

Tomorrow we had to come up with a plan.

Frank's truck made its way slowly up into the Rocky Mountain National
Park, Ian crunching through the gears, me navigating with a hangover, the
engine, weary and beaten, straining in the skinny mountain air.

Frank's truck had belonged to the eponymous Frank, a Spanish climber
who'd died soloing Fitz Roy in Patagonia a few years ago, leaving the old
truck he'd bought behind for all and sundry to use. Rolo had given us the key.

Although I'd never met Frank, or even seen his picture, I felt I knew
about him, and had thought a lot about this dead climber, a climber who
seemed to haunt me, his story drifting in and out of my life. I'd heard about
him setting off to solo the Californian route on Fitz Roy and never
returning, and being a fellow soloist I'd dwelt on this a lot: how easy it
would be to fall down a crevasse with no one to rescue you; to tumble down
the mountain with no one to see you fall; to just disappear.

To die quickly wouldn't be so bad. But to die jammed in an icy slot,
death taking hours or longer, knowing no one knew where you were, and
there would be no rescue, was unimaginable.

A soloist's mind can only be full of positive thoughts, but in their last
moments I wondered if every dark thought, saved up from a lifetime of
pushing them to one side, rushed in. In the moment of your death you
would see everything you believed was just an illusion.

And what about those who didn't disappear: parents, friends and lovers
– partners on the rope and in life? They had only their imaginations to
bridge the gap in their lives. You have to be selfish to climb, perhaps even
more so if you choose to take extra risks by soloing.

The story of Frank haunted me.

The night before I had been talking to Timmy O'Neill about Patagonia.
The subject of Frank cropped up. Timmy had known him. As a leading
American alpinist, Timmy had also climbed Fitz Roy by a new route and
at the top decided to abseil back down the seventeen hundred metre
Supercanaleta. I'd climbed the couloir in 1999 and it's a fearsome place to
be – a shooting gallery of loose rock and ice. As soon as Timmy and his
partner set off down they knew they had made a mistake.

To add to their growing sense of foreboding, a little way down they
found Frank.

Timmy had seen hair blowing from a wide crack and on closer inspection saw it was his old friend, jammed tight, a thousand metres up, trapped forever, or at least until Patagonia thaws out. He had fallen on his way to the summit, or on his way down, down the Super Couloir, the mountain catching him as he tumbled.

Stories like Frank's are not stories to dwell on.

But that's exactly what I did.

'What do you think?' asked Ian, nodding at the map on my lap, the key to our new objective.

'It looks like a long walk,' I said, tracing a zigzagging line up into the winter high country to the Diamond.

The previous night at the party, Christian informed us that the word on street was the Grand Traverse lay under deep snow and so was out. The next big objective was a winter ascent of the Diamond, the thousand foot vertical wall that led to the summit of Longs Peak, the highest mountain in the park, its summit sitting almost as high as Mont Blanc. In January it's seldom climbed, partly because it's hard to climb in such cold temperatures, but mainly thanks to the seven-mile approach walk, often through deep snow. Nevertheless, being cold, hard and big it ticked all our boxes.

'We're going to freeze our arses up there,' said Ian.

I couldn't wait.

It was mid morning by the time we started up the path, the snow lying knee deep. We took turns breaking trail. The first stop was to sign in at a wooden box at the trailhead, scribbling down our route and the date of our expected return. Being slow, we opted for caution, meaning if anything did happen we'd be long dead before a rescue party came looking.

The path zigzagged up and up through a thick forest named Goblin's Forest. It was totally silent apart from our breathing and our feet potholing through the snow. Ian and I had spent too long walking into climbs so conversation was minimal, a sign of deep friendship rather than a lack of anything to say as we took turns breaking trail.

Frank walked by my side.

I often wondered if Ian ever thought about dying, since he was the person I knew with the greatest chance of dying doing what we did. I considered asking him, there on the trail, but the question seemed so personal. It made me flinch to even *think* about saying it out loud. I thought about it a lot. Not death itself, but the guilt I felt about dying.

I had Mandy and Ella and Ewen, whereas from my point of view Ian had no one. If I was him I'd be free of guilt, free to do what I wanted. I often wondered what it felt like to be Ian. To have no one to worry about, to be fearless, free of the hurt you could bring, the lives you could destroy.

To have a life without consequences.

Then again, what did it feel like to come home after months away and have no one to greet you?

We emerged from the trees into the high country, a barren rocky plain swept clean by a wind that seemed much colder than anything in Patagonia. The Diamond came into view, steep, dark, cold, sitting above its frozen lake like a bird, wings wrapped around its frozen waters as though waiting for the cold to pass.

It was dark by the time we made it to the bivy spot, a flat area just before the lake and still a distance from the wall. I felt rotten, head banging, limbs aching, and assumed I was coming down with some kind of flu, forgetting we had raced up to three and a half thousand metres very quickly and therefore had mild altitude sickness.

I suppose the hangover also compounded things a little.

Pitching the tent in the dark we scampered inside and tried to stay warm in our sleeping bags, Ian looking after me as I lay there feeling pathetic. We were using a stove I'd made myself that could be hung from the middle of the tent, which although great for climbing had the nasty habit of melting anything that touched it. Soon the tent filled with smoke as holes appeared in Ian's brand new five-hundred-quid jacket.

At least it was warm.

The following morning I felt no better, wanting only to go down and get warm and eat food that wasn't as dehydrated as I was. Ian agreed, and decided we could leave all our stuff there, make a quick descent and come back a few days later once I felt better.

We made it back to Frank's truck before dark and drove over to Estes Park, a small mountain community not too far from Longs Peak, to visit Kelly Cordes, a young alpinist who was making a name for himself, who we'd met at the party two nights before.

Once again, although we turned up unannounced, the code of climbing bums kicked in and Kelly made some space for us on his living room floor. Or, more accurately, he made room for us on his girlfriend's living room floor, Kelly's place being, quite literally, a one-room chicken coop in someone's garden measuring five feet by ten. Luckily Kelly's girlfriend Bronson – as in Charles – was also a bum at heart, and happy to oblige.

Kelly was not a man to cross. Although he spoke with a slow drawl, as though he were slightly drunk, he was a boxer, wrestler and master of jujitsu.

Sat drinking small bottles of beer, Kelly told us a funny story about how a French climber had assumed that with a name like Kelly he must be a girl – and a hardcore climbing girl at that – and sent him some saucy emails. This was until Kelly put him straight.

After dinner Kelly took us over to a tiny homemade climbing wall, which, like Frank's truck, had been bequeathed – perhaps unofficially – to the climbing community by the previous owner, who died when an ice climb collapsed. Stripped off, Kelly looked like pure muscle; a construct of intense training over years, his physiology moulded into a climbing machine.

I thought about my own body, something I tended to conceal. I usually blamed being too busy, or the kids, for my lack of training, and although I thought it would be nice to be that ripped, that strong, I knew myself well enough to accept that I just couldn't be arsed. All I wanted to do was climb.

Sat watching Ian and Kelly bouldering, all I wanted to do was get up the Diamond.

Once more, we walked up through Goblin Forest, the trail now easy as we retraced our steps, this time without the tent, the idea to bivy right at the base of the wall, get up at four in the morning and climb it in a day. The idea was a good one. By making it to the base of the wall and digging a ledge to sleep on, we had every intention of cracking the route.

Passing our last bivy spot, we gathered up our rack and ropes, feeling smug at our good planning, then continued up to the lake, its ice a foot thick and crisscrossed with white cracks. The Diamond looked very impressive now, rearing up from the black lake like a wave of rock.

We plugged on to the next bivy spot, stamping down a platform as the sky grew dark, suddenly wishing we'd brought the tent as the temperature dropped quickly from bitterly cold to vindictively cold. Unpacking, we soon realised we had a problem.

In our haste we'd left most of the food in the truck.

Then Ian realised his headtorch had been left switched on in his rucksack, and the batteries were flat. We had no spares. All we could do was set Ian's alarm and hope we could cobble something together from the emerging disaster.

Of course we couldn't even do that.

And so we lay there, watching the sky lighten, cursing the missed alarm, yet secretly thankful we wouldn't have to climb in such cold. We had an excuse to go down. Yet retreat, instead of being a welcome respite from the cold, would be a hollow experience. We really hadn't done anything to warrant failure.

It was turning into one of those crap holidays; not fun enough to be a good time, not gnarly enough to be a great climbing trip. We were running out of time to get something done.

'I can't be arsed walking all the way back here again to do this route,' I said, knowing we had to get moving. 'Lets just give it our best try. We can climb up as high as we can and bivy,' I said, my plan overlooking the fact that we could only climb in the light, and that we had no food.

No matter. We got up, quickly packed and set off.

Our plan was to climb a line up the middle of the face, but out of time we opted for a system of chimneys and grooves that went up the side of the face with just four steep pitches to the halfway terrace, then snow and mixed climbing to the summit, with the odd patch of snow or ribbon of ice making it look like a winter route. Rolo's stories had inspired me to try climbing as fast as I could, my determination sharpened by the knowledge that Ian was filming me with the little video camera he had.

My pitch over, I belayed Ian, filming him in turn, then checking the footage of me. I expected to be dazzled by my speed. But instead of the slick and super-quick dude I thought I was, all I saw was a shuffling bumbler, who apparently had no understanding of the word 'speed.' I saw myself making a very small movement, then I would stop, think about it for a while and either reverse that move or make another very small movement.

I checked to see if the camera was switched to slow motion.

It wasn't.

Ian's pitch was also a slow one. He disappeared for half an hour behind a big flake. At first I thought he'd just stopped to have a crap, as nothing had happened for quite a while, and although the days were getting longer, they weren't going to be long enough at this rate until June. Then I saw a hand waving from inside a crack high on the wall, which was off-putting. It turned out the climbing involved a bit of caving, as Ian was forced to pass a huge chockstone before making a hard exit out onto the wall.

It was pure Parnell. With very little ice to help him, he indignantly bullied his way up, ignoring the fact that really he shouldn't have been able to do so.

You could tell it was hard as the wordage dropped with every metre gained, always a sign things aren't good, especially if the climber is a journalist.

'Watch me on this bit, Andy.' Pant. Scrape.

...

'Watch me here.' Scrape, scrape, pant.

...

'Watch me.' Pant, pant, scrape.

...

'Watch…' Scrape, scrape, scrape.

…

'… me.'

Scrape, scrape. Deep breath. Scrape.

…

There was total silence for ten minutes, before Ian suddenly bellowed: 'SAFE!'

The next pitch looked unpleasant, and very fall-off-able, with two ways to go: up a narrow icy choked slot to the left, or an off-vertical corner with a dribble of snot-coloured ice running down it to the right. Imagining myself getting upset on the latter option I traversed over to the left and started excavating a way of getting into the slot, which was too narrow to jam myself inside, but too wide to climb with my hands.

'It looks easier on the right,' said Ian, unconvinced by my struggle to get nowhere slowly. Neither was I, the difference being he thought I should go right and I thought we should just go down.

Half an hour later I'd jibbered my way up the corner, feeling like a mixed-climbing Homer Simpson. It seemed to me I'd put in a valiant effort and had got higher than I'd expected, but the next section looked like you couldn't wing it – unless that meant flying off the pitch. So instead I moved around a bit and groaned, putting in and taking out dubious nuts, hoping some protection would spur me on, but finding none that could.

Then I dropped my axe.

Off it went, having 'unclipped itself' from my wrist loop, spinning past Ian, and on to the bottom of the first pitch, out of sight.

I swore at my own incompetence, knowing that would be it. We'd have to go down now.

'I'll send up one of my axes,' shouted Ian, sounding helpful rather than annoyed.

I pulled up his axe on a loop of rope and carried on, but not before I down climbed – rather easily, I thought, considering how hard it had been climbing up – and reverted to my first plan, the slot, muttering, 'I knew I should have gone this way,' to excuse my poor performance in the corner.

The slot went slowly as well, but frustration is always a good boost to activity, and eventually I made enough progress to make it to easy ground, feeling a little more like a pro.

Then I dropped my other axe.

My heart sank, as no doubt did Ian's, as it slipped out of my hand and spun away towards him. This time fate felt sorry for me and instead of making a pair at the bottom, it speared a patch of snow and held fast.

'Bloody leashes,' I cried, which was about as fair as shouting at a car after crashing while speeding.

I was forced to climb back down, past hard-fought ground, retrieve my axe and climb up once again. I felt a total failure.

The pitch went on for what seemed like several more hours, at which point I was about fifty feet above the belay, poised beneath a dubious hanging pinnacle with nothing to clip into apart from a white sling that seemed to be stuck or frozen under a boulder. I was going far too slow, and so just clipped it and called it a belay.

Unconcerned, Ian came up and just yarded up the pinnacle with his axes, running it out to the wall and making what looked like a series of uncomfortably contorted and bold moves up the direct finish.

We'd done the hard bit.

By the time I reached the top of the route, there was about an hour left before it got dark. Our climb terminated a long way from the summit, which lay at the top of several hundred metres more of easy climbing.

It had taken us all day to climb four pitches.

With only one headtorch we'd have to bivy, something neither of us wanted even though we'd lugged our sleeping bags up the route. We just couldn't face a miserable night on the mountain.

We felt too old. We were on our holidays.

The desire for a warm bed, warm feet, warm food, warm anything was overpowering our desire to visit the summit of Longs Peak, but without it what would all the effort be worth? The only option was to descend once more, get some rest and food, then come back one more time. We discussed this miserable plan, which would mean yet one more trip back up here, the summit requiring twenty-one miles of walking. There was no paper, stone, scissors or tossed coins. The only things thrown were the rope ends. Down we went.

It was dark by the time we reached the tree line and began stumbling down the four miles of zigzagging trail back to Frank's truck. Ian lagged behind me in the dark, no doubt wishing he could see where he was going.

By the time we reached the signing-out booth, I was glad to be out of the woods. The sound of our boots on the tarmac was a relief. It meant we'd made it. At the truck we stripped off all our layers and threw the lot into the back, and with aching bodies slowly climbed inside for the hour-long drive back to Boulder, imagining the big Mexican meal we'd have as a reward for nothing in particular and thinking we could invite Rolo and Beth.

Ian turned the key.

Nothing happened.

Turned out he'd left the lights on.

It was great to be back at Rolo's house, just lounging around until the tiredness wore off and the guilt at doing nothing took hold again. Soon we'd be able to face the walk up one last time.

We spent the morning checking out secondhand shops in town for music and clothes, enjoying the kind of gigantic breakfast you can only get in the US.

Coming back to the house we found Rolo sorting through boxes of slides of Patagonia. Looking up he asked if we wanted to go climbing, which seemed strange as it would be dark soon, and outside the streets were thick with freshly fallen snow.

'We can go and climb the First Flatiron,' he said. 'It's a classic. It will be fun.'

Ian made an excuse about having to finish an article, so I felt compelled to say yes. It's not every day you get to climb with one of the best in the world.

'You won't need a harness,' Rolo said as I stuffed mine into a rucksack. 'Or boots. Or a chalk bag.'

'I'd better, just in case,' I replied, thinking, 'Just in case I'm as crap and unfit as I think I am.'

'Maybe I should take a rope?' he said, as if the same idea had just come to him.

'Yes. A rope. I think maybe that would be nice,' I replied, imagining his sadness at my untimely death.

We arrived in the car park below a small granite peak. Rolo donned his harness and grabbed a rope from the back of his truck, a rope that looked to be the same thickness as my shoelaces. I knew that Rolo was weight obsessed when it came to gear, noticing he'd weighed all his climbing clothing, then written down each item's weight in pen onto it. He obviously picked his ropes for their weight rather than their strength.

His skimpy rack consisted of three jumars and some karabiners and so wasn't really a rack at all.

'We'll put our stuff on here,' he suggested, 'then we can just take it easy and jog up to the route.' With that he proceeded to sprint up the steep trail as though being chased by a bear.

Seconds later we were below the route, a big granite slab about five or six pitches high, probably easy once you knew the way, and in summer. Now snow clung to big sections of it, and damp streaks testified to an unsettling lack of friction.

Rolo grabbed the rope, tied on and said, 'I'll climb the first three pitches in one, so don't bother belaying, just pay out the rope.' With that he literally ran up the cliff.

In his trainers.

You'd think that I had it easy. All I had to do was stand there until the rope went tight and then climb. Unfortunately I'd underestimated Rolo's speed and with only one boot on I was shocked to see how fast the man was moving, staring dumbfounded as the rope began to run out. It reminded me of that moment in the movie *Jaws* when the harpoon hits the shark and the shark speeds off, taking the rope with it at high speed.

I needed a bigger boat.

Within half a minute all the rope was gone and I was away, both shoelaces still untied, climbing, climbing, climbing, moving up the slab without skill or finesse, bullied by the insistent tug and only not falling due to sheer bloody-mindedness. There was no belaying, just simultaneous climbing. Moving together meant that if I fell, so would Rolo, and I didn't want the embarrassment of falling off a trade route and killing one of the best climbers in the world.

The holds were tiny, the easy-angled rock being climbed on friction, and the cliff became a blur as I pedalled my way up – sometimes literally. After every few feet I'd slip, only stopping myself by jumping upwards.

It seemed a joke, to be moving so fast I couldn't even see the rock, my hands and feet shooting out faster than I could think where to put them. I got to the first belay and found a jumar providing some small level of protection on the shoe lace, but before I had chance to even unclip it, the rope was pulling again and I had a split second to snatch it off the belay and carry on.

Seven minutes later I was five hundred feet off the deck at the third belay trying my hardest not to puke as I tried to unclip the jumars. Rolo was sat gazing out over Boulder. He looked serene.

'It's a great view from up here, isn't it Andy?' he sighed, looking as if he'd just awoken from a little nap.

'Y... y... yes,' I stuttered, pretending to admire the view, blinded by the blood pounding behind my eyes as my heart fought to keep up.

After half a minute Rolo stood up. 'Enough rest, I go.' And he did.

Fifteen minutes after leaving the ground we were at the top, a thousand-foot, six-pitch 5.6 rock climb below us. I swore I could see steam rising from Rolo's Nikes when I reached him for my second lie-down.

'I love it up here, it's just so peaceful,' he said, blue eyes shining, a breeze ruffling his raven hair, the sun burnishing his tanned cheekbones.

For a second I swore he was going to start singing.

I just knew he'd have a lovely voice but all I heard was the sound of my heart thumping.

'I need sugar,' I gasped. 'And the toilet.'

Rolo laughed, thinking I had made a joke. 'It's a few more pitches along the ridge then an abseil and we can jog back to the car. It won't take long,' he said, as my eyes recovered their focus.

I didn't doubt it.

Less than an hour after we left the house we were back. Ian sat at the computer, having barely started his writing.

'No luck?' he said without even turning to see my red face. 'Maybe we can all go and do it tomorrow.' Then he frowned. 'By the way, I've just seen that someone has made the first winter ascent of the Grand Traverse. They say it's been in perfect condition.'

We had to get back on the Diamond.

We slept in the car park, this time with three alarm clocks set, starting at stupid o'clock for the familiar walk in – zigzag, zigzag. We marched with earphones in listening to music, ignoring each other, oblivious to the wilderness. Ian was in front, saggy panted in my headtorch beam, my feet keeping time with his familiar quarter limp, like a pirate's. We shared just one thought – to get up this bloody route.

At dawn, we reached the frozen lake, knackered already as we tramped across its middle. Then we gathered up the gear we'd left behind last time – and the time before that – and went up, zigzagging across the steep snow slope, zagging and zigging, dividing effort by time. How much of both had we given to this lump of rock? It wasn't that appealing an objective or even that hard.

Why couldn't we just come on holiday and have fun? Like normal people did.

Having reached our highpoint, we slowly worked up the snow slopes, passing the odd rocky step that barred our way, the effort becoming greater the higher we got as the air thinned.

Snow became soft sand in our tired minds.

Sand then turning to porridge.

Porridge became cement.

We slowed even more, or at least I did, while Ian – the altitude expert – plugged on.

'I'm totally bollocksed,' I shouted up at Ian's arse, code for 'I'm having another rest,' knowing from experience that no rest would be long enough. All I could do was grit my teeth and move up.

The sky grew darker a few hundred feet from the top as storms clouds rolled in, wind and snow showers coming close behind.

This was the mountain's endgame. We plod on and my mind starts to wander.

I think about how familiar we are with this struggle, fighting every instinct to just sit back and be normal, content to do all that brings us pleasure. Instead, we do the opposite. We are drawn to everything that brings us pain. Maybe we're paying for something we did in a former life, or flagellating ourselves for some guilty secret. I thought about Kelly at home with Bronson, or Rolo at home with Beth, and wondered why they weren't here. Where were all those good climbers? If they're so bloody good, so bloody legendary, why weren't they up here with us?

I had every excuse not to be here.

And yet here I was.

'I'm really bollocksed now,' I said to Ian's arse again, the rope yanking me forward, every fibre of myself wanting to stop, wanting to have something to drink.

'Yeah,' said Ian, his answer open-ended, meaning either he was agreeing with me that I was indeed bollocksed, or that he too was knackered. Thankfully, his legs stopped moving and the rope stopped tugging, and in recognition of this fact I slumped down for a moment, one blissful moment, a moment worth all the effort required for its appreciation, a moment when all that becomes important is doing nothing.

To be still.

To be silent.

And thankful.

...

...

...

Nothing.

For a moment I find happiness.

Maybe that's what this is all about, this alpine winter climbing, the hedonism of suffering, to know the value of things we take for granted: body heat, a peanut, even nothing itself.

I looked down at the lake far below and knew we'd be on top within an hour, and that the way down, which we knew was complex, would be tough, and long, and knackering, just like the way up; that we'd get lost, and would be half dead when we got back to the car park.

Half dead, but happily so.

Content with nothing at all.

Ian cleared his throat and spat into the snow, his minute warning. He was about to start again. Looking at him, I felt I had let Ian down on this trip.

It wasn't like the Dru or Mermoz, where there had been only us, only climbing. Now my mind was full of dead climbers, and full of myself. I was weighed down. I couldn't keep up.

This was it for him and me.

I bent down and pretended to tighten my crampon strap, stalling for just one more minute.

Looking down the slope at our tracks, I wondered where we were going. I would have been content to remain slumped there forever. I guess that's how people die doing this kind of thing. I always imagined you'd fight, always thought of people who just sat and died as being weak, but maybe it would be easy, if it felt like this.

Bliss.

...

I was giving up.

I couldn't keep up with him anymore.

He was free.

...

Ian moved on.

I follow behind for the last time.

Sixteen

Post

I sat as usual in my tiny basement trying to write, trying to find a few hundred words about climbing gear for my column, trying to find a little magic in a dull piece of fabric or lightweight alloy.

Every day was pretty much the same in my life as a freelance writer: get up, get the kids up, take Ella to school, come home and look after Ewen until Jean the child-minder arrived, then go downstairs into the basement, sit in front of the computer and try to work.

It was like word constipation, day after day, just sitting there, attempting to write for *High* magazine or some other publication or website, struggling to force out the words. They never seemed to come easily.

Only with the approach of a deadline, and all its pressure, would the words start to flow, writing nothing for weeks only to bang out four thousand in a day. Most of it was crap, but I never missed a deadline, although my editor Geoff Birtles would have had a heart attack if he'd realised how close I was.

Geoff, the editor of *High* magazine, was a well-known old-school climber. He always scared me a little, probably a good trait in an editor. He had a whole host of funny stories and quotable sayings. On the first day I met him, he said: 'Andy, I'm a violent man, but...' It was a good start.

Geoff was a mine of advice on most subjects, such as why you should only have two kids: 'Because McDonald's only has tables for four.' He'd brought the house down at a slideshow given by Doug Scott, who had the tendency to disappear off on lengthy tangents. That night Doug had been talking about the seven summits, the highest peaks on the seven continents, which led his thoughts to a lengthy peroration on the number seven, which concluded: 'the seven wonders of the world, *Seven Brides for Seven Brothers*, the seven deadly sins...' at which point Geoff shouted out: 'Seven minutes till closing time!' Everyone burst out laughing and made a dash for the exit.

When you're working as a freelance writer there is always something better to be doing, with the biggest distraction being tea. A cup of tea is needed before each new chapter or article, and with each cup you need toast. The number of slices would increase in proportion to my boredom, thick white bread with marmalade and butter, maybe four slices, or more. I'd have a second helping if I found I still had tea left, although being lukewarm I'd probably make a fresh one, and have another four slices with that. The more I sat and ate and tried to work, the fatter and more frustrated I felt.

I'd discovered myself living a dream, making a go of it as a writer – me, with my stupid brain. Yet even though my words were full of climbing, summits and adventure, I'd never felt so far from these things, sat in that basement.

I missed working with the people at Outside, being immersed in climbing, even if it was often second-hand, listening to the stories or ambitions of customers, sharing and making plans. Working in a climbing shop in the heart of the Peak District was like being at the centre of a climbing universe. Now I felt banished to a distant star.

I also felt trapped, as anyone who's worked for themselves will know, having the freedom to go climbing when the sun shone, but not, feeling too guilty, and so just sitting there trying to work. Most of all I just wanted to go climbing, so not being able to do it, while forced to think about it all day, was like some slow torture. It was driving me mad.

And so I sat and looked at the screen.

As usual there was the logjam in my head, and nothing was arriving apart from my deadline.

Luckily, there was a knock on the door to disturb me.

It could only be one person.

The postman.

I walked upstairs as the knocking continued, wondering what he had for me, maybe some small bit of gear sent for review, or a book or video I'd ordered. Maybe it was a cheque? I could see him through the window, a blue Father Christmas, his bulk blocking out the light.

I felt privileged that he always wanted to stop and chat, usually me standing in my dressing gown, feeling a bit embarrassed at my idle appearance, a slice of toast in my hand, while he was obviously on the job, doing his round. He was a stout-looking man, solidly constructed from a lifetime's worth of walking and posting, his shoulders muscular and square, perfect for the huge red bags of post.

I'd always envied postmen and the physicality of their day, out on their own, not stuck inside like me, doing something solid and honest. I guess he envied me, sat at home everyday in my dressing gown, presumably watching daytime television and eating toast.

Being a postman wasn't for me though. The mental aspect, sorting post out down the depot, would be beyond me. As a kid, I'd had a paper round for a day, but lost it because I stuck most of the papers in the wrong letterboxes. I'd posted them in the correct doors, but I'd been in the wrong block of flats, a bit like getting the right house, but on the wrong street.

It also took me so long, running up and down stairs in a panic after I realised my error, that I was late for school, turning up looking like a chimney sweep, my face streaked with newsprint. I'll give things my best shot, but there are some things I just can't do, no matter how careful I am, a lesson learned from bitter experience.

I had a job collating sheets of paper in a printer's, which showed me that organisational tasks involving numbers had to be avoided at all cost. Doing them sent me into a funk that I was useless. By avoiding them, I could maintain the impression I was a competent and fully functioning human being. I guess my present situation stemmed from avoiding any sort of job that required I disturb what had become the off-limits part of my brain, boarded up for my own safety. The problem now was that I was employing myself. To be honest, I'd have sacked myself if I could.

I opened the door.

'Hello,' said the postman, tugging a big envelope out of his bag. 'Something to sign for.'

I took the large envelope and sticking it under my arm signed his little book with an illegible scribble, my name being far too long to ever complete, and passed it back. I could tell by its weight and shape the envelope contained some slides being returned.

'Can I ask you a question?' said the postman, as he stuffed his recorded delivery book back in his pocket. 'I need to buy some boots and thought you were the right man to ask.'

We chatted about the usual things, leather versus fabric boots, Gore-tex inserts, Vibram soles and how bendy a boot needs to be. It was a conversation I often had with strangers. I guess he'd spotted all the climbing magazines I got sent every month, and assumed I was an expert. I almost said, 'Come into the shop and I'll do you a dodgy deal.' But then remembered I was no longer in that line of work.

'Thanks for that' he said smiling.

'No worries,' I said, the full stop in our short conversation. But as he began to turn away, and I started to close the door, he stopped.

'By the way, did you know that climber who died this week?' he asked 'He was from Sheffield, wasn't he?'

I stopped, my hand resting on the door, caught out by his question, unexpectedly emotional, stirred, unable to speak.

He was talking about Jules Cartwright.

Jules, like everyone else I knew apart from Ian, had decided to become a guide, and had begun his training in the Alps. As was the case in most things, I was jealous. Here was another climber I knew who would be out every day, living in the Alps, probably ending up marrying one of their rich clients, a surgeon perhaps, living an ideal life in some amazing house in the mountains.

On hearing the news I'd wondered if this was a turning point for Jules, one of the most ambitious and uncompromising climbers I'd ever met. Now he'd be taking punters up mountains, going skiing, having fun. It didn't fit with the man I knew. To me, he seemed fuelled by more than a hedonistic escape from the real word, but something dark and noble, his life a project. Like Ian, for a long time Jules had no apparent connections to the world. He was a free agent, able to go where he wanted, and climb what he wished. Then something changed. He met someone, he mellowed, and that summer was working as an aspirant guide in the Alps.

Ian had emailed me the news a few days before. The subject line 'Jules Cartwright' popped up in my inbox. I knew straightaway he must have died.

I'd sat there and looked at it, read the words and imagined it happening: walking in to the North Face of the Piz Badile, walking along the top of some cliffs, either he or his client slipping on some loose stones, and, being roped together, both falling to their deaths.

It wasn't like when someone disappears or is stuck on a mountain, when there is hope they may reappear when all hope is lost. Jules was gone.

The news was a wall.

It stopped there.

He was dead.

It was tragic, but not for the usual reasons. There was always a good chance Jules was going to die climbing. It's something all climbers who push the limits accept, both about themselves and one another. When you hear they have died climbing it's never unexpected; not like being killed in a car or by a blood vessel popping in a brain. But for Jules to die simply walking to a climb, that was something shocking. It made you see that there was no line between extreme risk and safety.

I imagined Jules sat beside me, probably with a beer in his hand, his boyish face, his mind always turning, and imagined what he would say if it had been someone else: 'Stupid wanker.'

I'd known him for a long time, sat in pubs with him on lost winter afternoons, sparring, bullshitting, checking each other out. In my class-conscious mind he was posh, like a lot of people you find in alpinism, their love of the Alps stemming from skiing holidays as kids.

Jules' parents were doctors. I usually hated people like him, hatred of the worst kind, a mix of blind bigotry and envy. But I didn't hate him. I really liked him. He knew himself well, and had no reason to go looking for what was missing in others.

He'd once stuck up for me when I wasn't there and someone had said I was a crap climber. Finding this out made me more relaxed with him; I had nothing to prove. I thought back to him picking me up from work once and taking me to the pub where he grilled me with questions about my life. I just thought he was being friendly, but afterwards realised it was a sort of interview. Jules was always a man with a plan, and no doubt had a climb in mind. But if it was an interview, I guess I failed, as we never climbed together.

And now he was dead.

I always told people, when asked how dangerous climbing was, that none of my friends had died. It was a lie, the qualifications of friendship always growing stricter, any connection with the dead deniable. It kept my head straight.

The postman stood there, waiting for an answer, my face no doubt blank as I searched for words, as memories of Jules drifted through me like smoke, seeing him laughing at the table at the Sports Bar in Chamonix, so full of life – a force now entirely dissipated.

He was someone else's mate.

He was someone else's partner.

We'd never climbed together.

I hardly knew him.

He had nothing to do with me.

Just another climber.

'Yes, I knew him,' I said. 'He was a friend of mine.'

SEVENTEEN

Charlie

August 2004

'Do you fancy working with children, dwarfs and chocolate?' Nick said down the line from America. 'And Johnny Depp?'

It was obviously not your standard job offer, but I had an inkling what he was talking about: the remake of *Charlie and the Chocolate Factory*.

'It should be a month's work, maybe longer,' he continued, calling from the East Coast, where he lived.

'How come you're asking me?' I asked, knowing I'd never been invited to work on any other of Nick's film safety jobs: Batman, James Bond or Shackleton.

'I thought you would fit in well with the Oompa Loompas,' said Nick, laughing.

It was a once in a lifetime opportunity. Working on a film – proper work; not writing or talking about climbing, something almost grown-up.

And yet, as always, there was climbing.

I'd been scheming to go back to Yosemite, a place I knew could break my run of bad luck, where I could climb something hard, get back on track. My heart was set on a solo attempt of a route that had been tagged 'harder than the Reticent Wall.' If I took this job then there would be no climbing, and I'd have to wait until the winter to do something. Could I wait that long?

I needed to climb something.

Only then would I be right with myself.

I'd never let work get in the way of climbing before. I shouldn't start now.

'The day rate is two fifty,' said Nick.

'Two fifty an hour?' I replied, thinking it was a bit low.

'No,' said Nick. 'Two hundred and fifty pounds a day.'

…

'I'm in,' I said.

The last time I'd climbed with Nick Lewis was in Patagonia in 1999. It had been a life changing experience and my first expedition. I'd been asked along by Nick, Paul Ramsden and Jim Hall, all much more experienced than me, and who no doubt saw a masochistic streak in me that would come in handy.

The highpoint of the trip – if that's the right word – had been an attempt on a winter ascent of Fitz Roy up the seventeen hundred metre Super Couloir, the route where Frank had died. We'd got within a few pitches of the top, only to get caught in a major storm in a homemade tent lashed to a small ice ledge. We sat there for twenty hours, unable to sleep or go up or down, until the tent finally ripped apart. With no other choice, we began our descent, rappelling all night, exhausted, having not eaten or drunk anything for three days.

All the while I was convinced we couldn't make it, that we'd be swept away by an avalanche or our ropes would become stuck and we'd freeze to death. But we did make it down, reaching the base early in the morning, after fourteen hours of abseiling. Hardly believing we were alive, we staggered to our tent, staked out on the glacier, this tiny haven full of food and fuel, the focus of our prayers all the way down, only to find it had blown away.

Even though I felt I went to the brink in Patagonia, after that l knew I could cope with anything.

But for Nick I felt it was the end.

Nick was a very thoughtful climber, and on that trip you could tell he was grappling with what climbing meant to him, and whether the risks were worth it. Our Patagonia epic had come on the heels of a few other close calls.

How many times can you escape?

After Patagonia Nick focused his energy on work, and being highly motivated, with tons of energy and drive, he did well.

Always a great logistics man, learned from a wealth of expedition experience, he began helping oil companies access remote places, and then television and film crews. He was still going on expeditions, only now he was being paid.

Much of this work involved looking after people on ice, and so when the new Bond film featured a car chase on a frozen sea, Nick got the job as safety man and fixer.

At the time I was so jealous, especially when several mutual friends got work on the film, which was shot in Iceland. The wages were high and the work interesting, but for me the jealously stemmed more from missing a chance to work on a big movie.

All my life I've been a huge film fan. Beyond climbing, cinema has been my biggest passion. When you're a poor youth, going to the cinema is always a big deal, and many of my best memories revolve around going to the pictures. A dark cinema is as close to heaven as standing on top of a mountain.

I had never understood why I never got the call to work on any of Nick's projects, until one day I asked Paul Ramsden, racking up to climb an ice route in France, Paul having worked on many of Nick's projects.

'It's because he doesn't want you to take the piss out of him, or say something embarrassing to the director,' he said. I was shocked. Nick, although not much older than me, was my hero, the archetypal gnarly alpinist, climbing hard routes and always in winter.

The truth was I wanted to be just like Nick, but thinking back to our trip to Patagonia, I saw I had been quite merciless, taking the piss out of him, which was easy as he was always honest and sincere. In Patagonia he'd been the voice of reason, while I had been the voice of dangerous over-enthusiasm.

On our first route we'd come to an impasse, an icy slot that looked very easy to fall off. Nick had said that so far from help, we couldn't afford to climb anything we might fall off. To which I replied: 'What's the point of bloody coming then.' And with that I led the pitch.

Nick was my hero, but he disappointed me in Patagonia. My preconceptions let me down. The weaker he became, the stronger it made me. Every sly joke I made at his expense, every time I saw fear or hesitation in his eyes, I knew I was the better climber, better than my hero.

I was too blind and ambitious to see he was only human, and that he wasn't weak, only changing.

'You need to be down at Pinewood Studios next Wednesday, is that alright?' said Nick. 'There'll be five people running safety on the set, including me and Ramsden.'

My heart pounded at the thought of finally working on a film, working with the stars, the lights, the cameras, the five-star hotels.

'As it's in the United Kingdom we get no accommodation, so we'll be camping.'

'What's so dangerous about the set?' I asked, wondering if they'd built a chocolate Matterhorn, having heard on the grapevine that Nick had been teaching the guy who played the Oompa Loompa how to climb.

'No, it's not really climbing safety. In fact, it's probably going to be more like chocolate lifeguard work. Anyway, you'll see when you get there.'

The chocolate safety team stood outside the huge sliding doors of the 007

Stage at Pinewood Studios, dressed in climbing harnesses and helmets, badged up members of Tim Burton's *Charlie and the Chocolate Factory* crew. Everyone was wearing shorts and T-shirts, with a reflective safety vest over the top, the overall effect less 'safety' more 'Village People.'

Apart from me there was Paul Ramsden, Nick, Neil Bentley – a hulk of a man and one of the best climbers in the world – and Nick's business partner Dave Rootes, a former British Antarctic base commander, and the man who had looked after Michael Palin on his 'Pole to Pole' trip. You might say the team was more than qualified to handle anything that lay beyond the studio doors.

Nick and Dave's company was called Poles Apart, indicating the polar nature of much of their work, but had been renamed 'Legs Apart' by Paul, probably because they could turn their hands to anything for money.

'Right guys,' said Nick, everyone standing to attention, me especially, wanting to make a good impression. 'Is anyone on drugs?'

We all shook our heads.

'Good, because if anyone is on drugs then your brains may explode when you go inside and see the set.'

With Nick leading, we walked into the hangar-like building, the largest sound stage in Europe, big enough to hold a jumbo jet or two, and the location for just about every amazing set ever built, from Bond villain lairs to the Death Star from *Star Wars*.

I was expecting a huge white space of gleaming paint and technology, film types in turtleneck sweaters running around and actors swooning under the giant lights. Instead the first thing I saw was the crack of some builder's arse as he manhandled a length of rubber pipe, the space looking like a dilapidated shed or factory: dirty, smelly and full of cockney builders sat around drinking tea from Styrofoam cups and reading *The Sun*. Instead of an amazing set all I could see was a wall of scaffolding and plywood.

I was a bit disappointed.

'Right team, check this out,' said Nick, running up some stairs that led to the lip of the wall.

As I climbed after him, I spotted the top of something out of place in this dingy shed, in fact, something out of place in this world, a gleaming alien tree, its branches red-and-white-striped candy cane, limbs twisting around and up, up towards the giant lights that hung from the ceiling.

'That's got to be a snozzberry tree,' I said, but no one was listening. Looking over the wall, our eyes were transfixed.

Spread out before us in a space as large as a football pitch was the most amazing place I'd ever seen, a life-sized version of Willy Wonka's chocolate garden. Hills of brilliant green grass rose up from the far end, their heights covered in marshmallow trees and bushes hung with gobstoppers as big as your head. A huge tunnel was cut into the side of the hills from which emerged a chocolate river that ran through the middle of the set, its length spanned by two high-arching chocolate bridges, until it ended in a lake of chocolate below what seemed to be a chocolatefall – currently switched off – about a hundred feet high.

'Is it real chocolate?' we all asked in unison.

'No. It's more like washing-up liquid,' said Nick.

'Oh,' we all said, shoulders dropping in disappointment.

'They tried real chocolate but it was just a mess. There's two hundred thousand gallons of the stuff down there.'

The set was empty apart from some people scattering some giant plastic pumpkins.

'The grass is plastic and pretty fragile, the kind of stuff you used to get in butchers' windows. The hills and bridges are made of polystyrene and scaffolding, but the gobstoppers are real.'

We stood and gawped.

'Erm, I'm happy for the work,' I said, 'But what do they need us for?' Beyond getting diabetes from eating a gobstopper the size of a football, what was the problem?

Nick explained how there were lots of dangers on the set, beyond simply drowning in a river of chocolate. There were lots of unprotected drops, as well as the bridges. The stunt coordinator had worked on the Bond film with Nick, and on seeing the dangers on set called Nick, thinking that if he could manage safety on a frozen sea with cars skidding around, he could handle a mock chocolate factory.

'They start filming tomorrow, so we just need to check out belay points and come up with a plan. It should be more of a case of handholding and corralling the crew away from danger, as well as making sure no one drowns in the chocolate.'

'When's Johnny Depp arriving?' I asked.

'Oh, he'll be here tomorrow I think, I've met him and he's pretty normal.'

We spent the rest of the day wandering around the set, seeing what we could tie ropes to in case we had to haul someone out of the chocolate, not that easy when everything you think will be solid – candy cane trees, sugar lumps and marshmallow bushes – is in fact made from polystyrene.

Nick explained that the film had a budget of a hundred and fifty million, and that Johnny Depp was getting twenty five million of that, and so we'd better do a good job of keeping him alive, having only one million pounds each of insurance. I also fancied this sort of work, and knew that it would be both professionally amiss and also a poor start if I allowed Johnny Depp to fall off a candy bridge and break his neck.

In the evening we drove to our digs. On an overseas film, these would have been in a plush hotel, but being in Britain we had to pay for ourselves. So we just camped outside of London.

I'd bought a huge cheap tent that could fit about twenty people in it, so felt like a Bedouin sheikh as I sat drinking beer with the rest of the team. The campsite was filled either with elderly couples in caravans and loud football-playing barbecuing southerners, or people too poor to stay in London on their visit. The latter, which included us, were put in a big field out of sight of the former.

Sat there under canvas I felt as if I was on an expedition. I couldn't wait for the following morning for filming to start. I was a big fan of Tim Burton, who was directing, having seen all his films, and wondered what the man himself would be like. Paul seemed fairly unimpressed, but he'd worked on quite a few films already and knew what to expect. Being a Yorkshireman I'd expect if he met God one day he'd just say, 'Thought you'd be taller,' or something like.

'Andy, JD's coming,' Paul whispered, elbowing me. The two of us stood wearing harnesses, ropes tied to our backs, outside our gear cupboard beside the set.

'Who?' I said, as I fiddled with the radio earpiece that would be stuffed in my ear for the next two months, allowing the safety team to remain in contact, primarily to order cups of tea and sandwiches.

'Johnny Depp,' he said, pointing down the corridor to the main door, where a gaggle of important people were gathering.

Through the door a group of people entered. You could tell they were important because their arse cracks weren't showing over the top of their jeans, and they weren't drinking tea or reading *The Sun*.

'Bloody hell, he's tiny,' said Paul.

'I think that's actually the guy playing the Oompa Loompa,' I said, unsure if he was pulling my leg.

Johnny Depp appeared through the door, dressed as Willy Wonka, all in black, with a big top hat balanced on a smart looking bob haircut, a long walking cane in his purple rubber-gloved hands. He was shorter than I'd imagined he'd be, and also very skinny.

'God, he's got teeth like a Bee Gee,' whispered Paul, Depp's gnashers shining brightly even from our distant vantage point.

'I think they must be false ones,' I said, trying to sound like I knew about film dentistry.

He began walking down the corridor towards us.

We both tried to look busy and uninterested in one of the biggest film stars in the world. I started coiling a rope and whistling, a sure sign I was bluffing my indifference, while Paul fiddled with his radio.

As he passed I looked up and gave him a smile.

He smiled back.

He seemed normal enough.

'I'd give him one,' I said, under my breath.

'He's out of your league,' said Paul.

The crew assembled for the first scene, which would involve Willy Wonka, Charlie, Grandpa and the rest walking over one of the bridges. As we stood setting up, making sure no one toppled into the chocolate, Nick announced over my radio's earpiece that Tim Burton was on his way up to the set, and for us to 'stand by.' So far I'd been on my best behavior in front of Nick and not put a foot wrong – no jokes or daft remarks – and I stood to attention when I heard his warning.

I'd become fascinated by Tim Burton after seeing a photo of him, when his movie *Beetlejuice* came out in the 1990s, all crazy hair and long jumpers, looking just like one of the characters from one of his films. He'd left Hollywood and had settled in Britain, and although not all his films are great, they have all been visually thrilling. He appeared from behind a snozzberry tree looking a bit like Phil Spector, dressed in a big jumper and wearing dark glasses, his hair as crazy as the set he'd helped design.

A hush went through the crew as he approached, director, overseer, dictator and God all rolled into one. I soon learned the director is at the top of a rigid hierarchy that requires no one talk to the director apart from the cinematographer, assistant director and producer. The director's word is final, and woe betide anyone who does anything to stem their creative flow. Like the general of an army, the director is the tip of the spear and the shaft is the mass of tradespeople waiting for his orders.

As he walked down a line of steps, made to look like seaside rock, he tripped and took a tumble, rolling down a grass slope.

If it had been Johnny Depp who'd fallen I expect he'd have turned it into a flamboyant entrance, turning his tumble into an athletic flip back onto his feet, everyone applauding. Unfortunately Tim Burton just rolled down the hill like a barrel, in a loud and undignified manner.

Everyone tried not to laugh.

'Looks like he's gone for a Burton,' I whispered over the radio.
I couldn't help myself.

On location, I discovered, breakfast and lunch is supplied, and usually it's very good quality. We weren't on location, but did start early, so we got breakfast. We made the most of it.

Morning routine was to roll out of bed at six-thirty, get straight in the car, and arrive at Pinewood with enough time to have a leisurely and vast breakfast, involving several bowls of cereal and a big fry-up, followed by lots of tea and toast.

Being climbers – and so scroungers at heart – we overindulged with the free breakfast. Every morning I would sit opposite Paul as he stuffed his face, his new motto being: 'Eat your way to profit.'

Paul, being a no-nonsense northerner, always had a good motto or two. When, for example, we felt our day's work had not been up to scratch, he would just say, 'Well, we may not be good, but at least we're cheap.'

By the end of breakfast we'd be fit to burst, but seeing as all we were going to do for the next twelve hours was stand around it didn't really matter.

As I expected, filming was very boring, and although most takes were done in one, very often it would require half the day to get set up for that one take. The days were also very long, always twelve hours or longer. Work tended to revolve around either standing while waiting for something to happen, or sitting while waiting for something to happen.

The actual levels of danger seemed low, but with kids on the set it was good to play it safe. If they were my kids I'd want someone looking out for them. By and large the child actors seemed to take being stars in their stride, and never seemed to live up to the adage about children or animals. Plus, there was the bonus that legally they could only work four hours a day, so filming took twice as long as usual. It was all money in the bank.

A lot of time was spent just standing around next to the actors, meaning I had a window into their world. Everyone seemed very professional, never fluffing lines, while the job of direction seemed quite organic.

Grandpa Joe was played by David Kelly, who I remembered as the one-armed Irish dishwasher from the television programme Robin's Nest in the 1970s. When I heard it was him, my first thought was, 'Bloody hell, is he still alive?' I'd thought him pretty old when I was six watching him on television. It turned out that he was alive but very old and frail. We decided always to have a stool on set, so we could pull it out between takes and give him a rest. Beyond this being a nice thing to do, I also thought that being able to say 'I used to handle David Kelly's stool on set,' might be a useful gag.

Sat waiting for the next take, he turned to me and out of the blue started telling a story.

'I was in the pub with Pierce Brosnan, when a man came over and stuck his hand out, saying: "Put it there Pierce." Now, not wanting to offend the man, who was obviously drunk, Pierce shook his hand, at which point the man said: "That's the nearest my hand will ever get to Halle Berry's arse."'

Watching this old actor, looking like he'd sprung straight from one of Quentin Blake's illustrations, he always seemed very relaxed, as if there was no light between the character and the man, out-acting everyone by simply being there.

'Andy, I've been performing since I was eight years old,' he said one day, looking up at me as we waited for the next take. 'I'm nearly eighty now. It's a hard life, full of ups and down, champagne and ashes, but when you find something that feels right, you can never turn your back on it, no matter how hard the road.'

One of the worst jobs on set was grass planting. Paul named those responsible the 'grass fluffers.' There was plastic grass worth a million quid covering the stage, glued and stapled into place during a month of backbreaking work. The problem was as soon as anyone walked on it, the grass would break up, a real issue when you have a whole film crew camping on your handy work.

Every day there would be a call for the grass fluffers to mend an area that could be seen in the camera, a job that entailed the sort of care employed by minesweepers, as down on their knees they would patch and repair each strand of grass at a time. It was a thankless task. As soon as the shot was finished, some careless crewmember would walk across the same patch and ruin it.

One scene that stayed with me was Mike Teavee, played by young American actor Jordan Fry, having to smash open a giant candy pumpkin by stamping on it. The pumpkin was made of fibreglass and filled with KY jelly and sweets.

Each time the scene was set up, the pumpkin would break apart before he had chance to kick it, meaning the grass fluffers would have to come and clean up all the KY jelly and sweets, replace the grass, and stick another pumpkin in its place. They only had three pumpkins built for the scene, and on the third take, with the last pumpkin, he finally managed to break it himself.

'Jump up and down really hard,' shouted Tim Burton as Mike Teavee went crazy, his feet covered in KY jelly.

'I'm just imagining it's my sister's head,' the kid shouted.

'That's what I like,' laughed Burton. 'A method actor.'

It was great working with the other members of the safety crew, as most had very interesting stories to tell, and plenty of time to tell them.

Dave Rootes looked like a very ordinary middle-aged guy, sort of a cross between a dad and a school teacher, and was the public face of Poles Apart, giving the impression you were in a safe pair of hands. One day, stood at the edge of the set while the grass fluffers worked, I asked Dave what he'd done before this, always curious in how people became who they were.

'Well I worked for the British Antarctic Survey for many years as a base commander,' he said. Managing a team in the most hostile environment on earth was a very impressive job to have on your resumé.

'Did you ever winter over?' I asked, knowing that most bases were evacuated during the blackness of winter, when temperatures drop off the scale.

'Oh a few times,' he replied, as if describing how often he'd been to the Costa Brava.

'What was it like?' I asked, wondering what it was like waiting for months to see the sun reappear.

'Dark,' he said.

'What did you do before that?' I said, continuing to probe.

'Well, I managed a band, but I left before they got big,' he said. This was an unexpected answer.

'Really?' I found it hard imgaining Dave even being into music, let alone looking after a band. 'What were they called?'

'Genesis.'

I almost fell into the chocolate.

Beyond the film crew – camera operators, grips and sound engineers – there were Pinewood crew – painters, riggers, scaffolders, electricians and carpenters. All were being very well paid, and yet I'd never met such a bunch of miseries in my life. Everyone seemed grumpy about something, or someone, always backbiting and bitching, quick to put down or slag off any other trade, or any fellow tradesman. I guess it's the same on any factory floor, but I was naive enough to think that movie making was above all that.

We shared a little shed built into the wall of the set with the wire riggers, who told us that 'wire work' was one of the oldest trades in cinema, the pioneers being seaman looking for work between voyages in the days of the tall ships. Their skills with ropes, pulleys and knots were ideal for moving things around the stage. Back then they used to communicate up in the rigging by whistling, the reason why it is bad luck to whistle in a theatre, as tooting a little tune could easily lead to a beanstalk landing on your head.

The oldest wire rigger had worked on just about every big film in the last thirty years. He looked like he'd walked off the set of an East End gangster movie. He was obviously not a fan of cinema though, or actors, as every actor you asked about was described as 'a feckin' cant.'

One day I asked him what the biggest film he'd worked on was, and he'd told me it was *Superman*.

'What was Christopher Reeve like?' I asked.

'He was a cant,' was the reply.

A few days later I tried another tack. 'Who's the best actor you've worked with?' I asked, hoping that even this curmudgeon might have a little nugget of movie magic deep inside.

'Richard fackin' Burton,' he said.

'Why was that?' I asked, impressed, imagining that the great actor's talent had been so powerful it had reached even into the heart of this philistine.

'He was always fackin' drunk so we got loads of over-fackin'-time.'

It was bad form to speak to actors unless they wanted to talk, so autographs were out of the question, and the only time I talked to Johnny Depp was when he had to walk over one of the bridges.

I said, 'Mind that step. It's loose.'

I doubt I made it into his memoirs.

A lot of time was spent hanging around with Neil Bentley, another climber from Sheffield. Only a few years before Neil had been one of the best rock climbers in the country, having put up the first 'E10', a route called 'Equilibrium.' He was an intimidating character, both because he looked like he could crush bricks in his hands, and also because, being a Yorkshireman, he more often than not looked unhappy.

His hard climbing had been cut short by an accident on a climb well within his ability in the Dolomites. He'd pulled off a huge flake and been crushed, receiving terrible head injuries. It had only been the actions of his partner lowering him down the rock face and running for rescue that saved his life. Any normal man would have died.

The accident had left him with both a limp and a huge scar across his face, the accident putting an end to his hard climbing, physically and mentally. He'd done other film work before, including acting as Matt Damon's stunt double on *The Bourne Identity*.

'What was he like?' I asked, agog.

'Alright,' said Neil, his usual answer to most things, being a man of few words.

As the filming went on, people kept asking me how Neil had got his scar, not wanting to ask him themselves, perhaps because he looked intimidating.

I told the first couple of people the truth about the accident, but as time went on I started to embellish the story a bit, saying that his face had been ripped off by a rock and then sewn back on, which wasn't remotely true.

One day a timid camera assistant plucked up the courage to ask Neil if the story he'd heard was true.

'Excuse me,' he said, looking up at this scarred colossus, 'is it true that you once had a really bad climbing accident?'

Neil nodded, amazed that someone had finally got part of the story right.

'And did your mate lower you off the mountain?'

Neil nodded again, looking at me to check I wasn't feeding the guy the correct line via sign language.

'And then...' the man continued, speeding up now, as though sure he wasn't being wound up by his mates, '... he lowered you into a crevasse and had to cut the rope with a pen knife?'

Neil looked at me, but instead of the scowl I expected, I saw his stony face begin to crack and he burst out laughing.

The movie made progress, and we all settled into a humdrum routine of breakfast, standing around until the snack wagon, which was also free, opened, then taking it in turns to go for tea and smoothies and cheese toasties. In fact, life became one long round of cheese toasties. Time lost all meaning, as on the set the light was always the same, and very often I'd suddenly find I had no idea if I'd just arrived at work, or was just about to go home.

'Film work is always like this,' said Paul, an old hand in the movie business. 'But don't worry, it will get worse, and before you know it you'll be reading *The Sun* and moaning like everyone else.'

'I don't mind it, really,' I said, happy to keep my head down and do my time.

'That's good,' said Paul. 'What I find works on jobs like this is to break down your pay, so you know how much you make every minute. That way no matter how bad things get, you can always just say: "well, I just made myself thirty-two pence." If it gets really bad you can do it by the second.'

The only break from the tedium was going into the chocolate itself, either in a rubber boat or a dry suit. The chocolate was about three and a half feet deep and came up to your waist in a thick and viscous gloop. In your tiny rubber boat, complete with outboard motor, you would move at a snail's pace. Usually we'd go for a little trip down the river, find a spot hidden from everyone else, and play on our phones or read a magazine.

The river itself was home to the naval detachment of the safety men, also working for Legs Apart, who would cruise around waiting to rescue someone from the chocolate, an even more boring job than ours.

One of these bona fide chocolate safety crew was a South African diver and former bomb disposal expert. One day, sat moored together under the chocolate bridge, I asked him if this was the most boring job ever.

'No mate,' he said, 'this is nothing.' He had, he explained, worked for an oil company planning to run a pipeline across the Pacific. His job was to watch the footage from their robot submarine.

'The sub had filmed the whole length of the proposed route of the pipeline, and I had to watch to see if there were any bombs left over from World War Two. For two months I sat in a tiny room looking at hundreds of video tapes of the bottom of the sea.'

'Did you see any?' I asked.

'No,' he replied. 'But every week or so I'd see a fish.'

After a few weeks, the chocolate began to go 'off' and as it did so its smell intensified. At the start of filming, it had been a bio-free zone, and anything dropped in it had been scooped out immediately. But after a week or so the people with scoops disappeared and the trash built up: cups, sandwiches the odd floating rat. As soon as you entered the set the smell would hit you, a smell that is wholly indescribable, sort of how you'd expect an alien world to smell, but one where all the aliens had died and were rotting away – so not in a good way.

As the stench grew so did an unwillingness to go near the chocolate in the boat. Sat afloat this honking gunk you could see the whole surface shimmering with a new form of life, a polystyrene, chocolate, washing-up liquid hybrid. The smell stayed with us when we returned to the campsite, and people began to get ill, eye infections being the most common ailment. Happily, I seemed immune, no doubt due to growing up next to another chocolate river – the Humber. People started dropping out of the team, either because it was too smelly, or too boring – or too boring and smelly.

A member of the crew told me a story about how John Wayne had probably died of cancer caused by exposure to radiation while filming the Genghis Khan biopic *The Conqueror* close to Nevada's nuclear test sites. This led me to imagine that some time in the future, I'd appear on Panorama, unhealthy looking, maybe with Johnny Depp, as we discussed our terminal 'chocotosis' brought on by working on *Charlie and the Chocolate Factory*.

One morning at breakfast, I admitted to the rest of the team that the day before, while standing next to Johnny Depp, I suddenly realised I could stab him with my safety knife.

This, I suggested to them, must be the kind of thought that goes through the mind of unhinged celebrity assassins. I shared this though because

I'd found it quite worrying – the guy paid to keep Depp safe thinking about stabbing him.

Rather than greet my confession with shock, three of the team admitted they'd had the same thought, while the fourth said he been so bored he'd worked out a way of kidnapping Johnny Depp and holding him for ransom.

After a month, the first unit left and the second unit took over, filming Deep Roy, the actor playing the Oompa Loompa, doing a big dance routine. This required Roy to carry out a few short dance moves while miming to a music track, then moving a metre sideways and doing the same. Once this had been done twenty times, all the frames would be spliced together on a computer to give a Busby Berkeley dance routine, with dozens of identical Oompa Loompas dancing in sync.

At least, that was the idea.

In reality, Deep Roy had the rhythmic sense of a baked potato and wasn't helped by having two choreographers and a mime coach shouting at him as he tried, for the ten thousandth time, to do a few moves identical to those of his other selves now stored on a hard disk. This part of filming was only set to last a week or so, but due to its complexity, the job rolled on and on.

It was during this period that I thought my mind would snap.

Again and again, there would be a shout from the second unit director to 'Roll please!' followed by the booming words:

Augustus Gloop, Augustus Gloop,
The great big greedy nincompoop.
Augustus Gloop so big and vile,
So big and vile.
So greedy, foul, and infantile.

Adding together the dreadful smell, the misfiring Oompa Loompa choreography and the loud song, repeated over and over again, I felt I was involved in some appalling CIA experiment in brainwashing, pushing my grip on reality to the brink.

But for two fifty a day I held on tight.

I rarely went home, and while Mandy and the kids came down and camped a few times, the long drive to Sheffield and back was too much. There was a family day one Saturday, and the kids came for that, exploring the sets: Charlie's house, the inventing room, the outside of the Chocolate factory. It was a day they never forgot.

Mandy seemed happy enough me being away, but I felt bitter. It was okay if I was away working hard, but not if I was doing the thing I loved doing, which also made money. I'd once seen the line 'Do the thing you love, and love the thing you do,' written on a poster on the Underground, and it stuck with me, but I'd begun to see that if you loved something too much, it led to resentment.

The film stretched on for two months

There seemed only to be work, sleep, or travelling between the two, those twelve hours growing longer by the day. It had become a job.

I often wondered how people kept on working themselves so hard, head down, and not just step off when they realised they were selling their life and all its potential riches, even their health, for a wage, a wage you had no time to spend on anything meaningful, just stuff.

I'd seen this in the faces of many people I'd met when doing business talks, me presented as the bloke who never let work get in the way of experiences, talking to a room of people who gave everything to their companies. Now I knew it was really quite easy, especially when you're being paid half a pence a second.

As the filming dragged on I found myself sinking into the same chocolate funk as everyone else, complaining about the smell, Deep Roy's dancing, the lack of biscuits at break time, how horrible tea tasted when your taste buds were contaminated by the river.

I began to detest the big breakfasts, the sickly smoothies, the plastic taste of tea from polystyrene cups, hanging around with the riggers and scaffolders, gossiping, the whole while trying to manoeuvre myself into another job. In our shed I became the old-timer, bitching about people who didn't pull their weight, thinking I should get paid more, seeing as I'd been doing it longer than anyone.

I saw I was getting fat, fatter than I'd even been before, my harness no longer fitting properly. Fat, but not arsed to go for a run or do anything about it except eat my way further into profit, food hiding the boredom.

'I'm off, I can't do this anymore,' said Neil. 'There's more important things than this.' I thought he was crazy.

At the start I'd wondered if I should have gone to Yosemite, but now I was making big money, more than I had in all my life, my old weekly wage every day. Two fifty became my mantra, ironing out any worries about what I was doing. The longer I worked the more cash I'd have at the end. No amount of misery or discomfort could stand between my paycheck and me.

The only person I never heard bitching was Mike, an old guy who looked a little like a hippy and said 'man' at the end of every sentence. He dressed in a tatty leather waistcoat and faded jeans. Of all the people on the set, he had the most to bitch about, being the longest serving grass fluffer.

If there is a university of life, then there is also a university of sticking plastic grass to polystyrene, and if so, then Mike had earned himself a doctorate over the last two months.

Every day he'd been ready for the call, and when it came, he knelt down and mended the grass, without fuss or complaint. Job done, he would stand, not looking for thanks and resume his place, waiting to be called back, more often than not to mend the very same piece of grass, over and over again. While the others would pull their hair out, Mike would just look content, kneel down and do it all again.

Towards the end of filming, while standing beside Mike and guarding him from falling off a bridge into what was now a chocolate sewer, I asked him a question that had been bugging me for days: 'How do you stay so bloody cheerful?'

Finishing his work, he stood up and with a theatrical cast of his hand, like Willy Wonka introducing his guests to the crazy vista of this room full of snozzberry trees and giant candy pumpkins, he said something I could never forget.

'I can still see the magic.'

His words were like a spell.

I straightened up, and looked around me, at the brilliantly green grass, the red toffee apple trees, their branches reflecting the shimmering chocolate, the huge twisted candy cane trees, dazzling in their stripey-ness. I was standing in a place that in a few weeks would be torn down and never be seen again, constructed from the imaginings of a genius filmmaker, an experience as valuable as any summit of any mountain.

I was taking part in something unique and fabulous.

I had to hold on to the magic in this.

I had to hold on to the magic in everything.

'Now I see,' I said.

And I did.

EIGHTEEN

Grounded

I made the kids' breakfast – white toast and marmite – as they watched Dora the Explorer on television, the sun streaming in through the window. I hadn't climbed for three months straight.

There weren't many kids programmes I could tolerate, so I thumbed through the latest climbing magazines instead, their pictures only making me feel even more removed from it. Flicking to the pages where all the world's new routes were recorded, I pored over those recently climbed on the hardest mountains. I read the names of the climbers, knowing many of them, feeling jealous and bitter it wasn't me. This issue covered the latest news from the Himalaya, and after examining the lines drawn on photographs, traced my finger either side, searching for potential new routes.

I knew it was a waste of time. I couldn't be so long away, couldn't afford the expense, the porters and peak fees. It was just too much when you have kids. The big mountains were for the single and the selfish, those more selfish than me.

I knew I'd never climb in the Himalaya.

The kids sang along with Dora.

Where was I?

I tried to return to the living room, to Ella and Ewen.

They were growing up but I was too wrapped up to care, my head always full of mountains.

Why did I find it so hard to be here?

A friend had once pointed out that Ewen, even when he was a baby, seemed to crave my attention, but that I just wasn't there, my head always buried in a book or magazine, or else in front of a computer screen.

Why was my love so abstract?

'Come on kids eat your toast,' I said. Time was moving on, the credits were about to roll, the signal to get dressed.

The kids didn't move, but giggled instead, joining in with Dora.

'Ella, Ewen, eat your toast, I won't ask you again,' I shouted, only this time in a dad's voice.

Ella flashed me a look – 'Don't talk to me like that', as though I was infringing her human rights, while Ewen blindly felt around for his toast, eyes transfixed by the screen, and ate around the crust.

Maybe none of us are really ever where we seem to be.

I brought down the kids' clothes and got them ready, double-checking Ella was up to standard. Her school was only a short distance away, and was mostly a mix of lower, middle and upper working-class kids, the 'upper' meaning they were actually working. The less well-off parents dressed their kids in nice new clothes, made sure they combed their hair and had the latest trends.

The middle-class kids more often than not wore hand-me-downs, and looked more bohemian, as if they'd just come from a houseboat or a tree house. It seemed the richer you got, the more of a tramp your kids looked. I'd really noticed this when talking at private schools, where the kids often looked a real state with grubby uniforms and mad hair, something I put down to the fact that their parents must be skint after paying the school fees.

An army officer once told me it was fine to dress down as long as you wore polished shoes, just to show it was in fact a disguise, that the down-at-heel look was a choice, not a necessity. What broke my heart was seeing poor kids standing in the playground, or walking up the hill to school, alone and late, dressed in tat like the rich kids, only without their nice shoes or their self-confidence. I just knew they were unloved and uncared for, that they had a huge mountain to climb to have any kind of life.

I looked at Ella and Ewen as they half-heartedly got ready in front of the TV, finishing their toast.

How much do I love you?
Are you unloved?
Are you two just speed bumps in my way?
You tie me to this spot.
I never wanted kids.
I never wanted anybody.
...
I can ignore almost everything, but you.

I stood in the playground with the other parents, Ewen on my shoulders, Ella playing on a slide, waiting for the bell to ring. Looking around at the other grown-ups, I wondered how they felt, having to come here every day, juggling work and fun to be here at school, on time, twice a day. It was like being on parole, only for much longer. Most looked like parents should

– dumpy, peevish and knackered, as if they had been ready-made for the job, all elements of themselves as independent human beings sacrificed on the altar of childcare.

The bell rang, I kissed Ella goodbye, and watched her line up with the other kids, the signal for parents to leg it. Only I didn't, I stayed and smiled, as she smiled back, waving at Ewen, blowing kisses until they filed away through a set of old blue doors.

I felt a strange sadness at being unable to share every moment of her day.

Throwing aside such mawkish thoughts, I walked down the hill, gripping Ewen's chubby legs, as he bobbed on my shoulders.

'Pull my left ear to go left, and my right ear to go right,' I called up to him, a daft game for two Kirkpatricks who couldn't tell one from another. 'Dad? Where are we going?' he said, kicking his feet.

'Ian's house.'

Ian lived in a shared terraced house on one of the darkest and grubbiest streets in our part of Sheffield, a street overhung with dirty trees whose dead leaves never seemed to decompose, but stuck to the street like grimy glue. His landlord, another climber, lived upstairs. The other occupants were students, climbing students or ex-students.

'Hello,' I said as Ian opened the door. 'Are you up for a visit?'

Ian stood in jeans and his sponsor's T-shirt, looking tired and harried, the way he usually looked, seeming more dart-player than mountaineer.

'I've been up all night trying to finish an article before I go away, but I suppose I can take a break for you two.'

His room was through the kitchen, which you could tell was shared, because of the continuous presence of toast detritus. His own abode had all the ambiance of a garage filled with junk, only without the space, as if the contents of his entire life had been upended into this little cell, then trampled down to allow access.

If Ian's room had been placed behind glass, like Francis Bacon's studio, the public would have marvelled at how a person could live day-to-day like that and still be productive. The guided tour would be short: a bed, unmade and half hidden by stuff, its sheets the kind any decent mother would burn; a desk, buried under sheets of slides, broken cameras and their lenses; a grubby computer, the frame around the dusty screen a mosaic of post-it notes and to-do lists; and a wooden bouldering wall, made from a sheet of wood bolted to the plaster board with chains, a sign that this room had never been intended to be lived in, and was in fact just a large cupboard.

The climbing wall looked like it hadn't been climbed on in a long time, its dust and old chalk marks giving it the appearance of a long forgotten piece of school apparatus. Fall from its holds, and you would likely be impaled on an ice axe, crampon or ski pole. The room's floor was littered in climbing gear, the tools of Ian's trade.

You didn't walk through his room. You waded.

On the walls were pages from magazines, climbing posters, and route topos. His bookshelf held every book you could imagine on climbing. Standing in the doorway you got the feeling that this was either the dwelling of a climbing-obsessed teenager or someone who was mentally ill; in a way both were true. It was no wonder he spent so long away from home, and no surprise he didn't have a girlfriend.

'Got any romance at the moment?' I asked, as Ian put on the kettle, his sideways glance signalling the answer was a no.

'I haven't got time for such things,' he said, opening the fridge. 'Erm, do you like soya milk?'

Tea-less, we went back to Ian's room. While I kept an eye on Ewen to prevent him sinking into the mire, Ian tried to excavate a slide I needed for my column that month, Ian being my go-to man for images.

'It should be in this pile,' he said, sitting down and lifting a big stack of slide sheets onto his knee. Most conversations we had in the real world were undertaken through the lens of a sheet of slides.

I knew Ian was off the following day with John Varco to the Indian Himalaya for an alpine-style attempt on a brilliant line up a mountain called Saf Minal. If they pulled it off it would be a world-class climb.

'Is John ready for the off?' I asked, and got a repeat of his 'loveless' look again.

'Of course not, he's juggling even more than me.'

'What are your chances of getting up it?' I asked.

'It's two thousand metres high, loose, and capped by a big cliff of black shale. Oh, and the summit is just under seven thousand metres, so who knows?'

There was a brief silence.

'How are your teeth?' I asked.

A few months before, Ian had been soloing at Burbage, a gritstone crag above Sheffield, the routes just high enough to hurt yourself but perfect for soloing, which he'd been doing, and had thus proved the former point. He'd been near the top of a climb when his hand slipped and off he'd come. Ian had hit the ground many times before, so was something of a pro when it came to falling well. He had the presence of mind, in the split second left to him, to try and land on a ledge halfway down. Unfortunately, his plan backfired, and the ledge merely flipped him over, sending him headfirst into the ground.

Most people would have died, but not Ian, who had woken up, dazed, his face and jaw in agony, his arms cut and badly grazed by the rough gritstone.

Most people who had not yet died would have lain there waiting for rescue. Ian, on the other hand, staggered to the car park and found someone to give him a lift home, which can't have been easy, seeing as he was covered in blood.

Getting home, his face now throbbing, Ian went to the bathroom to check if he still had a face, and saw he'd not come off too badly, and that only one tooth was missing from the jawbone in the middle of his mouth. It took him a moment to recall that people tend not to have a middle jawbone, and he realised his was broken. To fall head first off a climb, the ground littered with brain-splatting boulders, and walk away with only a broken jaw showed the angels were with him that day. But Ian's angels had their work cut out.

Ian opened his mouth and showed me his impressive dental work, most of it caused by a diet of Haribo and Coke rather than climbing.

'Are you looking forward to it?' I asked, wondering how long it would take to pack.

'I can't wait to get out of here,' he said, turning away and looking at an email that had just beeped onto his computer, instantly distracted.

I looked around the room and considered both of our lives, what we had and what we didn't. Who would have missed him if he'd died that night? How long would he have stayed there till someone realised he was gone? Movie con artists always say that to avoid capture a good grifter must be able to drop everything and just walk out of their life at any moment. Maybe this was why Ian was so good at what he did. But what was the price?

'Dad can we go?' asked Ewen, untangling himself from a rope that looked like it had seen its best days.

'Okay, we'll be off and leave you to it,' I said, standing up and lifting Ewen into my arms, distracting Ian again. 'Sorry for disturbing you.'

'I'll see you out,' he said and walked us to the door.

'Don't eat any yellow snow or die,' I said, turning to see him standing in the door. Another email beeped in, and his head turned back towards his room, then back to me.

'Are you up to anything?' he said.

Lifting Ewen back onto my shoulders, I said, 'A bit of this and a bit of that... but mainly this,' and bumped Ewen up and down until he laughed.

We both laughed, probably both thankful for what we had and what we didn't.

It was time to go.

'See you soon,' I said, wondering if I would.

'You too,' said Ian, closing the door, leaving us to walk home, Ewen's small hands twisting my ears.

NINETEEN

Magic

January 2005

For as long as I'd been climbing in the Alps I'd dreamt of spending a winter season in Chamonix, as so many of my friends had, to go and not come back, if only for a month or two. Being there for more than three weeks meant I could get fit on a hard route and carry that fitness over onto something harder still, instead of coming home. It was something I'd seen many good climbers do, stepping from one summit to another, never having to descend again to the real world.

For most of us, doing a whole season remains just a dream, lived by those rich enough to take a few months off and rent a flat in the valley, or those poor enough not to care, sleeping on floors and eking out their savings, making ends meet with bar work or emptying bins.

I'd always been envious of climbers who'd done the whole season. I'd turn up for a brew on my first day to get the beta on conditions at a flat where every inch of floor space was sub-let to other climbers to get the rent down. Their faces would be suntanned and wind-blasted, with panda eyes from goggles and glasses. They had the look of ski bums, weary from nonstop fun, but also as fit as butchers' dogs.

Often they arrived as climbers, with ambitions for long gnarly climbs, only to turn to the dark side, and start skiing. Before you knew it, skiing took over, and climbing ambitions shrank to day routes, which wouldn't get in the way of fun on the slopes. Instead of tales of epic bivvys on the Grandes Jorasses or mad soloing escapades, I'd hear stories of the 'best powder ever' or off-piste adventures, big drop-offs and runs through the trees.

All this made me grumpy. One of the biggest factors in the slow demise of British alpinism has been the metamorphosis of climbers who could hardly ski, into skiers who climbed. Part of the reason for that was the number of

climbers who'd become alpine guides, a qualification that required a high level of skiing proficiency, turning them, body-snatcher style, into skiers.

But there was still something fabulous about turning your back on normal life and going to live in such a place for the whole winter.

Now it was my turn.

All summer the Alps had been my focus. The promise of winter helped me ignore the fact I wasn't climbing and was instead living a normal – for me – nine-to-five existence. I pushed that queasy feeling of time slipping by to the back of my mind, telling myself that come winter I would pack up my stuff and finally get to grips with climbing. On *Charlie and the Chocolate Factory* what kept me going was the thought of using the money I'd earned to spend six weeks in the Alps.

Throughout the summer I made plans, found a tiny flat just outside the Chamonix valley that was cheap, and sorted out climbing partners. Six weeks was too long to be away from the family, so Mandy and the kids planned to come out for half the time. It seemed the perfect plan – but, as usual, reality got in the way.

Mandy decided she wanted to move house, thinking ours too small. She complained it didn't have a garden, which didn't bother me, as in my experience gardens were just overgrown jungles for those people like us without the time or money to tend them. Having grown up in a block of flats, whose balconies grew only lichen and mould, I didn't see the point of a garden anyway.

Mandy was on a mission though, and so I went along, not bothered either way when I discovered moving day was in the middle of my trip to the Alps.

It wasn't far to go, just two hundred yards down the road, but I knew I should be there. I was too selfishly attached to my dream, and left it to Mandy's friends to help Mandy move.

My selfishness didn't register, so complete was my focus on what I wanted. Sometimes it's shaming to understand the reality of letting nothing stand in your way. I packed the car with everything I could possibly need for routes on north faces and big walls, kissed the family goodbye and set off for the ferry and the long drive out to the Alps. I reached France that evening and drove through the night, the temperature falling as I drove up into the mountains at dawn.

I knew that really I was running away from my family, going to my other life. I often thought about this, about just running. When people told stories of dads going out to the shop for a packet of biscuits and not coming back, I totally understood it. The idea of disappearing on a mountain sounded a little nobler, but there was very little between the two.

Driving into the Chamonix valley in my own car felt special, as if finally I was planning on staying for a while, bringing a big chunk of one world to another, my stuff, my car, my family; as if the barrier between the two worlds was finally breaking down. Looking through its grubby windows at the Dru and the Aiguilles, snow trails blowing from the sunlit summit of Mont Blanc, I could see that high pressure was coming.

This was going to be amazing.

I found my flat in the tiny village of Servoz and settled in, sorting out my gear on the porch in warm sunshine. Paul Ramsden was flying out in a week's time, and before he arrived I planned to solo the Walker Spur on the Grandes Jorasses, and so spent the afternoon packing my kit, my head full of excited thoughts, choosing the gear, spraying my cams with lube so they wouldn't stick in the cold.

I went into town and photocopied a topo, bought my hill food and told the rescue team where I'd be if I didn't return, feeling the confidence rushing through me as I walked through the streets of Chamonix, knowing that nothing could stop me.

A week later I'd done nothing but lie in bed.

A virus had been touring the valley all winter, and as soon as I arrived it found me, starting on my throat, then spreading through my body, knocking me sideways and dashing my plans.

I lay in my bedroom for a few days, curtains drawn, feeling sorry for myself and only managing to make it to the living room with a supreme effort. I sat there watching French television, looking longingly at my gear packed and ready to go in the corner.

My one consolation was I had time, lots of time, and that I would soon get better.

Then it started to snow – and snow.

And snow.

Four days went by and I pulled myself together and went for a walk up a trail through the woods, wading up to my knees, feeling weak. I prayed that by the time Paul arrived I'd be fit and the weather would have improved.

Snow covered everything. I thought about being up on the Grandes Jorasses now. I'd probably be near the top if I'd managed to set off. I'd expected a storm might come, but just thought I'd deal with it if it did, not wanting to be put off. I'd been in plenty of storms. They always rage hardest in the mind.

A wind blew through the treetops, showering me with snowflakes, big white patches on my red jacket.

I imagined being up there now, high on the Walker, feeling this wind cut through me, the snow shifting and sliding under my feet.

There was nowhere to bivy up there.

The wind blew stronger and the trees creaked, large clumps of snow dropping to the ground.

I wished the kids were here.

I met Paul at Geneva airport, pleased to see his familiar hangdog expression after a week in solitary confinement. We seemed to have so many failures under our belts I hoped this time we'd have a bit of luck.

Driving to Servoz, Paul admitted to feeling fat and unfit, with too much work taking its toll. Having taken up Pilates, his back was feeling better, apart from the odd twinge. Pilates seemed a bit New Age for Paul. I told him I was also under the weather, but should be fit to climb tomorrow.

'We've got to climb something this time, no matter what,' said Paul.

'No matter what,' I replied.

Wanting something challenging, but not too extreme for unfit men with jobs and children, we chose the Messner route on the Northeast Face of Les Droites, a mixed line that was rarely climbed in winter, but would allow us the luxury of going slowly and doing what we did best: Scottish mixed climbing, suffering and camping.

I'd climbed the North Face twice before, and had made a couple of attempts that came to nothing, so knew the way down, often reason enough to try a new way up.

The face was broad, split into two angled faces by the Northeast Spur, twelve hundred metres long, the faces on either side a kilometre high and angled at sixty degrees with the odd steeper section.

We packed in the morning, erring on the side of caution by taking food for four days and a small bivy tent. The Messner was mainly a rock buttress, meaning we could get on the route and climb it to the top no matter how slow we were.

The familiar walk down from the Grands Montets lift went swiftly on solid snow, the new stuff blown away in the previous few days. But instead of crossing the glacier to the Argentière hut, with its dank winter quarters, we opted to bivy in our tent at the base of the face, putting the route on our doorstep. Walking up the easy-angled lower slopes to a flat spot a hundred metres from the bergschrund, my legs seemed leaden. I was still weak, not quite over the virus.

Chopping out a platform for the tent with our axes, we paused to rest and scope out the route in front of us. It began with some moderate ice that led to a big snowfield, before rearing up a granite pillar.

'It looks like a meaty route,' said Paul, looking up as he fitted the tent poles together.

'Weather looks set as well,' I replied, the evening sky empty of clouds.

'Maybe this time we'll be lucky,' Paul said, as he slid the poles inside the little yellow tent. We crawled inside as night came on and curled up in our thick sleeping bags.

'How did your virus start?' Paul asked after a while.

'I had a sore throat and a temperature,' I replied. 'Why?'

'Either this sleeping bag is warmer than I thought or I'm coming down with what you had,' he said.

I lay there in the dark, still not recovered myself, knowing that in the morning we'd be going down.

We woke before the alarm to the clink-clink of climbers passing by, shouts in French echoing from the face as they negotiated the bergschrund and began to climb. I guessed they were heading for the parallel Koenig-Suhubiette route, and felt guilty and lazy for having a lie-in when others were up and climbing. I guessed it was probably still only three o'clock. They must be expecting to climb the route in a single day.

Lying in my warm sleeping bag, in my tent, it felt good to be going slowly, lying in the river, waiting for the flood, unsure if the drought would continue.

'Are you awake Paul?' I whispered.

'Yes,' he whispered back, as if we didn't want the French to know we were there.

'How are you feeling?'

'Not bad,' he said, by which, being a Yorkshireman, he meant terrible.

The alarm went off at five and I lay there for a moment waiting for Paul to cancel our plans, something not too hard to swallow at that time of the morning. Instead he unzipped himself and leaning on his elbow, lit the stove.

'How you feeling?' I asked, still laid on my back.

'I've got a headache. Feel a bit crap,' he said, not sounding too good either.

'Are you okay to climb?' I asked, concerned he might kill himself on my behalf.

'I'll give it a go.'

With so many disappointments over the last few years I guessed he wasn't going to let anything stand in his way.

By the time we'd packed up the tent and closed the gap on the face it was dawn. The first few pitches were steep but not too steep, the going slow, with plenty of stops along the way. As the sun lit up the glacier we could look across to the French team, as they made equally slow progress a few hundred metres to our right, their shouts echoing back and forward, removing all sense of isolation from the face.

The only memorable pitch was a steep ribbon of snow and ice leading up a blank granite slab, one of those pitches where there is no gear, but the ice feels secure. It was an exercise in mind control where fear was the only enemy.

As I led, I tried to work out the last time I'd led an ice pitch, thinking it must have been the Lesueur a year ago. I felt intimated by the pitch, the weight of my pack, the sensation my crampons might slice through the snow at any moment and leave me hanging by my tools.

I forced the feeling back, telling myself that I led harder pitches when I knew nothing, and I could lead this now, with many tens of thousands of metres between that novice and me. It was like riding a bike, only downhill and fast along a potholed road. All I had to do was concentrate on positive action, not negative emotion.

The ice got thinner, probably three inches thick, thick enough for ice, but thin for snow-ice, which had the resistance of over-frozen ice cream.

I kicked my feet hard, wanting the most metal and boot possible in the ice, feeling all my weight bearing down, each step a little act of faith.

My pick struck the rock and bounced off and instantly I felt as if I was only balanced on my feet.

My sack felt heavy, pulling me backwards.

My attention was suddenly down at my feet, feeling them about to rip out.

'Bit thin this bit, Paul. Watch me.'

I breathed in and out, and focused on that.

In and out.

In and out.

I tried higher with my pick, the only chance I had to make progress.

It bounced off again.

I reset it beside the other tool, my arms now getting tired and my calves sore.

In and out.

In and out.

I chopped the ice away in front of my face to create a little shelf, the rock beneath blank, then rotated my axe by ninety degrees so the whole length of the pick hooked against it.

Then I kicked hard, first left then right, and stepped up, pulling down on the shelf I'd cut.

I tried higher with my other tool, just a little tap, scared another rebound might topple me off.

The pick bit by an inch.

I kicked again, keeping both axes in place, left then right, stepping up.

'If anything pops I'm off,' I thought.

How often had I thought this?

One day something would.

I placed the other pick a little higher, a little harder, its tip biting an inch deeper. Lifting my foot up to the little shelf I'd cut, and praying to the angels, I stepped up.

'How's it going?' said Paul cheerfully.

The day went quickly, and darkness caught us moving up the big snowfield beneath the buttress of rock, perhaps a third of the way up the climb, still below the hard stuff. Luck was with us, and our line bumped up against a small rock buttress, the size of a small garden shed, but offering the chance of a good bivy with good protection if we could cut a ledge below it.

Attached to a couple of nuts we hacked away with our axes, stopping every so often to rest, both dying for a brew.

'I feel fucked,' said Paul, stopping and resting his head on the boulder.

With the snow and ice chopped away, we had a ledge wide enough to take the tent, which we pitched, attaching it to the rock as well as us. It was quite a camping spot.

Paul crawled in and I passed him the bivy gear, listening to the echoing calls of the French team, who, out of time, were abseiling back down their route, their headtorches flashing back and forth.

Inside the tent we could forget we were on the side of a mountain, that is until we ventured too far from the side of the tent pressed against the mountain, and felt only the void on the other side. Since he was ill, Paul got the inside berth, and I made a mental note not to roll over in the night.

As the stove purred away, Paul lay on his back looking at the ice crystals grow on the tent ceiling. It was obvious he wasn't feeling well.

But then I wasn't feeling much better.

My heart seemed to be beating very hard and very fast. Unsure whether altitude was the cause, I unzipped the door of the tent a few inches in case the stove was asphyxiating us.

My heart raced on.

'There you go Paul,' I said, passing him a cup of noodles, then listened, between the thumps of my beating heart, to a helicopter moving below us in the dark. It was odd for a helicopter to be out at night, so I poked my head out of the tent and saw its flashing red light moving over the glacier below us. The beam of a big searchlight shone down, the helicopter transformed into a UFO about to scoop up some hapless climber, the white light sweeping across the ice as it neared the bottom of the face, where it began to creep up the wall below us, seemingly following our tracks.

'What's it doing?' asked Paul, sucking down noodles.

'I think maybe it's looking for us?'

The chopper rose higher and higher until the searchlight illuminated the tent, which I guess must have been a bit of a surprise, pitched there, seemingly defying gravity, like a limpet to the side of the mountain's hull.

The chopper hung there for a moment, no doubt taking us in, and I gave a little wave to say we were okay, wondering if there was a signal meaning: 'We're camping.' I guessed someone had seen our lights on the face and imagined we were in trouble.

'Ask if they've got any paracetamol,' said Paul.

With a whoosh the chopper swept away and dropped towards the glacier, its beam of light growing smaller, and then picked its way back down the valley. We were alone with our noodles again.

The following morning it was light by the time we'd packed up. Everything was done in slow motion.

Paul looked in pain as we stuffed our gear back in our packs, and I felt even stranger than the night before, my heart still pounding.

We really had to go down, and we both knew it.

'We could traverse over to the Lagarde couloir from here,' said Paul, pointing over to the left side of the face. The Lagarde was an easier route up the edge of the face, nothing more than a big gully. 'It would be easier and we could get to the top today.'

Paul was not going to give up.

'Sounds like a plan,' I said and off we went.

After a series of traverses we broke into the Lagarde couloir and began climbing up its edge, placing more gear than usual, aware of the state we were in. Each pitch seemed to take an age.

My heart now began to act very oddly indeed, beating hard but then seemingly skipping a beat, going bu-boom bu-boom bu-boom, falling silent for a beat, and then recovering with a boom-boom, before continuing as normal, as if it was taking a breather. Feeling it pounding like that, as if at any moment it could just stop, was scary. Very scary. A sane person would immediately go down and rush to a doctor. I did neither. I just pressed on, convinced that at any moment I could simply drop down dead.

While climbing a pitch, something caught my eye on the side wall, something I mistook for ice for a moment until I realised it was a fist-sized crystal, a huge lump of beautiful quartz.

I climbed up to it, took off my glove and ran my fingers over it, so perfectly smooth and geometric. The last crystal I'd seen like this was on Poincenot in Patagonia. It was a tiny hollow of rock I'd stumbled on filled with stones just like these. My instinct had been to smash one out with my axe and take it with me, but as I lifted up my hammer I had stopped, believing that if I stole it, the mountain would punish me.

The same thought came into my head again, as I stood there on Les Droites, that the mountain would punish me. That the mountain cared.

I lifted up my hammer and smashed it out and stuck it into my rucksack.

We swapped leads until night was nearly on us, believing we could get to the top, but knowing we probably wouldn't.

The gully petered out and we broke right up a wide chimney, looking for a spot to sleep.

'I think I've found something,' Paul croaked, and I climbed up to find him sat on a large wedged block the size of a wheelie bin laid on its side. It was plenty big enough for us to sit out the night, but within a minute a slight wind picked up, dumping spindrift onto us from the summit slopes.

'Let's see if we can get the tent perched on top,' Paul suggested. He looked pale in my torchlight, as though he too could drop dead at any moment.

We worked hard, chopping away ice and fiddling with frozen poles until the tent hung half on, half off the tiny perch. It was another improbable campsite.

Squirming inside, both on our sides, we fought to get our shoulders and arses on something solid, while the rest hung over the drop. Spindrift poured down now, pressing on the tent, building up on the fabric, pushing us off our spot until we punched it clear.

'This is pretty grim,' said Paul, quite a remark from the master of tough bivys.

'It could be worse,' I replied, which was no comfort at all.

With great care we got in our sleeping bags. Then Paul fished out the stove and fired it up. As soon as it lit, a foot-long flame flared out.

'Don't shake the stove, Paul,' I gasped with alarm, judging the tent about to go up in flames.

'I'm not,' said Paul, as another huge belch of fire burst out of it.

'You bloody are,' I said, flinching backwards. 'Don't move it.'

'I'm not bloody shaking it, there's something wrong with it!' he said, his head held back from the rocket-like flame.

'Give it to me, you're wobbling it,' I said, taking it from him, showing him the correct way to hold it.

The stove immediately flared again, the flame an inch from the tent fabric.

'Told you,' said Paul, looking smug as the snow hissed down hard on the tent.

The stove settled down at last, and after a brew and more noodles we tried to get comfortable, not easy in such a cramped spot. The sound of hissing spindrift, my beating heart and Paul's groaning were far from conducive to sleep.

Lying half on, half off the chockstone, I felt unable to move an inch, as if even the slightest alteration in position would see me slide over the edge, trapped in a pocket of tent until its seams bust. My feet were stuck in Paul's face, his in mine. Our bivy had all the comfort of a shared park bench. It was one of those nights when you keep feeling for the rope, making sure you're still tied in, giving it a little tug to check it's not too slack and that you'll not fall too far.

As the snow continued to pour down on us, we began to realise that the chimney was its usual path and we had camped midstream, the tent a logjam flexing under the onslaught. Just as quickly as we cleared it with our fists and elbows, the snow pressed down again.

I worried about the pole snapping, or that the spindrift would push us off our block, and so lay there half awake for much of the night.

'This is *really* grim,' mumbled Paul, his voice sounding muffled and faraway.

I flicked on my torch and saw his head was trapped under the bulging fabric. It looked as though a big fat person had parked their backside on his end of the tent.

'I concur,' I said.

And I did.

There was no desire for a lie-in next morning. Just after dawn we broke out of the chimney and made our way up the final snow slopes to the East Summit of Les Droites, moving together in a light wind, watching the snow catch the sun as it blew from the summit ridge. We sped up the final few metres, just wanting it to be over.

At the top we sat down and shook hands.

The whole of the range was spread out around us.

I'd seen it before.

It took two days to make it back to the valley, my heart settling down as we lost altitude, Paul getting more ill and looking like he was ready to check into A&E when I drove him to the airport.

A few days later I was back at the airport to pick up Mandy and the kids, my heart taking another kind of leap as I saw them coming through customs, the kids running up to the glass partition and waving madly.

This was it, the two sides of my life about to meet.

Ella and Ewen had never seen so much snow in their lives, and they made the usual comic errors kids make, like making snow balls with their bare hands, or not making sure their snow suits were zipped up before tumbling into a drift. The result was their first hot-aches, standing dumbfounded and tearful as they held out their hands, their clothes soaked with melted snow.

Yet they were fast learners and soon when they fell over in the snow without gloves they would always fall with their hands held clear.

'Just think of snow as radioactive poo,' I told them. 'Only touch it if you really have to.'

I wasn't due to climb for another week, so we did family things, my main exercise pulling the two kids in a sledge around town, which was good, as my system felt strained after climbing Les Droites.

Mandy was keen to ski, so we headed over to the nursery slopes in Argentière. I'd barely skied myself, but gave Mandy and the kids the benefit of my limited knowledge, confined to shuffling along the flat on borrowed skis and then taking them off to walk downhill.

It was the usual British ski farce, with kids falling off the tow and crying, or speeding off into the trees without being able to stop. Being the one in charge, by necessity I improved fast and soon found myself skiing down with Ewen and Ella taking turns to stand between my legs, their skis trapped between mine.

I'd come to realise that the one thing I could do well was deconstruct complex tasks and understand how they worked. It's how I'd learned to climb, to write, and take photos. So I applied the same method to skiing, looking at how the French did it. I guess it's called copying.

Judging that being able to ski was a good thing for a middle-class family, we booked Ella into ski school, and Mandy took lessons, leaving me with Ewen. Only being three, it was easy for him to travel along with his skis braced between mine, lifting him up when we needed to turn, and the number of crashes caused by his skis catching mine was quite small.

Anyway, he had a helmet.

My long-anticipated climbing holiday became a family skiing holiday: chocolate croissants and hot chocolate for breakfast, collecting our skis, queuing, skiing, more hot chocolate, then home.

All day, I watched Ella go by in a long line of kids, learning the basics. The French skiing instructor kept calling her Ellek all the time, which confused me. It was only on her last day – her new silver snowflake badge denoting snow-ploughing mastery pinned to her red ski suit – that I asked him why he called her Ellek. He said it was the name we'd written on her skis – Elle K.

After her first lesson the three of us skied a very long green run, Ewen between my legs and Ella sliding hesitantly behind me, coaxing them down each little steep step.

'Throw yourself into it Ella – be bold!' I told her. 'Try and relax, enjoy it, don't be scared.'

We reached the bottom of the slope, and a long queue for the button lift, the kids shuffling along beside me like penguins.

'You cannot go on,' said the ski patroller, holding up his hand. 'They are too young, you will have to walk up the hill.' He obviously had no children, I thought to myself, otherwise he'd know how likely that was. 'Or you can go down that blue run over there and get the chairlift back,' he said pointing to a trail that led through the trees.

The safe option was to walk all the way down, but the more exciting one was to try the blue run. If we couldn't do it, we could always just walk down.

Plus, I'd not been down a blue run yet.

As soon as we set off I could see there was a big difference between green and blue. The piste, as narrow as a road, zigzagged through thick forest, the trail dropping off steeply in places.

It was obvious Ella's snow-plough skills were not going to cut it, so the only way was to hold Ella's hand and keep her steady on one side, while holding the scruff of Ewen's neck as he zoomed along between my legs.

It was a little taxing, to say the least, juggling both kids, dodging other skiers, trees and pylons, while skiing my first blue run. Thankfully the kids stayed calm, and they trusted me, even if I didn't trust myself.

Down we hurtled.

By the time we reached the final stretch, and I was at last able to let go of Ella and release my death grip on Ewen, I was in a state of nervous exhaustion.

'Can we do that again?' said Ella, beaming.

Sat on the chairlift, slowly rising through the trees, the kids pressing hard against me on both sides, scared of the drop while swinging their skis backwards and forwards, I realised that maybe one day the three of us might go on a proper adventure together.

That just being a dad was an adventure in itself.

After a week it was time to climb again. This time my partner was a German called Robert Steiner, a man I'd never met, but had heard a lot about from other climbers.

He was famous for an epic on the Grandes Jorasses, falling seventy metres near the top of the Colton-MacIntyre route and ripping out half the belay. Having broken his pelvis and ankle, Robert was unable to move. His partners were forced to leave him on a tiny ledge – this was in the middle of winter – and climb to the top to get help. It took them a further two days to make it down to Italy where they'd raised the alarm.

Robert had lain there in terrible pain, without food or water, waiting for a rescue.

On the second day he'd been so desperately thirsty he'd drank his own urine, only being so dehydrated it had simply burned his throat.

On the third day Robert saw a big storm approaching, knowing that when it hit the Jorasses there would be no rescue. He had held on, but now time was running out.

Yet as the first snowflakes began to fall he heard the rattle of a helicopter and saw the tiny red machine flying ahead of the storm as it closed in on the mountain.

The crew had one chance to save Robert. The winch man swept in at the end of the cable, clipped him in, cut away his belay and then kicked them both clear of the face.

The accident had left Robert with a fused ankle, but this hadn't stopped him becoming one Germany's premier alpinists. I'd never seen a picture of him, however, and only knew him through email. We'd made loose plans to climb on the Grandes Jorasses, and perhaps repeat the Japanese route, and agreed we'd meet at the Montenvers railway station in Chamonix before heading up to climb.

I'd heard a lot about Robert's exploits, and his many solos. He seemed very much like a German version of me, always getting into trouble. I'd once asked Alex Huber, Germany's greatest alpinist, if he'd heard of Robert. 'I think Robert is a bit crazy,' he said, a real compliment coming from Alex.

I packed my kit under the gaze of Mandy and the kids, Ella and Ewen packing my sleeping bag, Ella in fits of laugher when Ewen tried to put it on his back, the sack twice his height.

After breakfast I kissed them goodbye.

'Be careful, Dad,' said Ella, as she stood at the door.

Meeting Robert at the station, I half expected some monster of a climber, limping perhaps, but gigantic nonetheless. Instead, the man I met in the car park stood beside a ramshackle car full of tatty gear looking more like a schoolteacher, appropriately enough, as that's what he was in the real world.

'It is very good to meet you,' Robert said, holding out his hand. Perhaps he had also been expecting some hero climber, and was now disappointed. 'I've read a lot of your writing Andy, I think we will climb together well.'

As we shook hands I noticed that half his index finger was missing.

Although no monster, it was evident Robert was hardcore.

We boarded the train up to Montenvers and the start of the long walk-in to the Jorasses, our big rucksacks dumped on the seats beside us.

'What happened to your finger?' I asked, a little self-consciously. It must be a question he gets asked a lot.

'A bear ate it,' Robert said, his face stern.

I looked down at it and shuddered, not sure if I should ask any more.

'I am joking,' he laughed. 'I was soloing The Sea of Dreams on El Capitan. I pulled on a block that was loose. It came down and chopped off my finger,' he said, holding it up for me to see, as though describing a bad blister he'd once had.

Soloing a route like The Sea of Dreams was bad enough, but being alone on a big wall with a chopped off finger must have been serious, not to mention painful.

I suddenly wondered what I was getting myself into.

Robert described how the finger was dangling from some tendon, and how he'd nevertheless managed to abseil down and make it to the road. Holding up his bloody hand he'd stopped a car, which took him to the small local hospital.

'An amputated finger can be sewn back as long as it's within four hours of the accident,' said Robert, looking down at his hand like a bride admiring her ring. 'The problem for me was I had to be flown to a bigger hospital and they wouldn't do that without a credit card. I had left mine on the wall.'

Finally a friend vouched for Robert and the chopper whisked him to Merced, only to find the surgeon was off for lunch.

'My finger was sewn back on, and I was told not to take the bandage off for two weeks, but after a week there was a stink. My finger was dead, and so it was cut off,' Robert explained. 'It is bad to lose your finger,' he laughed, 'but worse when you owe nineteen thousand dollars for a late helicopter and a bad operation.'

The train arrived and we headed down to the glacier. I put on my snowshoes and Robert his skis, and then we began shuffling towards the Leschaux hut, the same hut I'd visited so many times but never successfully.

Maybe this was the trip where I would break with tradition?

Leaving the Mer de Glace, we trudged slowly up the Leschaux Glacier, the mighty Jorasses filling our view, until we reached the ladders that led up to the hut. I felt intimidated climbing with such a legend so went first up a short section where the ladder had torn away, hoping to show I could climb, only to have my crampon pop off.

Dumping our gear inside, we sat on the balcony and looked up at the face, tracing the lines.

'Once I stood here and saw stones falling down the couloir of the Colton-MacIntyre,' said Robert. 'They were tumbling from top to bottom.' I looked at him, wondering what the significance of the story was. Perhaps it was a warning, since the Japanese route ran next to the Colton-Macintyre. 'Then I realised they were people,' he continued. 'Three Spanish climbers, falling all the way to the bottom.'

'Want a cup of tea?' I asked.

It was getting chilly.

I busied around the hut, melting water and chatting while Robert lay in the bunk bed that ran the length of the room, the same bed I'd shared with Paul Ramsden, Ian Parnell, and many others.

'I don't feel well, Andy,' said Robert, sitting up. 'I think I have caught this virus.'

The next day we slogged back to the valley, me walking, Robert skiing, but visibly ill, stopping and starting, his head bowed, his weight resting on his ski poles.

At Montenvers, I said the usual stuff, the stuff you say to partners who have let you down. 'Not to worry, we can try it another time.' Inside I was seething at my continuing bad luck.

'You must be careful with a virus not to push yourself,' said Robert, as the train slowly descended to Chamonix. 'It can damage your heart. It is not worth it.'

I told him about my heart palpitations on Les Droites, laughing them off, but Robert looked concerned.

He was right too. For two years I had chest pains when I exercised.

Back at the car we sorted out our gear and shook hands once more, still only strangers who climbed.

'I can come back in a week perhaps,' he said. 'We must climb something Andy,' said Robert.

'I hope so,' I said.

And he was gone.

I got the train back to Servoz and walked back to the house, knocking on the glass of the door, seeing the kids inside watching television, sat on the settee under a blanket, messily eating a baguette.

'Daddy!' they both shouted, leaping off the settee in a shower of crumbs, unlocking the door and both hugging my legs.

'Oh Dad, we've missed you so much,' said Ewen.

'What happened?' asked Mandy looking irritated that I'd not climbed anything. The sale of our house was not going smoothly, and I felt some pressure to make this trip worth all the expense and hassle. At the time, I resented her question, that now she wanted me to perform. The reality was that as usual she had found the strength to see me go, and hold it together, knowing I might not come back. She wanted me to go and climb and feel normal, that one hard route would be enough. Coming home like this solved nothing. She knew I'd have to leave again.

The following day we went skiing, Mandy going off for some one-to-one instruction while I skied with the kids, Ella snow-ploughing, while I skied with Ewen between my legs again, the technique advancing in leaps and falls.

The day started badly. Ella had built up a phobia about the button lifts, scared she couldn't get off at the end, that although she could grab the seat and stick it between her legs before being yanked forward, she wouldn't be able to reverse the process at the end.

To get round this, I took Ewen on the lift, then once we jumped off, plonked him down to wait for Ella and help her.

On the first trip of the day I arrived at the top, parked Ewen, then turned to grab Ella. But when I turned around, Ewen was not where I'd left him.

Instead, to my horror, I saw him in his red ski-suit sliding down the piste at high speed.

Mustering everything I knew about skiing, which wasn't much, I suddenly developed enough skill to hurtle after him like an Olympic champion.

In my head I had visions of him hitting the trees, or being wiped out by another skier, each scene playing out in my head as I raced after him.

Ewen hit a flat spot and slowly came to a halt just before another drop off.

When I reached him, he was standing dead still and crying.

Ella swooped in behind, laughing so hard she could hardly stand.

We met Mandy for a hot chocolate at the top, the kids sworn to secrecy about Ewen's near-miss. Mandy was thrilled by skiing and loved the mountains, all of which was a surprise. For all our lives together, the mountains had come between us, a place she didn't understand that she was forced to share me with. I wondered if it all made sense to her. 'Why don't you ski down the mountain instead of getting the cable car down' she said. 'We'll meet you at the bottom.'

The way down was a long blue run, and without a child between my legs I found the going much easier, sweeping down in long turns, exhilarated. It suddenly made sense why people like skiing. It was fun. It wasn't like climbing, with all its doubt and fear and death. It was simply fun – intoxicating, lighthearted fun.

I thought back over the last few years, trying to recall moments that stood out like this one did: sliding down from the Dru sat on a haul-bag, standing in a frozen river in Norway, and all my time with Ella and Ewen.

Halfway down I came to a big drop-off marked as a black run, the blue zigzagging down in another direction. I came to a halt and looked at its steep angle, feeling like James Bond. It looked terrifying and dangerous. One slip and you'd go for miles. I'd only been skiing for a few days but assumed I was now good enough to do a black run.

'I'll learn on the way down,' I thought, and just dropped in.

The slope was icy and the edges of my skis barely gripped as I tried to make a turn and slow down. Skittering across the ice, my focus was intense as I drew on everything I knew, while filling in the gaps. There really were only gaps.

I must not hesitate.

I must be bold.

I must imagine I am a great skier.

I made the turn and swept on down again.

Two more turns and I was down.

I turned around on shaky legs and looked up at the stupid thing I'd just done.

Mandy and the kids were waiting as I whooshed towards them, feeling like a pro now.

'Wow you look like a proper skier,' she said, as I clipped off my skis.

Sat in the car on the way back to the flat she turned to me and said how at home I was such a fuckwit, forgetting everything, unreliable, distant, not there, while here I was in my element, capable, dependable – 'a real man.' Maybe that's why I liked it – because I was good at it.

Feeling better, Robert returned a week later with another strong German climber named Martin, an engineer who worked for BMW with whom Robert had climbed a hard route on the Eiger.

They only had the weekend, so we planned another route on the North Face of Les Droites, the Maria Callas Memorial Route, aiming to climb it on Saturday and Sunday. It would be a tight schedule.

The forecast was fine apart from the temperature dipping down into the low minus twenties. There was also a lot of snow in the mountains, so Martin had brought a pair of mountaineering skis for me to use and so speed our approach.

We fiddled with gear in the morning outside the flat, the kids looking on, fascinated by Robert's missing finger.

'What happened to your finger,' asked Ella shyly.

'A shark bit it off,' came the reply, and forever after Robert was the man whose finger was eaten by a shark.

I tried to get the skis to fit onto my soft mountaineering boots, then Robert had a go, but to no avail.

'Here let me try,' said Martin 'I'm an engineer.' Within a minute he'd broken the binding in half.

'Don't worry, I won't be able to ski in my boots anyway. I'll just shuffle down, it'll be fine even if its broken.'

Saying goodbye to the family was even harder than the last time. There had to be some separation between one life and the other. It was like gearing up for war with your wife and kids looking on.

'Be careful, Dad' said Ella – again.

'I will.'

The journey up the Grands Montets was so familiar now, the smell of the cable car, the smell of the people, the view, the sun dazzling through scratched windows. I looked around and saw the faces of all those climbers I'd shared this little box with, the living and the dead.

Clumping down the metal stairs to the snow, the vast slope leading down to the Argentière Glacier looked easy enough to ski in rigid boots, but not soft ones. No doubt born on skis, Robert and Martin clipped their skis on and within a minute were several hundred metres away, skinning up the glacier.

'I'll catch you up,' I shouted after them.

I soon found that a heavy rucksack, compounded by having the wrong boots, meant going in a straight line proved impossible. Any acceleration caused me to fall over backwards.

Each time I hit the snow, which felt quite hard by the twentieth repetition, I'd take off my heavy rucksack, get up, put it on again, then zoom off uncontrollably again, desperate to keep the skis on because if the broken one popped I'd struggle to get it back on. I was quickly exhausted.

Having almost reached the bottom of the slope, I took a hard fall and lost the broken ski. Without the usual brake, or a strap to attach it to my ankle, my ski quickly picked up speed.

Resigned, I watched it slide away without me, powering down the slope, over a small ice cliff, and out onto the glacier, where it stopped like an obedient dog that's roamed too far.

Now I was really in trouble, as the snow was too deep to walk in, and skiing on a single board was beyond me.

I took off my remaining ski and sat on it bum-shuffling down the slope, knowing full well that there had never been a more pathetic sight in the history of ski mountaineering. To make matters worse, a French guide swooshed down to me, looking like skiing's answer to Mikhail Baryshnikov, asking if I was alright.

'I'm British,' I said looking at the floor, trying hard not to burst into tears.

'I understand,' he said, no doubt embarrassed for me, and then skied off.

I made it to the glacier an hour after setting off and picked up my missing ski, only to lose more time as my skins fell off with the cold, almost as soon as I put them back on.

I took it as good manners that neither Robert nor Martin asked where the hell I'd been.

We sat in the dark hut sorting out gear again before getting to bed. Due to our tight schedule we had to get up at one. It hardly seemed worth going to bed at all.

I lay in the same bunk I'd slept in many times before and wondered what our chances were. I was nearly out of time on my dream holiday, and it was turning out to be far from what I'd imagined. Maybe there was something to be said for having your dream in installments.

The alarm went off. We packed and walked over the glacier to the start of the face. Spindrift poured down making it seem a lost cause, but Robert tried anyway while Martin and I stamped our feet at the bottom.

It was too cold.

It was too dark.

It was too grim.

'This is no good,' shouted Robert, his way blocked by a never-emptying bucket of powder, and with that another climb came to naught.

Down he climbed, jumping back over the bergschrund.

'Maybe we can wait till it gets light,' I suggested, happy to fail, but wanting to know we were failing because we couldn't climb, not because we didn't want to.

We pulled out a bivy bag and sat side-by-side, shivering, frost covering the fabric. Our breath fought and died against the cold. No one spoke. I felt the cold creep into my soul, the cold that had been eating into me for so long, its nails buried deep and never letting go. The feeling of freezing to death was a familiar call to arms. But as I sat there, I felt all my fight had gone.

'Once,' said Robert, bent over and hugging his legs 'I climbed the Messner route on Les Droites with a friend. Halfway we found a small cave filled with tools and chemicals left behind by the crystal hunters and the crystals they had been searching for, all lying there, waiting to be fetched once their chemicals had done their work.'

'What did you do?' I asked.

'We filled up our rucksacks and took all we could carry,' he replied. 'We were very poor, and knew the money from these stones could pay for many more holidays.'

'How heavy were they?' I asked, knowing that on such a route every gram mattered at the best of times.

'This was our mistake' said Robert, his face still bent towards his boots, as he hugged his legs, fighting to keep the cold from entering his chest. 'The higher we climbed the more crystals we had to throw away, until we reached the top and found we only had one small stone each.'

'Why didn't you just abseil down?' I asked, knowing this way they could have kept the lot.

'We are climbers. The route meant more.'

We were silent again, and I recalled the span of time between that moment and the Lafaille route, the routes and the people between. Someone once told me that you never know when you're standing on your greatest summit until you look back many years later, that although you believe that there will be better and harder climbs to come, in reality you are simply climbing slowly down. You will never hold those heights again.

The thought that this was true was almost too much to bear. All those years, I'd been struggling to return to those same heights.

Where had it gone wrong?

When had I begun this descent?

I knew the answers. We'd not gone to the summit from the top of the Lafaille. I'd retreated from the Devil's Dihedral on Fitz Roy. I'd backed off from the Troll Wall. A hundred moments when I was too weak to push, too scared of death to risk it all.

It was all over.

...

I wanted to go skiing.

'It is nearly light, maybe we can climb a little way up then come down,' said Robert, pulling up the corner of the shelter.

Martin and I were quiet.

'Let's just go home,' I said finally. 'There's is nothing left to discover here.'

This time Mandy was pleased to see us back safe, and I knew she knew we would be back empty-handed. Maybe she saw what I had become, that even superheroes couldn't keep their masks on forever.

The kids hung around Robert as we sorted out the gear, their eyes fixed on his missing digit right up to the last moment he waved us goodbye.

'Are you going climbing again, Dad?' asked Ella, holding my hand as we walked back to the house.

'No,' I said.

We sat down in front of the television and I flicked through the channels, looking for something kid-friendly, catching for just an instant a banner headline scrolling under a BBC newsreader.

'Breaking news: RAF Hercules shot down in Iraq. Ten crew believed killed.'

I sat there, stunned.

No one had my number in the Alps.

What if it was Robin's aircraft? He flew to Iraq almost every week.

I found a cartoon for the kids and went to the bedroom to call the

Ministry of Defence helpline.

'If you are the next of kin you will be informed shortly,' said a woman's voice.

I rang my brother's number.

There was no reply.

I dialled my mum's number.

'Hello,' she said in her normal cheery voice.

'Hi Mum, are you okay?' I said, my voice close to trembling, my mind racing out of control, my brother's life flashing before me.

'I'm fine, are you enjoying your holidays?' she said. I didn't know what to say. I wondered if Robin's wife had been told but Mum hadn't heard yet, unsure of how these things worked.

'Just checking you're okay,' I said.

I put down the phone and rang Robin's number again.

It was a UK dial tone, meaning at least his phone was at home.

I imagined it sat in his locker, left behind, ringing.

The whole room would be filled with phones ringing.

Images of him as a kid raced through my mind, all the good times and bad, how I had hardly seen him for the last ten years. I thought about his kids, the same ages as Ella and Ewen.

The phone rang.

I thought of him as a child, as my child.

'Hello,' said the voice of my imagined dead brother.

'Robin,' I said, lost for all words but his name.

'I'm okay,' he said.

I knew he'd been crying.

'They're all dead,' he added.

I put the phone down and lay on the bed and cried my eyes out, cried and cried and cried. I cried with relief, but also because now I knew, knew what it felt like to lose someone you love.

The following day, the last of the holiday for Mandy and the kids, we went to the top of Les Houches and made the most of our newfound love of skiing, feeling like a family for the first time in what felt like forever.

The slopes were full of people having uncomplicated fun, going up, coming down, never going anywhere, connecting with that childlike whoosh of speed.

I looked over at the Dru, cold and distant, shuddering at the thought of being up there. It seemed so long ago since the Lafaille, my high-water mark, a thousand years ago, not four.

Through it I'd been granted access to an ideal life, a semi-pro climber, free to do whatever I wanted, a small window of fame. But this wasn't the life I'd imagined it would lead to. I guess I didn't have the foresight to see that climbing is always the easy part, and that normal life is the struggle.

By late afternoon Ewen was flagging.

'You and Ella keep skiing and we'll see you at the cafe at the bottom,' said Mandy. 'Just be safe,' she added.

'I will,' I said.

We skied along together, father and daughter, Ella's skills now sufficient for her to manage blue runs without me holding her hand. We had a ball, and our shared exhilaration seemed to rub away the cloud that had hung over me for a very long time.

Taking the chairlift back up, I would ski ahead, then wait for her, Ella drawing up beside me each time with a smile.

We got to a steeper section than normal, dropping through a patch of trees, the other skiers slowly making a few careful turns. Ella hesitated.

'Don't be scared, just focus and you'll be fine. Be bold,' I said, half joking, but taking my advice, she charged down, barely in control.

On the way back up, I told her that unlike skiing, when you're climbing coming down is always the most dangerous part of a climb, and it was then, when your guard is down, that you must focus the most.

'You're always careful aren't you dad?' she asked, looking up at me, flecks of snow sticking to her eyebrows.

'Always.'

It came to me, as we rose up through the trees, that I'd been descending for a long time, since that moment on the Devil's Dihedral on Fitz Roy. Four years of coming down.

Was I at the bottom, on safe ground?

Was it safe to stop?

The day was almost over, so we headed for the cable car with the rest of the skiers not confident of skiing safely all the way down the mountain.

'Ella,' I said as we prepared to enter the queue, 'why don't we ski down instead?'

She gave me a look, the kind of look that said she knew better, that sensible parent look I should have.

'Come on, you can do it.'

Down we swooshed, me going first, looking for the easiest line, Ella just behind me.

Within a few hundred metres we passed a skier being treated by medics and ski-patrollers, which helped focus the mind. With a child the blue piste suddenly seemed much steeper, and as evening fell, the light became flat and the slope more difficult to read.

With each drop, I could sense the anxious grind of Ella's tiny skis as she ploughed harder. A few times she stopped because she feared it was all beyond her, the gathering darkness adding to the sense of dread, but each time I told her she could do it, and she did.

The whole descent was nine hundred metres through the trees, and her tiny legs soon grew tired.

'When you do something impossible, Ella, you've just got to do one bit at a time until it becomes possible,' I told her as she looked down nervously.

'Anyway, we're nearly down,' I told her, wondering how far it really was.

At last the valley lights grew bright and we were on the final slope down to the cafe, skiing side by side, father and daughter, Ella's shoulders slumped with fatigue, her arms by her sides, ski poles dragging as the mammoth snow plow drew to its end.

'Stay focused, Ella,' I warned her. 'You're not down yet.'

I knew we would never forget this moment.

I swept down to the car park amongst the last few skiers, stopping with a quick sideways slide, clicking off my skis like someone who knew what he was doing. Ella came to a wobbly half-stop, running over my skis and grabbing my arm just before she carried on to the tarmac.

I looked down at her, her face raised up to mine, her eyes closed in mock-exhaustion. I was so proud.

I lifted her up and gave her a big hug, her skis bashing my knees, whispering 'Don't bloody tell your mum you did that.'

The cafe was hot and noisy, the floor running wet from a thousand stomping snowy boots. My glasses instantly steamed up. I took them off and stood at the threshold, wiping them dry, all the faces suddenly indistinct, apart from Ella's at my side.

'There they are,' she cried, pointing, leading her half-blind father through the crowd to Mandy and Ewen. Ewen's red ski-suit was round his ankles, his face covered in hot chocolate, utterly content.

'Where have you been?' asked Mandy, relieved to see us, her hands held to her chest. 'I was about to call the mountain rescue.'

She always seemed to be relieved or anxious. I allowed myself to believe that now I knew how it felt, that I could empathise. That I knew how it felt to watch someone go and worry that they might not come back. In my life there had been people who had gone and not come back. I had learned the trick of placing them in boxes, and putting them away. Each time my father drove off, his box would close. It was the only way.

But now there were people who could not be hidden – and it was me who was always leaving, just like my dad. I wanted them to put me into a box, but they wouldn't, and so they paid the price.

'I was so worried,' said Mandy as she helped Ella unzip her suit, her little face flushed.

'We were having an adventure,' I said, my hand on Ella's shoulder, her face also beaming at our secret as she shuffled up next to Ewen.

I took my place at the end of the table, Mandy at the other, the kids between us.

'Will you miss drinking so much hot chocolate?' I asked Ewen as he tried to scoop out the dregs with a teaspoon, most of it missing his mouth.

He was too focused to answer, and simply nodded.

'He really missed you two,' said Mandy.

'Not Ella,' added Ewen, looking up from his drink.

I ordered two more hot chocolates in terrible French.

'I hope you take up skiing rather than climbing,' Mandy told Ella, wiping Ewen's face with a tissue.

'I'll disown her if she turns into a skier,' I replied, only half-joking.

'I want to be a climber like Dad,' she said, shuffling over to me and hugging my arm.

I saw her life pass before my eyes.

'Maybe being a skier wouldn't be so bad,' I said quickly. 'At least it's better than golf.'

I noticed the room was beginning to thin out, as the skiers boarded buses for home, or hobbled to their cars in their clunky boots.

'Did you enjoy your skiing holiday?' asked Mandy, sounding a little like a teacher, our kids now officially middle class.

'Was alright,' said Ella.

Tomorrow they would be gone, and I had a week left on my own. But I knew this trip was over. I'd not climb another route this winter. I wondered if I'd ever climb another route again. Maybe if I'd climbed something hard this trip it would have been the end. I could have finished on a high note. Summits had never been that relevant, just way-marks on the road, but I needed one more, to round off the story. Life's never like that though.

'Let's have one last drink,' I said, happy to just sit in the warm. 'This is always the best part of any adventure, the bit I like most.'

'Which bit?' said Ella, looking around the room as if I had seen something she hadn't.

I stared out of the window through the gathering darkness at the last ember of sunlight on the mountaintop above us. Then it faded, leaving only my reflection.

'I like the end,' I said, turning back to Ella with my answer. 'When it's over and I'm human again. And I can see the magic.'

Climbing 101

A short non-climbers guide to climbing

I once read a book about a guy sailing single-handed to Greenland in a tiny yacht, his story full of terrifying storms, ship-sinking icebergs and waves big enough to smash an aircraft carrier. It was great little book as it gave me an insight into something I had no real understanding of until then, having always seen sailing as the sport of toffs. The only problem was for much of the book I had absolutely no idea what he was talking about, the story full of technical details: spars and booms and mainsails; strange knots and hanks and sheets; not to mention all the usual bewildering nautical terms for things we already have known names for, like back and front, left and right.

Reading this book it suddenly occurred to me that non-climbers might find my stories equally confusing, and although I endeavour to keep such techie stuff to a minimum, sometimes even the most basic things may prove a little confusing.

So here are a few answers to the fundamental questions a non-climber may ask.

Q: How do you climb?

A: Most climbers use just their hands and feet (free climbing), climbing the rock as you would climb up the side of a building or tree. If the holds become too small to use, you either have to stop or alternatively resort to artificial means (aka 'aid'), pulling yourself up, or standing on protection placed in the rock. On ice, spiked crampons attached to your boots are used to gain traction, and an ice axe is used in each hand to aid balance, allowing vertical ice to be climbed.

Leading   Belayer holding a leader fall   Seconding

Q: How do you stay safe when you climb?

A: Climbers usually work in a team of two, joined by a single or double length of rope (fifty to sixty metres long). This is tied to each climber via a harness around the waist. The climber who goes first is called the 'leader,' while the one who holds their rope (using a metal belay device that locks down on the rope in a fall) is called the 'belayer.' As the leader climbs the belayer slowly pays out the rope, giving the leader just enough slack so they can move. The leader places protection in the rock as they ascend (rocks, cams or pegs), clipping this into their rope(s) via karabiners. This way they create a safety chain through which the rope slides. If one piece fails in a fall, then there should be another piece not far below, climbers generally placing a piece of gear roughly every five feet.

Q: What if you fall?

A: If the leader falls their rope will be held by the belayer (via their belay device), with their weight coming onto their highest piece of protection. This means they should only fall twice the distance above their last piece of protection. For example, if the leader is twenty metres above the ground, places a solid nut in a crack, climbs one metre higher and then falls, they will fall two metres. As long as there is plenty of protection then the climber is safe: the less protection there is the greater the danger.

Q: How do you carry enough gear for a long route?

A: The leader places the protection to safeguard themselves, and on reaching the end of the rope (the pitch), they secure themselves and now belay their belayer up (the belayer is also know as the 'second' for this reason). As the second climbs they remove all the protection placed, allowing the next climber to lead.

Q: What about jumaring?

A: Jumaring is used on very hard routes, or aid climbs, where it would be too slow for the belayer to re-climb the pitch which the leader has just completed. In order to speed things up they simply use two mechanical clamps on the rope – one attached to the harness, the other to one foot – allowing them to climb up the rope.

Glossary

Abseil	To descend a rope using a *Descender*.
Aid Climbing	Climbing using gear for resting or making progress.
Aider	A ladder-like sling used to climb up when *Aid Climbing*.
Angle Peg	See *Peg*.
Arête	An outward pointing bit of rock: a ridge or rib.
Ascender	A device for climbing a rope when all else fails. Also see *Jumaring*.
Axe	Climbing ice axe that can be swung into ice or turf. Used in pairs.
Beak	A tiny *Peg*, the thickness of a credit card.
Belay (noun)	A place where you attach yourself to the rock.
Belay Device	A piece of equipment which you use to control the rope when *Belaying*.
Belaying	Fixing a rope round a rock, pin, or other object, to secure it.
Bergschrund	Crevasse that forms between a mountain face and the moving glacier at its base.
Beta	Prior knowledge of trick moves, protection or just about anything about a route available before you start climbing.
Birdbeak	See *Beak*.
Bivy Bag	Gore-tex sleeping-bag cover.
Bolt	An expansion bolt fixed permanently into the rock face to protect a climb or form a *Belay*.
Break	A horizontal crack.
Bulge	A small rounded overhang.
Cam	A complex expanding nut with three or four opposing camming lobes, used in cracks of all sizes.
Chalk	Magnesium carbonate used to dry the hands when climbing.
Chickenhead	American term for a small lump of intrusive rock which sticks out of a slab.
Chimney	A crack wide enough to fit your whole body into.
Chockstone	A piece of rock which is jammed immovably in a crack.
Choss	Soil, dirt, rubble, stones, vegetation, in fact anything other than good clean stable rock.
Cleaning	The act of removing protection placed by the leader, performed by the second as he/she follows.
Copperhead	Alloy or copper *Nut* that can be hammered to fit in seams and flared cracks allowing progress but not protection.
Crux	The hardest move on a *Pitch* or the hardest pitch on a climb.
Daisy Chain	Long sling with multiple places to clip into, and used in conjunction with aiders.

Deadhead — Fixed *Copperhead* with broken clip cable.

Descender — A friction device used when abseiling, such as a figure of eight or a *Belay Device*.

Étrier — See *Aider*.

Expanding Flake — A flake that moves when pulled on, or which looks as if it might move or even detach completely if pulled hard enough.

Figure of Eight — The most commonly used knot to attach a climber to the rope.

Fixed — See *In Situ*.

Flake — A partially detached section of rock which will often yield good holds along its detached edge.

Free Climbing — Progressing up a route by using your body rather than the gear.

Hammer — Wooden-shafted hammer used to place *Pegs*.

Haul-Bag — Large heavy-duty rucksack (150+ litres) used to hold all your big-wall gear on the climb.

Hauling — The process of dragging up your *Haul-bags* after each pitch.

Head — Short for *Copperhead*.

Hex — A large alloy nut. Sizes range from finger to fist.

Hook — See *Skyhook*.

In Situ — Latin for 'in place'. Used for protection that is found on the climb, placed by a previous climber, including *Pegs* and *Bolts*.

Jamming — The technique of inserting part (or all) of the body into a crack to make progress.

Jug — An excellent handhold.

Jumaring — The technique of climbing a rope using jumar clamps.

Karabiner — An oval metal hoop with a springloaded 'gate'. Rope and protection are attached to karabiners. Also known as a 'krab'. Karabiners come in many forms, and arguments about which is best occupy many hours in gear shops.

Knifeblade Peg — See *Peg*.

Leader — The person going up the route first: the one who solves the conundrum of 'how do you get the rope up there then?' hence 'lead a route' and 'leading a route'. Is followed by the *Second*.

Mantleshelf — Technique used to establish yourself on a ledge below a blank piece of rock. Often shortened to 'mantle.'

Micro-wire — The tiniest of climbing *Nuts*, being the size of a large pinhead, with an equal amount of strength.

Nut — The simplest form of protection. A metal wedge threaded on steel wires, intended to go into cracks and stay there. The name comes from the practice of 1950s climbers, who used motorcycle nuts.

Offwidth — The most awkward width of crack: too wide for fist jamming, but too narrow to *Chimney*.

Peg	A simple length of steel, either u-shaped (*Angle Peg*) or flat (*Knifeblade*) with an eye in one end for clipping the rope to. Hammered in place.
Pendulum	Swinging on a length of rope in order to obtain a distant hold.
Pitch	A section of a climb, usually close to a rope length.
Piton	A *peg* or spike hammered into a crack to support a climber on a rope.
Placement	The place in the rock face where *Protection* is actually positioned.
Portaledge	Folding bed made from alloy tubing and nylon and used on a big wall.
Pro	Abbreviation of *Protection*.
Protection	Also known as gear. The devices that climbers use to prevent themselves from hitting the floor.
Pulley	Metal wheel used to increase the mechanical advantage when *Hauling*.
Quickdraw	Two snap-gate *Karabiners* linked by a short sling equal one quickdraw.
Rack	A collection of gear, usually attached to loops on a harness.
Rappel	Another word for *Abseil*.
Rivet	A 5mm x 50mm machine *Bolt* hammered into a drilled hole on blank sections of rock.
Screamer Sling	A shock-absorbing sling.
Screwgate	A locking *karabiner*.
Seam	A very thin crack, one too small for any protection wider than a *Knifeblade* peg.
Second	The person who belays the *Leader*, and gets the fun of taking out their protection on the way up. Being the second is generally less dangerous than leading, because you have a rope above you – except on traverses, when it can open you up to big swings if you fall off and the leader has not put in enough protection.
Shit-tube	Plastic tube used to store bodily waste when climbing on El Cap.
Skyhook	Small steel hook that will hold a climber's weight when placed on a small flake or flat edge.
Sling	Loop of rope or tape, useful for racking gear or looping around chockstones for protection.
Solo	To climb without ropes, or to climb alone with ropes.
Static Rope	Compared with a dynamic rope, a static rope does not stretch significantly when loaded.
Torque	Technique whereby a climber places the pick of an ice axe in a crack and twists it.
Wire	Short for a *Nut* on wire.